Introducing Intersectionality

look at past papers to see if theres anything you want to expand on

Possible paper topics

- Pro-choice/abortion after thoughts vs Pro-life/abortion after in USA, maybe UK   look for sources that (they home intersectional views (race, class, religion, gender identity, gay?)
    • Maybe something about access to it and Roe v W

- Violence in the military

Introducing Intersectionality

Mary Romero

polity

First published in 2018 by Polity Press
Reprinted: 2018 (twice)

Polity Press
65 Bridge Street
Cambridge CB2 1UR, UK

Polity Press
101 Station Landing
Suite 300,
Medford, MA 02155
USA

ISBN-13: 978-0-7456-6366-1
ISBN-13: 978-0-7456-6367-8(paperback)

A catalogue record for this book is available from the British Library.

Library of Congress Cataloging-in-Publication Data

Names: Romero, Mary, author.
Title: Introducing intersectionality / Mary Romero.
Description: Malden, MA : Polity Press, [2017] | Series: Short introductions | Includes bibliographical references and index.
Identifiers: LCCN 2017013088 (print) | LCCN 2017035338 (ebook) | ISBN 9781509525287 (Mobi) | ISBN 9781509525294 (Epub) | ISBN 9780745663661 (hardback) | ISBN 9780745663678 (pbk.)
Subjects: LCSH: Intersectionality (Sociology)
Classification: LCC HM488.5 (ebook) | LCC HM488.5 .R65 2017 (print) | DDC 305–dc23
LC record available at https://lccn.loc.gov/2017013088

Typeset in 10 on 12 pt Sabon
by Toppan Best-set Premedia Limited
Printed and bound in the United States by LSC Communications

For further information on Polity, visit our website:
politybooks.com

Contents

Detailed Contents

Introduction

Intersectionality's focus on social inequality has its roots and development in social justice research and struggle. As an activist project, intersectionality provides analytical tools for framing social justice issues in such a way as to expose how social exclusion or privilege occurs differently in various social positions, and it does this by focusing on the interaction of multiple systems of oppression. It is important to emphasize, however, that the concept is not just about poverty and those of lower socio-economic status. Intersectionality also helps us to understand privilege, riches, and access to higher education. It is a useful concept for understanding what the media have been calling the "1 percent." Access to inherited wealth, admission to Ivy Leagues (especially as a legacy student), and social networks of upward mobility form just as much "an intersection" as the school-to-prison pipeline and the father-and-son construction union or plumbing business.

In the early 1980s, the phrase "race, class and gender" was popularly referred to as the "holy trinity"; a growing number of researchers in the sociology of race and gender called attention to the explanatory power gained by analyzing interactions among these three systems of oppression and privilege. Research demonstrated that the inclusion of systems of power and social location were central to understanding everyday social interactions between individuals in society. Black feminists were at the vanguard of developing this new approach which challenged older theories that analyzed only one social category, for instance gender, without acknowledging that the experience of gender is not the same for a white woman as it is for a Black woman or a woman of color. In studying class inequality, intersectionality insisted that both gender and race power relations were instrumental in comprehending the dynamics of class oppression and privilege. Race, class, and gender had long been treated as *variables* in sociological research. Intersectionality criticized the notion that these were simply variables to be controlled for. It also criticized the emphasis on one of these power systems, without taking into account the other two, as "essentialist."

Clearly, neither racism, sexism, nor classism in the US can be fully explained by, for example, only analyzing the circumstances of elderly married poor Black women in the rural South. Treating the experience of this group as representative of all Black people, or all women, or all poor people is an essentialist view. Critical race scholars contributed to the understanding of systems of class oppression by documenting the ways in which race had always been a primary division in law, economics, and education in the US – and all other multicultural countries with histories of colonialism, conquest and immigration. Thus, neither class nor gender dynamics can be explained without figuring out the impact that racial differences have on oppression and/or privilege that individuals and communities experience. Without considering the interaction of systems of oppression and privilege, one might assume that racism, sexism or classism is the same experience regardless of your position in society. As social science came to recognize the different ways members of society experience oppression and privilege, it became important to explain how multiple systems of power interact in different times and locations.

In the past few decades, an increasing number of sociologists have come to accept that an intersectional approach was the key to under-standing how inequality, privilege, and oppression worked. More sociologists came to recognize the limitations of one-dimensional approaches to social inequality. Class alone does not explain all aspects of poverty or housing segregation. Gender alone cannot account for wage disparities and occupation segregation. Race by itself does not provide a complete understanding of health disparities or college retention rates. Intersectionality, as an intellectual project, delves deeper into the nuances of social equality by pushing researchers to analyze the various manifestations of inequality. The holy trinity has been complicated by additional power systems: sexuality, ableism, ethnicity, citizenship and age play important roles in social identity and economic status – their reproduction and maintenance.

Among the social sciences, sociology has been a leader in developing the concept of intersectionality, both in theory and in research methods. Sociologists began using intersectionality to frame teaching as well as research addressing social inequality. For instance, growing numbers of scholars are contributing to disability studies by examining intersections of race, class, gender and sexuality. Sociologists specializing in the sociology of immigration are incorporating race and gender, to understand how racism has shaped immigration legislation and law enforcement. Research in the sociology of family includes the intersection of systems of inequality – sexuality and citizenship, alongside race, class and gender. While intersectional approaches in sociology are gaining wider acceptance, not all fields of study embrace the concept or consider that only focusing on one category is an essentialist approach to the sociological imagination. Many sociologists embracing intersectionality are engaged in conversation with interdisciplinary programs and committed to social justice research.

The word "intersectionality" is frequently used as a noun describing inclusivity in social justice movements, organizations, and campaigns. In student services and human resources, the word appears alongside "diversity," "multicultural," "tolerance" and "difference." However, "intersectionality" has a particular meaning and use in sociology. I developed this book as an invitation to engage students and inform them about the significance of intersectionality as a concept to help a sociological imagination. As C. Wright Mills explained the sociological imagination, it is the power to connect private troubles with public issues. In each of our lives, thinking about the interactions of race, social class, and gender in everyday life and in the political and economic arena does exactly that. My hope is that this book stimulates students' curiosity about the many complexities of systems of privilege and oppression we encounter on a daily basis.

To begin, I will introduce intersectionality by drawing from experiences we are all familiar with – parenting and childhood. While not all of us are parents, we do recognize the ways our own childhood may not have always reflected the family life depicted in sitcoms or experienced by our friends. What happens when we attempt to plan programs aimed at children but we do not recognize diversity? What limitations are there to providing childcare and other assistance to parents if we assume that all families are the same and have the same needs? Why do some parents and children always seem to fit in, while others always appear as misfits?

Chapter 1 introduces intersectionality by examining the complexities of the interaction of race, class, gender, sexuality, citizenship and age in the diversity found in parenting and childhood. The discussion of parents and children sheds light on why an intersectional approach is significant and what we miss in attempts to capture universal truths in sociology. I introduce how systems of power are apparent through social policies and the institutional practices in the law, education and economy that oppress or privilege certain types of sexuality, citizenship status, class and gender positions. Subsequent chapters break down the major components of intersectionality, social identity and interlocking systems of oppression, and apply the perspective to everyday life and social issues. However, before tackling these topics, I turn to the question, "Where does inter-sectionality come from?"

Chapter 2 traces the critiques of one-dimensional approaches to explaining social inequality. Black feminist scholars and activists writing in the 1970s and 1980s called attention to the way they were excluded from the Black Power Movement, which primarily defined race from the position of Black working-class males, and a Feminist Movement that defined gender primarily from the position of white middle-class women. Scholars traced the roots of race, class and gender intersectionality to Black women's writing by Maria Stewart, Sojourner Truth, and Anna Julia Cooper as early as the 1830s. Early writing and speeches contained a critique of political platforms that did not articulate their social position at the intersection of all three systems of inequality – gender, race and class. This chapter chronicles the major contributions to the development of intersectionality within sociology, which also highlights why certain concepts emerged as scholars aimed to understand social inequality. Actually, the concept "intersectionality" was born from activism and social justice struggles like the Civil Rights and Feminist Movements. Scholars joined with these to develop frameworks that incorporated marginalized voices.

I then explore ways of using intersectionality in a sociological approach to everyday life. Chapter 3 focuses on everyday life experiences on campus. I illustrate the complexities of lived experiences through the narratives of deaf African American college students, and working-class women, predominantly women of color, employed as janitors. I draw from Reshawna Chapple's (2012) and Becky Petitt's (2008) dissertations to analyze how the intersectionality of everyday life functions on university campuses. Both scholars' ethnographies capture experiences of everyday life that usually go unnoticed and unacknowledged. Chapple's and Petitt's research identifies social practices and rituals experienced by Black deaf college women and women custodians to demonstrate the ways in which systems of social inequality are reproduced and maintained.

Social identities are the key aspect of mapping an intersectionality perspective. A visual way of conceptualizing intersectionality is by imagining a multi-dimensional graph with axes of gender, race, class, citizenship, ableness, age, sexualities and the like. These characteristics are part of our identity and everyday experiences. Even if one doesn't want to be identified in this way, it is often impossible to control how others see you. Moreover, these identities are not fixed but fluid: which ones are central at any particular moment depends on the time and setting. How family members see you is different from how you are perceived by classmates, fellow workers, teachers or managers. Thus, in a suburban high school class where all the students are white and more or less the same age and social class, gender or sexual identity are more likely to be the central elements identifying your coordinates. Similarly, in a mixed crowd protesting about civil rights, age, race, and social class may be very important axes.

To further illustrate the interaction of systems of oppression and privilege on identity, I will focus on gender identities (which we do not experience apart from our class, age, sexuality or ableness). Chapter 4 provides a framework for understanding why a young masculine middle-class Black man's gender is not socially constructed in the same way as that of a young poor homeless white man. While both may share a heterosexual masculine identity, when confronted by police in the inner city investigating a robbery, the social construction of their male identity is likely to place the Black male in harm's way. However, entering a business office, the Black middle-class male is more likely to gain entrance without any disturbance because his social class is primary. This chapter provides the tools for analyzing these experiences and recognizing power structures intersecting and shifting as we move from one social setting or one point in time to another. By examining gender through an inter-sectional lens, I will show the ways in which one identity may be salient in one social setting and another in a different setting; and at the same time, multiple identities are experienced simultaneously. This chapter prepares us to return attention to a more comprehensive overview of systems of oppression and privilege, which were briefly presented in chapter 1.

The question posed in chapter 5 is: "How are systems of oppression and privilege interlocked?" To answer that question, I focus on immigration and the social construction of citizenship. Examining the history of immigration legislation in the US makes evident how citizenship is socially constructed. It is important to recognize that citizenship status is complicated. Having a birthright to citizenship, becoming a natural-ized citizen, having the right to live and work in the country but without full citizenship rights, or undocumented persons who have no rights to be in the country – these different citizenship statuses are linked to power systems interacting with forms of racial, class, gender, and sexual denomination and disability. Examining the legal history of citizenship and immigration in the US makes apparent the interconnection between systems of white supremacy and the complexity of systems of oppression surrounding citizenship, such as nationality, sexuality, gender and age. For example, there was a time when Irish, Italian, Jewish, and Greeks were not considered "white," and Blacks were considered three-fifths of a citizen. Examining the policing of citizenship by laws, the state and other citizens will illustrate the practices and rituals used to produce and maintain privilege and oppression.

Chapter 6 further explores the type of sociological imagination that intersectionality brings to the study of social interaction, institutions and society by analyzing social issues. How does intersectionality examine social issues differently from one-dimensional approaches that consider each social identity as a variable to be controlled for, or simply adding race and gender together rather than all the complex multiple identities of lived experience? Why is this perspective important in understanding social issues? I approach the answers by using contemporary social issues: the wealth gap, the care crisis, and the Black Lives Matter (BLM) Movement. One might assume the wealth gap to be solely a class issue. However, an intersectional approach illuminates ways in which social class alone does not explain the wealth gap between rich and poor. Analysis needs to consider the history of gender, race and citizenship that determined property rights and inheritance laws. I then explore the care crisis which recent sociological literature tends to present as a relatively new social issue concerning families in the last two decades. However, an intersectional perspective demonstrates that issues currently classified as "the care crisis" actually date to an era before middle-class white women entered the labor force. I end this chapter discussing the Black Lives Matter Movement and its use of intersectionality.

The final chapter summarizes important points of intersectionality and highlights the significance of an intersectional sociological imagination in searching for solutions to social inequality.

It is important to note that "gender," "race," and "class" – as well as many other terms we will refer to in this book, such as "sexuality" and "social justice" – are themselves not fixed concepts. They do not have universal, undifferentiated meanings, and much sociological work involves breaking these ideas down to explore what they mean in different settings as social constructions. For instance, the sociology of gender teaches us that it is simplistic to treat gender as a crude categorization of "male" or "female." Scholars of race have shown that racial categories do not exist in "nature," but are social identities assigned to individuals and groups with real outcomes in their life experiences and opportunities. There is a long history of sociological work which tries to define what "class" is and how we measure it: is it about income, is it about tastes and lifestyle, etc.? And the same is true for many of the terms used in this book. This book does not explore each individual concept but what it means to put these categories together – but do bear in mind throughout that each of these social categories is fluid, contested and open to debate.

My goal in writing this book is to introduce intersectionality to students beginning their journey into the field of sociology. I also hope to inspire our future scholars and activists to use an intersectional approach in their research on social inequalities and strategies for building social justice coalitions.

I am indebted to the scholars cited in this work for leading the way with their scholarship. I thank Enobong Hannah Branch and Light Carruyo for inviting me to be a discussant for a panel on Intersectionality. This began my work with Jonathan Skerrett, who has been a tremendous and patient editor to work with. Along the journey to writing this book, Zulema Valdez invited me to co-edit a special issue of *Ethnic and Racial Studies* on "Intersectionality and Entrepreneurship." The project pushed me to read new literature and consider new ways scholars used the concept and the reshaping of their method and analysis. Thanks, Zulema, for the invitation to collaborate. Reshawna Chapple and Becky Petitt, your intersectional analyses of higher education are inspiring! Thank you for sharing your scholarship with me. I thank Eric Margolis for his encouragement and support, especially his willingness to postpone holiday and summer vacations so I could devote more time to research and writing. I appreciate his careful reading and suggestions that greatly improved the final project. He enriches my daily life.

1

Identifying Intersectionality

In 1992, Ms. Foundation launched their project "Take Our Daughters to Work Day" as an effort to counter the impact of sexism, sex discrimination and gendered occupational segregation. Planned activities aimed to build young girls' self-esteem, expose them to male-dominated professions, encourage them to enter highly paid and prestigious fields, and boost girls' self-confidence by exposing them to women employed in nontraditional professions. In 2003, the Ms. Foundation incorporated boys into their educational program "Take Our Daughters and Sons to Work Day," which occurs on the fourth Thursday in April in the US and around November 7 in Canada. The foundation designed the program to enrich the educational experience of children by exposing them "to what a parent or mentor in their lives does during the work day" (http://daughtersandsonstowork.org). For sheltered children of the well-to-do, the world of work is often a hidden and mysterious realm – one that keeps their mothers and fathers working late into the evening or demanding overnight travel. However, for girls and boys whose parents are among the women and men laboring in the low-paid service sector or the underground economy, going to work with mom and dad is more likely an everyday experience and one that will probably lower self-confidence, reduce expectations and damage self-esteem.

Some mothers and fathers have a long history of taking their children to work – sponsored not by the Ms. Foundation but by low wages and the lack of after-school care. This was immediately evident to me in my research on the children of domestic workers. One interviewee from this research project, Olivia, recounted going to work with her mother as a small child. Her mother worked as a live-in maid but, eventually, she negotiated room and board for weekend work and did paid day-work as a housecleaner throughout the gated community her employers resided in. Olivia's childhood memories of going to work with her mother contain stories of learning rules, which she had to do quickly.

> My mother took me to work with her. After a while, I started to realize that I was being taken every day to somebody else's house. Everybody's house had different rules.... My mother says that she constantly had to watch me. She tried to get me to sit still and I'd be really depressed and I'd cry or I wanted to go see things. She didn't want me to touch anything. She was afraid that I was going to break something.... The first thing that I learned was "No touch. No touch." "Don't touch. Don't touch." "Don't touch this. Don't touch that." I told everybody, "Don't touch."

I interviewed other adult children of domestic workers who recalled going to work with their mothers during the summer and holidays when school was not in session. Sometimes they accompanied their mothers in lieu of staying home alone, but, many times, they went to work alongside them. Sometimes their mothers' employers recruited their sons to do yard work and their daughters to babysit. However, like other immigrants and parents of color employed in minimum-wage dead-end jobs, their mothers did not want to make their employment attractive to their children, nor did they want their children to be ashamed that their parent(s) worked hard to make ends meet. Immigrant Mexican fathers were employed as landscapers, construction workers, underground miners or shop mechanics working around toxic chemicals, in male-dominated occupations that offer higher wages than most female-dominated occupations but that can be extremely dangerous jobs. Fathers do not want their daughters working under hazardous conditions and frequently encourage their sons not to follow in their footsteps.

As in the stories I collected in my interviews, there are boys and girls in cities across the United States who wait at the end of the service counter until their moms finish their shift at cleaners', restaurants, and beauty salons. In immigrant and refugee neighborhoods, girls and boys too young for work permits may help their parents doing piecework in their homes; they work as food vendors in the evening and on weekends, or wait for their mothers in sweatshops, garment factories or nail salons at the end of the school day. Often these same children serve as important interpreters for their parents negotiating working conditions and pay with mono-English-speaking employers or clients (Park 2005). In tobacco-growing states in the US (Human Rights Watch 2014) and corn-producing areas in western Quebec, Canada (Kielburger & Kielburger 2011), children as young as 12 and 13 years accompany their parents to the farms during the summer to work the fields, just as they did generations ago.

Celebrating a "Take Our Daughters to Work Day" makes sense in the US if we assume that the experiences of boy and girl children and their parents are universal, and only gender shapes and influences their childhood. However, assumptions around universal experiences of childhood and parenthood ignore the ways in which class, race and citizenship privilege some and disadvantage other families, neighborhoods, schools and workers. Only by denying these significant differences can one expect all girls and their parents to experience "Take Our Daughters to Work Day" and related activities similarly. Only by assuming that parents share the same gender-segregated working conditions, income and status in their occupations can an educational program aimed at exposing children to career opportunities advocate that children accompany their mothers and fathers to work. From its inception, the program focused on sex stratification and sex discrimination in the labor force and assumed a universal experience of girlhood and parenthood. Fundamentally, the "Take Our Daughter [or even our sons] to Work" program is flawed by the assumptions not only that parents taking their daughters to work will expose them to higher-paying male-dominated careers but that gender socialization is the major or sole source of social inequality that limits children's aspirations, ignoring class privilege, immigrant status or disability. While occupational segregation by gender continues to be a salient characteristic of the labor force, there are other forms of oppression intersecting in paid employment.

I will examine parenting and childhood to identify the insights intersectionality provides into the activities, experiences and people that most are familiar with on a daily basis. One place to begin is by identifying the barriers, obstacles and disadvantages some parents confront while caring for their children. The ability to fulfill society's social expectations is largely constrained or enhanced by parents' economic, educational and other social positions in society, which in turn determine access to privilege or the degree of oppression they encounter.

The Rubik's Cube Metaphor

A helpful metaphor we might use is that of a Rubik's cube, which has six faces each covered by nine stickers. This visual of six solid colors, white, red, blue, orange, green and yellow, arranged in various combinations in which each face turns independently to mix up the colors, helps in conceptualizing different intersections. A Rubik's cube may be useful to conceptualize the rotating mix of identities and shifting systems of domination which result in certain social identities being more salient than others at a given time and place. A Rubik's cube does not capture the fluidity of systems of domination but it may be useful in visualizing multiple layers of domination and the intersection of systems of oppression.

The Rubik's cube might also serve to demonstrate ways in which sociologists use an intersectional approach to analyze the social dynamics of multiple identities interacting with societies' social hierarchies. Of course, actual lived experience is not static but our analysis requires us to identify social identities and the interaction between different systems of inequality. We begin by recognizing each system of inequality as represented by one of the different colors (though the intersectional Rubik's cube is not necessarily limited to six systems). Once we assign a color to race, class, gender, sexuality, citizenship and abilities, we can begin to analyze the intersection of different dimensions of an individual's personhood. They are all social identities that increase privilege or disadvantages, and position one's access to opportunities. Our positions in various social settings determine the systems of inequality we face and the intersection of individuals' statuses.

Begin to consider the combinations of race, class, gender, sexuality, citizenship and age. What obstacles do gay middle-class Latino fathers face in volunteering at their daughters' first-grade activities? How does this differ from the situation of a heterosexual working poor white mother who is single? What are the different ways in which parents experience their daughters' school's expectation that they volunteer? How do systems of inequality privilege some parents and disadvantage others? Intersectional analysis involves identifying social identities or social hierarchies and examining the systems of inequality that dominate particular social settings and social relationships. Power relationships in settings differ between individuals and groups, and at times privilege race, but, in another setting, class privilege is more pronounced. Intersectional analysis requires uncovering power, privilege and opportunity structures and examining their link to social identities.

Intersectional Analysis of the Inequalities in Parenting and Childhood

A single-axis analysis of inequalities experienced by parents or children only examines one category of a person's identity and results in a limited, one-dimensional and incomplete understanding of inequality. It is impossible to understand the effects of gender, age and class as the sum of "-isms." For example, we do not understand the constraints a poor grandmother might face in caring for her grandchildren by adding up sexism, ageism and classism (i.e., sex + age + class). This grandmother experiences all aspects of her identity simultaneously rather than separate dimensions summed up. One-dimensional approaches have the consequence of creating specific aspects of personhood as the norm, such as being a middle-class grandmother. This erases important differences in the experiences of being a grandmother that occur when class interacts with gender and age. Consider, too, the experiences of 12-year-old children in school. Obviously, not all 12-year-old children experience the same personal rewards in school. White middle-class 12-year-olds may relate better to traditional textbooks based on their experiences of family life. Some working-class immigrant children of color may not relate to textbooks that describe a nuclear family with a father who leaves to work dressed in a suit carrying a briefcase. If these immigrant children are from a non-English-speaking country, it will be difficult for them to confront teachers speaking only English. It is essential to untangle the effects of many dimensions interacting simultaneously. Children who share the same social class but not the same religion, race or sexual orientation are not going to have experiences identical to those of other children the same age. The different social identities people have in society are complex but intersectionality provides a standpoint for making sociological sense of broad categories of people.

Race, class, gender and sexuality differences have real consequences in people's lived experiences and life chances for acquiring access to healthy food, quality education, excellent healthcare, and housing that provides a safe environment. If parents can afford to live in affluent neighborhoods, they are likely to have local grocery stores that carry fresh fruits and vegetables. Others live in what are termed "food deserts" – frequently, they shop at the corner store that does not have fresh produce. Increasingly, the working poor are isolated in suburbs, lack personal vehicles, and are faced with inadequate public transportation to get to shopping centers to purchase food. Affluent-neighborhood schools receive more funding, hire teachers that are more experienced, have the latest computer and science technology to offer students a college preparatory curriculum and provide course materials that confirm their white privilege. Upper- and middle-class parents are able to access good health and dental care and do not experience the inefficiencies in the healthcare system. The working poor find access limited to overcrowded emergency rooms. This is true for the majority of poor workers who are white. Populations of the working poor who are Asian, Muslim, African American or

Latino/a face additional discriminatory treatment based on phenotype or dress.

Understanding parenting and childhood through the lens of intersectionality presents a more nuanced understanding of social inequalities. Intersectionality makes visible dynamics of privilege and subordination in changing circumstances. For instance, an African American father driving his daughter to a private school before heading to his office on Wall Street will probably not encounter the sexism, racism or classism that an African American mother faces while taking her daughter on the subway to an inner-city charter school before heading to her job as a dockworker. Race alone cannot explain their differences. Gender alone cannot describe their circumstances, nor can class. Being an upper-middle-class Black father is not the same racial experience as being a working-class Black mother. Similarly, their daughters' experiences, if explained by only one or two of their social identities, are not complete. In addition, they share other social positions, such as being a citizen and non-disabled, among others.

Now, consider focusing on sexuality and intersectionality. Gay fathers, lesbian mothers or transgender parents experience a legal system that questions or denies their rights as parents, particularly custody or joint custody rights when divorcing straight partners. Low-income LGBTQ parents are frequently discriminated against when they participate in school activities designed for white middle-class heterosexual parents. If one or both of the parents are men or women of color, these social identities position them differently on the axis of privilege or subordination and they would also be concerned about protecting their children from homophobic forms of racism they may experience when engaging with family members, classmates, teachers and others. Forms of discrimination experienced in their neighborhoods, families and workplace depend upon access to race, class, and gender or citizenship privileges.

Another example would be intersectionality and citizenship status. During periods of strong anti-immigrant sentiment, racialized Latino parents encounter frequent citizenship inspection and humiliation in front of their children as they attempt to participate in school activities. This is compounded in interaction with police officers and access to social services available to other families. Latino families who have been citizens for generations are frequently profiled as undocumented and treated with disrespect. Undocumented immigrant parents with US-born children risk their livelihood and deportation if they participate in school activities or even drive their children to school. Thus, US-born children of undocumented parents may never experience a family trip or vacation because their parents avoid being in public together out of fear of deportation – if one parent was deported, the other must remain to care for their family. Jobs for poor working-class males, such as landscaping and construction, expose them more to law enforcement than their wives, who may be working in the homes of the middle and upper-middle classes as domestics and nannies. Gay and lesbian immigrants of color are likely to confront more barriers in reuniting with deported partners or sponsoring their relatives.

The intersectionality of class, gender, race and citizenship differences shapes people's experiences every day, and limits and constrains the choices they can make. It is a form of psychological reductionism to limit discussions to individual choices; individual choice blurs social structures and hierarchies of power which privilege or subordinate parents in different ways. While individuals do have agency, social institutions constrain and limit their choices. Identifying and examining these institutions reveal the ways that social identities interact, and the privileges and oppressions within which choices are made. Seeing parenting as a universal activity overlooks the unequal circumstances individuals face as mothers and fathers living within different intersections of religion, race, ethnicity, class, sexuality, gender and disability. In the next section, I will explore the significance of intersectionality in identifying the range of differences found in research on parenting.

Examining Parenting through an Intersectional Paradigm

Parenting is an activity mothers and fathers engage in with their children that is generally recognized as "universal," but research shows that the specific types of tasks they carry out are frequently not at all identical. In the US, mothers are the chief caretaker, even when employed outside the home; and fathers are most commonly the main breadwinners. Mothers are more likely to be the parent who makes sure the children bathe and provides them with clean clothes, as well as the parent who stays up at night caring for a sick child (Coltrane 2000; Gottzén 2011). Fathers frequently spend their time with their children playing (Segal 1990), tending to participate in fun time rather than the everyday tasks that involve feeding, cleaning, laundry or shopping (DeVault 1991). Fathers do excel at assuming responsibility for their children's sports, however (Root & Wooten 2008; Shows & Gerstel 2009; Gottzén & Kremer-Sadlik 2012). Parents further perform gender identities through their involvement with these sports – mothers tend to volunteer as team moms, and fathers as coaches or assistant coaches (Messner 2009). Coaching or supervising their sons and daughters in sports activities are more public types of childcare than that of team moms. The increased popularity of "family values" further enhances gendered approaches to parenting. Here, men's roles are perceived as those of protectors, providers and leaders while women are caregivers – both roles are represented as natural, universal and unchanging (Coltrane & Galt 2000). While gender goes a long way in explaining differences between mothers' and fathers' activities, intersectional perspectives offer a more complex and nuanced understanding of parenting.

What type of parenting occurs in families with only fathers? Think about the way parenting changes when not divided between mothers and fathers. Men in single-father households do not limit their interaction with their children but engage in all the gendered activities traditionally characterized as "mothering," without the assistance of women (Doucet 2006). This finding suggests that "mothering" and "fathering" are gender performances and are not inherent characteristics of either men or women. Thus, gender performance appears to motivate the continuation of the traditional division of household labor between husbands and wives (Shelton 1992). However, traditional gendering roles in caretaking are far from a fixed experience. Interestingly, working-class fathers tend to take a more egalitarian approach to parenting than middle-class fathers (Shows & Gerstel 2009). There are increasing numbers of stay-at-home dads, which further challenges traditional gender roles (Chesley 2011). In the case of race and ethnic differences, Latino fathers in dual-wage families (where both mother and father are in paid employment) are more likely to do more household work (Coltrane & Valdez 1993). African American fathers employed full-time do a larger portion of household labor than those who work part-time or are unemployed (Shelton & John 1993). The patterns are the same among white fathers.

Different systems of parenting interaction become visible when considering the intersection of sexuality. Gay and lesbian families may or may not engage in similar gender performances in parenting. The division of labor among gay couples with children tends to divide the primary housework from childrearing, which may be a form of "degendering parenting" (Silverstein et al. 2002). Mothering and fathering outside heterosexual norms, gays and lesbians are less likely to assign tasks rigidly and are more flexible in the division of labor, including childcare. Lesbian mothers who adopt children engage in more egalitarian practices than lesbian mothers who create biological families (Ciano-Boyce & Shelley-Sireci 2002). Additional differences appear if you consider that gay and lesbian families do not generally share the same class privileges as heterosexual couples, which also shapes the options involved in making decisions about family roles. As men, gay fathers are likely to earn more than lesbian mothers, and thus have more options such as working fewer hours or hiring a nanny (Downing et al. 2012). White lesbian couples do not appear to exhibit different employment patterns, decision-making processes, parenting or division of care and household work from white middle-class heterosexual couples (Biblarz & Savci 2010). However, Black lesbian couples tend to have different parenting roles if there is a biological mother (she is the one to do more housework and childcare and to have a greater role in decisions about raising the children). Nevertheless, couples do share the role of provider because they value financial independence (Moore 2008).

In considering the range of differences in parenting, it is important to keep in mind the prevailing ideology of motherhood prescribed by childcare experts – it has become a gendered middle-class model of "intensive" or "competitive" mothering, which involves a tremendous amount of time and energy. Some call it "helicopter" mothering. The approach advocates child-centered living, emotionally demanding time and activity, and labor-intensive and financially draining methods of parenting (Hays 1996). This type of mothering is also referred to as that of a "mother–manager" (Rothman 1989). Sharon Hays (1996: 6) created a list characterizing intensive mothering that captures the essence of the mother–manager approach and points to why social class is important:

> Why do many professional-class employed women seem to find it necessary to take the kids to swimming and judo and dancing and tumbling classes, not to mention orthodontists and psychiatrists and attention-deficit specialists?...Why are there aerobics courses for babies, training sessions in infant massage, sibling-preparedness workshops, and designer fashions for two-year-olds? Why must a "good" mother be careful to "negotiate" with her child, refraining from demands for obedience to an absolute set of rules?

While middle-class parents promote their children's self-esteem, provide choices, and negotiate rules (Hays 1996), they rely on class privilege to purchase extracurricular activities and healthcare. Parents employed in high-status professions are in a position to provide their children with private schools and an extensive list of extracurricular activities: private tutors and cultural experiences, including travel and "volunteer" work that prepares them for admission to an Ivy League-level university. Parents' class, race and religious networks can place their sons and daughters in highly competitive internships and provide the educational background to assist their navigation of college and career opportunities (Kendall 2002).

In the global arena of the parenting spectrum, because of the globalized economy, new forms of parenting emerge in response to scarce employment opportunities. Denied access to high-paying jobs, mothers and/or fathers may seek employment in another country, leaving their children in the care of others, usually a female relative. In this case, their major parenting activity focuses on the financial needs of their children, which they fulfill by sending remittances home. This type of activity, recognized as transnational parenting, is more visible as mothers and fathers work abroad to earn enough money for their children's survival and education, and to assist with the needs of their extended families remaining in the homeland. Transnational fathering is a successful strategy for fulfilling a gendered parenting role as breadwinner, which enhances their children's opportunities for continuing their education (Dreby 2010). Unable to engage in face-to-face interaction with their children, mothers and fathers working abroad express their love and parenting role by fulfilling their children's economic needs.

Under these conditions, providing material goods, such as schoolbooks, new clothing and electronics, becomes symbolic of emotional attachments between child and parent (Pribilsky 2007). Like migrant mothers, migrant fathers have found many of these innovative ways of maintaining a presence in their children's lives while they are working abroad (Roer-Strier et al. 2005). In some cases, such as those documented in a study on Ecuadoran fathers, they might rely on traditional ways of keeping in touch with their children through letter-writing and photographs (Pribilsky 2007). However, technology has transformed transnational parenting by creating the means for more contact between mothers and fathers working abroad when their children reside in their homeland. Communication across national borders is increasingly available through better mail services, cell phones, and the use of less expensive calling cards, social media and Skype. Parenting activities include sending remittances, making phone calls, and posting on Facebook and other social media for mothers and fathers who are part of the globalized workforce. Recognizing the different activities that transnational parents use to engage with their children debunks the strongly held belief that absent or nonresidential fathers are not part of their families. Among these parents are workers in the gig economy that includes jobs in the tech, oil and engineering fields, and the military. Intersectional research approaches identify the different strategies used by migrant workers as transnational parents, demonstrating that their parent–child relationships are strong and are important (Arditti et al. 2014).

The work involved in parenting is not the same for everyone; and, even though childcare experts espouse a universal definition of required activities, parents fulfilling their childcare obligations engage in a wide range of diverse activity influenced by a combination of gender, race, class, sexuality, and citizenship. However, only parenting practices such as competitive and intensive mothering are dominant forms by which society evaluates other parenting. Differences marked as inferior (such as being a nonresidential father) or superior (such as taking part in all the activities listed by Sharon Hays above) indicate that there are systems of oppression in operation. To further aid understanding of intersectionality, I'll provide a more detailed description of the complexity of choices and constraints that working parents face in finding childcare.

Childcare for Working Parents

To examine parents' decisions surrounding childcare, let's begin by looking at the constraints that employment hours have on choices of childcare. In the case of two parents working different shifts in a hospital as a nursing assistant or a physician, each may have complex schedules to juggle sleep and childcare. However, salary differences between nursing assistants and physicians offer completely different economic resources for addressing childcare needs. Physicians are able to afford to have a partner who is a stay-at-home parent or works part-time, or have the option to hire a live-in nanny. A nursing assistant with a toddler or young child cannot afford to hire a nanny and must find other solutions, relying on kin care or a partner with a different work schedule. Physicians and nursing assistants who are single parents face other obstacles in acquiring reliable childcare if they work late and cannot rely on another parent. If they live with or near extended-family members, kin care may be an option on a weekly basis or as back-up. However, if the hospital provides on-site care facilities for working parents, the search for childcare becomes a much more level playing field, whether for physicians or nursing assistants.

If parents are not white, English-speaking, Christian, and non-disabled, they are likely to encounter additional constraints assessing the care their children need even when on-site care is provided. For example, parents of color seeking childcare, regardless of economic circumstances, are likely to include a concern about racial diversity to protect their child from treatment as an inferior, a token or exotic by the other children or adults. If the family's religion restricts their diet or activities in ways different from the larger society, their search will include a caretaker familiar with these religious practices. In the case of gay and lesbian parents, their search for childcare, as well as the process of choosing schools, will assess the likelihood of discrimination against their children based on their parents' sexuality (Biblarz & Savci 2010).

Disabled working parents encounter other obstacles in their search for dependable, reliable and adequate childcare. Deaf parents or children are limited to caretakers who have the ability to communicate with them. If a disabled person uses a wheelchair, they may need to find day care that is physically accessible for them. Parents' searches for childcare include a mix of social identities that facilitate or disadvantage their efforts.

In a related example, consider the choices and constraints that working immigrant parents of color might face in finding affordable, safe, reliable and adequate childcare. Their search for childcare might include a requirement for a bilingual and bicultural environment (Utall 2002). Parents who are monolingual in a language other than English will need to find a caretaker who speaks the same language. Immigrants employed in low-wage jobs are likely to piece together caretaking among relatives and older children in the household. If you work nine to five, churches, mosques and community organizations may offer after-school programming that assists in covering childcare needs. For parents who are undocumented workers, the burden is further complicated by the fear of leaving their child with anyone who is not a close family member because of the possibility of an immigration raid at work or being stopped by the police on their way to or from work (Yoshikawa 2012). If stopped by immigration, these parents may deny being parents in fear that the state will place their children in protective custody and they will never see them again. Therefore, the person placed in the caretaker role must be someone who not only can care for their child while they work but also is committed to caring for the child if the parent is deported. This type of caretaker needs to be able to maintain communication with the parent until completion of arrangements to unify the family. As these various cases demonstrate, a mixture of race, class, gender, sexuality, and more present advantages and disadvantages that influence parents' decisions about childcare.

Without considering the interacting systems of power, it is easy to miss the variations in the living and working conditions mothers and fathers face in their daily lives. In poor communities, parenting incorporates efforts to keep children from the harms of substandard housing, such as overcrowding, city blocks filled with diesel exhaust fumes from nearby highways, and unkempt sidewalks neglected by the city. Parents might also confront illegal "red-lining" restrictions preventing them from buying or renting in affluent neighborhoods because of their race, religion, or the number of children in the household. Parents without reliable cars confront inadequate public transportation to take children to the doctor or extracurricular activities, and for other parenting errands. Low-income neighborhoods are isolated from major grocery stores, parks, libraries and museums. Some of these neighborhoods are under intensive police surveillance, and in others soliciting police assistance or receiving immediate emergency services when calling 911 is difficult. Having access to these "opportunities" has consequences for life expectancy and well-being.

As demonstrated at the beginning of this chapter, Ms. Foundation programming highlights the assumption that the lived experiences of parents are universal and only shaped by gender, rather than a mixture of a wide range of forms of privilege and oppression. Focusing on childcare through an intersectional approach further demonstrates how the social positions of mothers and fathers present diverse sets of circumstances for caring for and educating children, and preparing them for adulthood. Moving on in the exploration of intersectionality, consider the interacting systems of power at play as parents face limited abilities to shape socialization processes, such as schooling.

Parenting, Choosing Schools and Socialization

Schooling is as much about socialization – the reproduction and passing on of culture – as it is about acquiring knowledge. All parents are concerned about the culture children learn, including big things like religion and language, and smaller things like table manners and polite forms of interaction. Hindu, Muslim and Jewish parents may prefer religious schools that embrace non-Christian religion and culture. Immigrant parents might seek schools that offer students a choice of learning in more than one language. Single, white poor mothers may well want their child socialized to middle-class norms. LGBTQ parents may seek out schools that offer a learning environment promoting diversity and inclusion.

Socialization occurs through parents' networks – perhaps an active temple or mosque group, a country club, influential clients or customers, generous relatives, or an engaged community. Parents' networks are gendered, class- and race-based. An African American father who is a barber with his own shop is likely to have a predominantly Black male clientele. Given continued racial and class segregation in US neighborhoods, his shop is highly unlikely to be located near a neighborhood populated by judges, the state senator or a university president. In contrast, an African American father who owns his own law firm is more likely to be a member of a country club and play golf with a federal judge, the CEOs of major companies in the state or the owner of an investment company. Both of these fathers are able to assist their teenage sons and daughters with summer employment but their networks are so vastly different that the "opportunities" obtained from the summer job will not have the same effect on their résumés when applying for scholarships, grants or college. These networks are vital in obtaining knowledge about choosing colleges and careers. Single, white poor mothers employed in minimum-wage jobs do not have the social network to assist their sons or daughters in selecting college-prep classes. They are unlikely to have the flexible work schedules required to attend parents' night or to have the education to assist their children with homework in high school, particularly if they are high school drop-outs (Chaudry 2004). While these parents are no different in caring deeply about the educational success of their children from parents with more resources, access to "opportunities" are structurally constrained in multiple intersecting ways.

The constraints on parents' choices and decisions can appear obvious and solely class-based – either you can afford to purchase a commodity or service or you cannot. However, economic circumstances are not only a class issue. Women still earn less than men do. Parents entering the labor force without documented status are usually restricted to low-wage work without benefits. Parents of color continue to encounter discrimination in the labor force and are likely to earn less than their white counterpart does. Disabled parents also face limited opportunities in the labor market. Nevertheless, like middle-class parents, working-class and poor parents "share a set of fundamental assumptions about the importance of putting their children's needs first and dedicating themselves to providing what is best for their kids, as they understand it" (Hays 1996: 86). This is true for undocumented mothers and fathers, parents of color, disabled parents, single mothers and other parents lacking the resources of white professionals.

The challenges faced by working parents constrained by economic circumstances are many. Parents working full-time in low-wage jobs frequently juggle more than one job to make ends meet. Working-class and poor parents cannot afford private lessons to enable their children to excel in music, dance or the sciences. In 2016, the federal-government-mandated minimum wage of $7.25 per hour had not changed since 2009. Arizona, Colorado, Maine and Washington approved gradual increases to $12 an hour; only California and New York are gradually increasing the minimum wage to $15 an hour; and 42 percent of workers, nationally, make less than $15. More than half of Black, Latino, and women workers make less than $15; many of these workers are 35 years and older. Employers avoid benefits by not allowing workers a 40-hour week. Generally, a single low-wage worker requires $15 and a 40-hour week to make ends meet (Tung et al. 2015). Today, women in the US make only 77 cents for every dollar earned by male workers, which is a 23 percent wage gap. However, African American women only make 64 cents, and Latina women only 55 cents, for each dollar earned by men.

However, employment and family wealth are only two of the structural constraints, and additional obstacles exist. Working poor families of color, for example, are frequently limited to schools in their poor and working-class neighborhood, which tend to lack adequate funding and are staffed by inexperienced teachers who are likely to emphasize discipline rather than teaching because their classes are overcrowded. When school funding becomes tied to student performance measured through standardized tests, teachers focus their time on teaching to pass the exam rather than sparking students' creativity, developing a love for reading, or encouraging innovative thinking. Whether rural or urban, underfunded schools lack the resources for an education that prepares students to excel in math and sciences or other highly valued skills in order to succeed at a competitive university. They are unlikely to provide safe environments to protect students of color, or gay or transgender children, from bullying, or to provide programming that enhances the self-esteem of girls. Cutbacks in public education resulting from reallocation of monies to charter schools result in eliminating art, vocational shop classes, and music, which are courses that connect students to school. In the case of Arizona, every family can donate $1,090 to a school and subtract the entire amount from their state tax bill. Establishing a charter school, and reaching out to inform a social network that this is a "Jewish, Mormon, Christian" – or whatever – school, drains money from the public school system, further impoverishing it; at the same time it provides riches for the rich. Even in school districts that allow school choice and open enrollment, mothers living in low-income communities are likely to face long commutes to access additional resources for their children.

The first priority for working-class and poor mothers is the physical survival of their children (Edin & Kefalas 2005; Romero 2011a). They stress children's formal education, establish rules and emphasize obedience (Hays 1996). These parents make hard choices to secure a good education for their children, and they expect their children to be more responsible and more disciplined than do wealthier parents (Nelson 2010). Unlike middle-class parents scheduling children's activities, these parents are more likely to allow children "long stretches of leisure time, child-initiated play, clear boundaries between adults and children, and daily interactions with kin" (Lareau 2003: 3). This "free-range" type of parenting emphasizes independence and self-sufficiency (Pimentel 2012), which accommodates poor and working-class parents' work schedules and the lack of money for activities such as music or sports lessons. At the same time, parents of self-sufficient children have been turned in to the authorities for "neglect" when they allow a 10-year-old to take his 6-year-old brother to the park. Researchers studying families of color note that these findings based solely on class do not always consider that parenting in low-income Black families involves the belief that "it takes a village to raise a child," and other-mother (e.g., Collins 1990) and other-father (e.g., Billingsley 1968; Stack 1974; Hamer 2001) roles are taken on by extended kin and community. Poor and working-class Latinos, and many immigrants, live in households with extended-family members, particularly multi-generational, which is an important strategy for caring for children and the elderly (Blank & Torrecilha 1998).

In the overview of parenting activities and sexuality discussed previously, the intersection of sexuality raises other circumstances that must be addressed by mothers and fathers. Gay, lesbian and transgender parents face challenges confronting their children's school activities structured around heterosexual relations. Like single mothers, lesbian mothers and their children experience exclusion in such school functions as the yearly father-and-daughter dance. Like many remarried parents, the majority of lesbian mothers (84.4 percent White mothers; 84.9 percent Black mothers) become parents through marriage to or cohabitation with people who already have children (Morris et al. 2002), which does not fit the traditional family model. While schools are becoming more aware of the diversity among families, administrators and teachers are not doing enough to address the bullying that the children of LGBTQ parents confront. Reflecting on their own experiences of homophobia, LGBTQ parents attempt to find neighborhoods and schools that offer a safe environment for their children. Gay and lesbian parents try to protect their children from discrimination, particularly bullying from classmates (Biblarz & Savci 2010). For instance, Catherine Nixon's (2011) research on working-class lesbian parents found that these parents use their own negative experiences of marginalization when students as emotional resources to protect their own children from bullying, impart life skills, and advance values of equality and acceptance of others. Nevertheless, class position limits the economic resources available and restricts the range of choices that middle-class LGBTQ parents have in finding an inclusive school that values acceptance and diversity. As children reach adolescence, their own sexuality becomes an issue for straight as well as gay and lesbian families. Old-fashioned physical bullying is amplified and made even more toxic in cyberbullying. It is estimated that "3 million kids per month are absent from school due to bullying. 20% of kids cyberbullied think about suicide, and 1 in 10 attempt it. 4500 kids commit suicide each year. Suicide is the No. 3 killer of teens in the US" (www.cyberbullyhotline.com/07-10-12-scourge.html).

Parents of color also face concerns about their children's safety and confront different circumstances in raising their children. For most non-white parents, they cannot rely on schools, media or other social institutions to provide positive role models or images to develop strong self-esteem. Two examples that illustrate parents' concerns are the controversies over teaching ethnic studies in high school in Arizona, and the demands for more textbooks on Mexican Americans than the one proposed by the school board in Texas. Parents instilling racial pride have done additional work to expose their children to their own histories, which are all too often isolated to the school textbook section on slavery, the American Indian wars, the Mexican–American War or the annexation of Hawaii, Alaska or Puerto Rico. The additional parenting may be difficult for those parents working long hours or lacking the educational background in their own formal schooling. Along with the absence of their history and culture, for some Blacks, Latinos/as, American Indians and Asian Americans, parenting involves addressing colorism. Research on parenting in Black families indicates that fathers are more likely than mothers to address colorism aimed at their daughters' dark skin, which is a form of discrimination (Wilder & Cain 2011). Parents from communities with histories of colonialism must also confront color socialization that may hurt their children (Glenn 2009). Socializing children to celebrate their non-white racial features is a challenging parenting activity because it runs counter to whiteness normalized in commercials, television and film.

Latino and African American parents face the difficult conversation with their sons and daughters about the ways to stay safe in police encounters. Following the fatal shooting of 17-year-old Trayvon Martin in Florida in 2012, by a neighborhood watch coordinator, President Obama reflected: "this could have been my son. Another way of saying that is Trayvon Martin could have been me 35 years ago" (The White House 2013). The Black Lives Matter Movement calls attention to the risks people of color face when confronted by the police, and the realities parents face in socializing their children. The war against drugs and the war against gangs have demonized young men of color more than white adolescent teenagers. Communities of color have a long history of "being policed" rather than "being protected and served" by law enforcement. African American fathers need to converse with their sons about understanding how society – and the police in particular – socially constructs their physical presence as a menace and dangerous. This conversation becomes particularly crucial when young men of color begin driving, because police stops can be extremely dangerous. This is not a new phenomenon: more than 20 years ago, Jerome McCristal Culp Jr. referred to the conversation as "the rules of engagement of black malehood" (1993). Parents reported coaching both their sons and daughters how to behave: "don't hang out in crowds, be polite, don't make any sudden moves, carry identification, ask to make a phone call, refuse to answer incriminating questions" (Lee 1997). Black and Latino/a mothers and fathers know that teaching their children to be calm and polite while having their civil rights violated may one day save their lives in police encounters.

The above examples show that a combination of parents' social positions interact in various times and places, presenting advantages or disadvantages for childcare and for accessing quality education and socializing processes that are inclusive of families' racial, sexual and class history. However, education is only one of the social institutions that attempt to establish standardized patterns of behavior. Other social institutions shaping our interactions include the economy, law, politics, religion and the family. Institutional practices shape our families in the policies and laws passed, governing eligible partners for marriage, lawful sexual practices, reproduction, state-recognized kinship, and eligibility for family social services. The intersections of systems of domination are visible if one considers the various social identities that position individuals differently in social institutions, maintaining power structures. The next section moves to a more in-depth examination of these social institutions and the way they structure people's daily lives.

Discussion questions

1   Compare and contrast a one-dimensional with a multi-dimensional analysis of social inequality in analyzing childhood experiences.
2   Map out and explain how the intersection of your own social identities privileges or disadvantages you in different social settings.

Recognizing Institutional Practices at Work

Who can marry and raise a family? Regulated by the state, marriage is the primary institution that legitimates parenting. The significance of marriage, as recognized by the state, is evident in the benefits, rights, and privileges gained through marital status. These are particularly important for parents' ability to care for children. In the US, marriage ensures that spouses have rights to benefits including Medicare/Medicaid, veteran's disability, insurance, and social security payments. The institution allows the surviving spouse access to inheritance. Marriage also carries the responsibility for financially supporting and raising children. Benefits include lower rates for federal and state income tax, insurance policies for automobiles, coverage on employment health insurance plans and access to "family only" services offered by clubs, organizations and neighborhood centers. Spouses get officially recognized kin that includes mothers-in-law, fathers-in-law, sisters-in-law and brothers-in-law. Family law regulates gender and sexuality by defining marriage and family, and establishing paternity and child support (Hamer 2001; Hobson 2002; Orloff & Monson 2002; Kim 2011).

When a parenting unit is sanctioned by the state through marriage, this provides extensive benefits for couples and families, but the institution also establishes the norms of parenting, mothering, fathering and family arrangements:

> Throughout Western societies, motherhood has long been seen as women's "natural" function and even duty, yet the *right* to mother is not firmly established in the law, nor do social arrangements guarantee women the wherewithal to fulfill their socially and culturally ordained obligations. These conflicting values are nowhere more evident than in contemporary America, where motherhood continues to be extolled but where individual women must claim the right to actually *be* mothers. (Michel 1999: 37)

Traditional norms of good mothering implied the biological mother who was a stay-at-home mom. However, this is no longer the majority situation: in 2012, only about 29 percent of all mothers were stay-at-home moms (Cohen et al. 2014). Mothering – and, more generally, parenting – occurs in living arrangements that legal, religious and cultural systems were not structured to promote or support. For example, decades after the landmark case *Loving* v. *Virginia* (1967), making interracial marriage legal, interracial married couples faced barriers and challenges to parenting their mixed-race children. They were the targets of racist attacks, shunned in many communities, and denied housing in White-dominated neighborhoods. Until recently in the US, only a heterosexual man and woman could marry but now the privileges and rights have been extended to same-sex partners in another landmark Supreme Court decision, *Obergefell* v. *Hodges* (2015). For most of this country's history, no state allowed or recognized same-sex marriages. However, the legalization of these marriages in 2015 did not automatically change all state, educational and religious practices that benefit heterosexual marriages, families and parents, or eliminate the disadvantages same-sex couples face. A closer look at the parenting and family experiences of same-sex couples illustrates the institutional practices maintaining the beliefs that people are either a man or a woman and that there is a natural tendency to adopt traditional gender roles and a heterosexual orientation. This viewpoint, known as heteronormativity, is built into many institutional practices.

To begin the examination of LGBTQ parenting experiences, it is important to confront the traditional assumptions that mothers and fathers have always implied heterosexuality (Bigner & Bozett 1990). Working-class lesbian parents face middle-class heterosexual constructions of mothering that exclude them and often perceive them as "deviant mothers" (Nixon 2011), or even worse – as a "sexual threat to children" (Richardson 1996: 280). Stares or actions of avoidance from neighbors and other mothers at school are daily experiences that convey lesbian parents' violation of heteronormativity. As noted earlier, working-class lesbian mothers may emphasize protecting their children from the bullying experiences that they encountered in schools, and worry that their sexuality may be the cause of bullying their children endure. Middle-class lesbian parents with access to more progressive schools are more likely to focus solely on promoting their children's educational achievements (Nixon 2011). Nevertheless, like gay fathers, lesbian mothers confront heteronormative institutional practices that invalidate their families. School, social services and other forms and documents used to enroll students require the name of the mother and father, typically allowing the listing of one mother or one father. While LGBTQ mothers and fathers challenge these categories, these actions may bring unwanted attention to the parents' sexuality and create discomfort and an unwelcoming environment for their children (Vinjamuri 2015).

Gay fathers are not immune to heterosexual constructions of parenting and fatherhood, particularly if their children are not from a former heterosexual marriage. "Even though desires for parenthood may be similar in some situations to heterosexuals' feelings, lesbians' and gay men's access to adoption is mediated by a bureaucratic apparatus that affects the conditions under which they can parent" (Berkowitz 2009: 118). Some state laws still limit or prohibit adoption by gays and lesbians. Gays encounter similar bans in international adoptions that exclude single men, or encounter restrictions on the age of the child available to them (Lewin 2009). Gendered workplace practices, such as maternity leave rather than parental leave, make it difficult for working gay fathers (or straight fathers for that matter) to spend time home with their new child without fear of losing their jobs. Although some gay fathers may benefit from the Family and Medical Leave Act (1993), which is a job-protected leave for caregiving, the Act excludes many workers. Since the leave does not require pay, employees working for companies that do not include paid leave in their benefit may not be able to afford to take an unpaid leave or may only afford a few weeks. Some companies only provide paid leave for mothers but not fathers.

Gay fathers committed to hands-on parenting are likely to experience work–family tension (Goldberg et al. 2012). Gay fathers who adopt children frequently encounter everyday interactions that call attention to the absence of a female partner or mother, and general confusion and surprise that they are gay fathers – fatherhood runs counter to the stereotypes of gay men as having uncommitted and unstable intimate relationships (Ryan 2007). Encounters with authority, such as police officers, nurses in an emergency ward, or airport security inquiring about the absence of the child's mother are all too common. Questions about "Where is mommy?" become embedded with assumptions that children are unsafe without mothers and only mothers can parent competently (Vinjamuri 2015). Gay men's parenting abilities are always suspect rather than assumed. A framed family photograph on an office desk, of a father walking hand-in-hand with their child or pushing a baby carriage, may generate expressions of confusion or disapproval.

Gay and lesbian families with children do not fit the heteronormative structure of the nuclear family. The range of configurations of these families may include biological as well as non-biological relationships. Lesbians and gays may be parenting children living in another home, may be single parents, parenting foster or adopted children, or co-parenting with a partner (Allen & Demo 1995). Lesbians joining families with children from previous marriages may choose to be step-parents (Patterson 2000), though these women may struggle to assert their rights as step-parents because of the father's and paternal grandparents' objections (Hequembourg 2004). Family arrangements among gay families may also include ties that cross class, racial and national boundaries, not frequently found in heterosexual families (Stacey 2004, 2005, 2006). Many gay and lesbian families develop an extensive social network that parents can call upon for support through illnesses and periods of crisis (Dewaele et al. 2011).

Heteronormativity functions to identify family structures that are not based on the nuclear norm as deviant "through racialized, gendered, classed, and sexualized discourses – and subsequently denying these family structures certain rights and privileges granted to the heteronormative subject" (Battle & Ashley 2008: 8). Ideological and institutional practices treat not only gay and lesbian families negatively, but all family arrangements with persons outside the heterosexual nuclear family. Examining other family structures reveals ways they too encounter opposition. Members of diverse family structures confront norms that advocate and support middle-class families that place value on "autonomy, including autonomous relations between generations and siblings once they reach adulthood" (Newman 1999: 192). Cross-generational or extended family activities, such as meals, attending school events, going to church, picnicking, playing basketball or biking, that regularly include cousins, aunts, uncles, grandparents and fictitious kin, such as godparents, do not fit this model and are more likely found among the urban poor, communities of color, and immigrant neighborhoods. Informal adoptions of relatives' or neighbors' children are common in some communities (Hill 1977, 1993). Asian American and many immigrant family households frequently include grandparents (McLoyd et al. 2000). In these families, extended kin are important networks for job opportunities, assisting in childcare, and sources of potential economic survival, but they are often invisible in traditional interpretations of the family. For instance, mainstream society classifies the men in single mothers' lives as absent, focusing only on the traditional nuclear family model – but this does not capture the complexity of daily interactions with uncles, fathers, brothers, sons, boyfriends, and husbands and ex-husbands: "Family responsibilities, including financial and emotional support, elder and child caretaking, and other household duties are frequently shared through support networks that may involve extended family and friends' participation in a variety of familial roles" (Cahill et al. 2003: 87). In her study of working poor families in Harlem, Newman (1999: 198) found some of these men "support the households they live in and often provide regular infusions of cash, food, and time to the mothers and their children with whom they do not live."

Intersectionality helps us to begin to understand the role that laws, religion, schools and other social institutions play in positioning parents and children in different social locations, which provides disadvantages for some and advantages for others. In the next section, I will explore how state–market–family relations shape families.

Discussion questions

1   How have various social institutions, such as the law, economics and religion, shaped social relations among people you identify as members of your own family?
2   Explain, with examples, how heteronormativity is part of economics, religion and education.

State–Market–Family and Institutional Practices Shaping Family Structures

Institutional practices established by law and the market reproduce race, class, gender, sexuality, age and citizenship privileges. Employment conditions created by the state and market have consequences for mothers' and fathers' abilities to parent, and create both opportunities and barriers. Fulfilling the "ideal mother" or "ideal worker" standards assumes access to privileges and opportunities, but despite a century of civil rights changes, a brief overview of the laws regulating marriage, labor and immigration reveals past and present legal restrictions that benefit white, upper-middle-class, heterosexual male citizens. Institutional structures locate fathers and mothers in different social positions enhancing or denying access to privileges.

The nuclear family is peculiar in human history, where family had been organized around kin, tribe and type. In the middle ages, with such a high death rate, the "commune" or village was the center of caregiving for peasants, as well as nobility. Under capitalism, the enclosure of common land pushed men into factory work, which made breadwinner and caregiver roles mutually exclusive. Previously everyone, man, woman and child, performed both roles. That was still common on the American frontier: children took care of children while both parents worked the land. The history of the institution of marriage is important in understanding the development of social policy enhancing and maintaining the nuclear family, as well as structuring benefits around a complex combination of social identities. This history explains the strong hold that the gendered "breadwinner–caregiver" model has in making parenting decisions between men and woman appear natural and inevitable (LaRossa 1997). However, the normalization of a heterosexual nuclear type of parenting and family life is produced by institutional arrangements (Lewis 1997). State–market–family relations in the US hold parents responsible for the care of their children but the state does not provide citizenship-based benefits or publicly supported employment to assist in meeting this responsibility.

The intersectional dynamics of race, gender and class systems of domination are evident in institutional practices that oppressed Black mothers. Dating back to the early days of slavery, unlike middle-class white women, who were perceived as unemployable because they were mothers, Black women were perceived as "employable mothers" and had no privileges granted to them for motherhood. Even while pregnant, they had to labor alongside men. Public officials controlled Black women's labor by treating unemployed Black mothers as idle when supported by their husbands; and during times of labor shortage, being unemployed and being a full-time mother were grounds for arrest (Glenn 2004). In most regions of the country, Black men were unable to find full-time employment during the Jim Crow era from 1877 to 1954 as criminal laws, vagrancy statutes and rigid segregation of occupations after emancipation frequently tied Black men to debt peonage as sharecroppers, and enticement laws restricted their ability to seek other employment. Consequently, many Black women who were mothers sought work as domestics, nannies, cooks, or by taking in laundry. Jim Crow kept wages low and opportunities scarce outside domestic work, and workers were vulnerable to dismissal without cause or cheated of their pay. Given the limited employment options for Black families, mothers had little choice other than working outside the home for wages, usually laboring to care for white families. Unlike immigrant women, they did not leave the labor market after marriage but remained employed to keep their children in school and delay their children's entrance to wage labor (Glenn 2010). Later, numerous states excluded women of color, particularly Black women, from laws protecting labor rights.

An examination of labor and immigration laws quickly demonstrates the legal institutionalization of race, class, gender, age, citizenship and non-disability privileges in the workforce. The following short list of the early laws demonstrates the state–market–family relations that insured white male workers' advantages over workers of color, especially if the latter were also immigrants (Johnson 2004):

- the Foreign Miner's Act (1852) forced Mexican, Mexican American and Chinese miners to pay a monthly tax to mine;
- the Anti-Coolie Act (1862) passed by California legislation imposed a tax on Chinese business;
- California legislation (passed 1876) denied Mexican and Chinese employment on county irrigation projects;
- immigration law (1882) prohibited entry to disabled individuals;
- the 1885 Alien Contract Labor Law criminalized the recruitment and hiring of immigrant labor.

Other institutional practices used to protect the privilege of white male workers involved establishing a dual-wage system and a segregated labor market. Dual-wage systems maintained a white wage and a lower wage for non-Whites working in similar jobs, such as those found in mining, agriculture and ranching. A segregated labor market hired only Whites for higher-paying skilled labor, and non-Whites for lower-paid jobs defined as unskilled and usually involving more dirty and dangerous working conditions. Of course, today, we still experience sex-segregated occupations, which pay higher wages to male-dominated jobs: construction workers, truck drivers and garbage collectors; and lower wages in female-dominated positions: grade school teaching, secretarial work and childcare. Unskilled workers, as well as workers facing discrimination and legal restrictions, often fill the lowest-paid and most dangerous jobs. The practice used to be so common that jobs identified the race, class and gender of the worker; for example, agricultural field workers as "Black and Mexican men's work," laundry as "Mexican women's work" or domestic service as "Black women's work," and Irish police and firefighters. Job discrimination against Black, Mexican American and immigrant men meant that the "family-wage" was a white-male privilege and they were unable to fulfill the breadwinner–caregiver model. Thus, formal discriminatory practices institutionalized by law were buttressed by informal discriminatory practices of excluding certain workers from the highest-paid positions and from social benefits.

Men fighting for a "family-wage" and labor unions during the first half of the twentieth century relied on women providing unpaid "reproductive" labor – care work and housework in the home. Reproductive labor during this time was hard and involved hauling water, washing clothes on the washboard, preparing all food from raw material in days before canning and refrigeration, maintaining an extensive garden if not on a farm, and raising chickens for meat and eggs. As capitalism developed and men fought for the eight-hour day, they simultaneously created the nuclear family: "The wage operates as an interface, or mediating agent, between production and the reproduction of labor power" (May 1982: 399). Providing for one's family and being economically independent became the hallmark of fatherhood and masculinity, which linked their citizen, gender, class and sexual identities as workers and fathers. Therefore, women came to depend on their husbands for the primary source of income, which they might supplement with additional market activity such as bringing in laundry, sewing or ironing or selling produce. Social insurance policies passed in the 1930s provided white male workers with some assistance during periods of unemployment. Disability, unemployment and retirement benefits, as well as sick pay, provided an economic buffer for white fathers to retain their ability to fulfill a breadwinner role. However, policies explicitly omitted agricultural and domestic workers (major sources of employment for Blacks and immigrants of color). During the economic crisis in the 1930s, the largest New Deal Program established was the Works Progress Administration (WPA), which employed millions of workers, mostly white men. This was a rare event in that the state protected male workers against market conditions. However, after the Depression, instead of keeping similar provisions to assist unemployed workers, welfare focused solely on those considered unemployable, such as the elderly and single mothers, particularly widows and spouses previously supported by white heterosexual wage earners (Orloff & Monson 2002). Included in the eligibility requirements of welfare policies developed during the New Deal were ones that excluded the majority of Black workers (Roberts 1997). Welfare programs established gendered systems for providing social insurance and assistance based on the breadwinner–caregiver model (Orloff & Monson 2002). However, the gendered system also included privileges and disadvantages based on race, class, sexuality and citizenship. An intersectional analysis uncovers these systems of domination operating in family life.

A closer look at government policies and programs initiated in response to the Great Depression reveals the significance of race, class and gender in understanding today's state–market–family processes.

- The National Industrial Recovery Act (1933), aimed at stimulating economic recovery, excluded unskilled workers, which resulted in thousands of Blacks losing jobs in the South.
- While the Agricultural Adjustment Act in 1933 assisted farmers by reducing farm production and raising food commodity prices, the legislation negatively affected poor Black sharecroppers who faced less work and higher food prices (Kelly & Lewis 2000).
- The Wagner Act (1933) was central to legalizing labor union democracies, which raised wages and improved working conditions for workers. However, many unions denied workers of color access to high-paying blue-collar jobs by practicing a rule of father–son membership. States excluded other workers of color from the benefits and legislation coverage by excluding the occupations they dominated.
- The National Labor Relations Act (1935) was crucial in protecting the rights of workers and encouraging collective bargaining. However, this Act excluded from coverage and protection agricultural and domestic workers, who were primarily Black, Mexican, Filipino and Japanese men and women.

The most significant federal statute passed was the Fair Labor Standards Act (FLSA) in 1938, also known as the Wages and Hours Bill. This Act aimed the first labor protection legislation passed in the US at male workers, introduced the 40-hour week and an 8-hour day, and established a national minimum wage for men. However, women's rights, like those of children, became "protective legislations" for what were seen as vulnerable workers, which mandated maximum hours to preserve maternal health and to prevent employer abuse. Contractual relations for men framed their argument as a fight for a "family wage." Women's employment policies framed women as mothers and wives, with statutes and safety regulations directed at motherhood. We should keep in mind that, during this period, the state motivation was to regulate working hours for women to protect their reproductive capacity. Yet domestic workers were not covered. Racism and its influence in regional politics prevailed and the federal government excluded immigrant and predominantly Black women from labor protections passed under the New Deal (Glenn 2010).

New Deal policies generally denied poor and working-class men of color access to the labor market as a high-wage earner or "good worker." Importantly, these policies and laws excluded them from being an "ideal" or "good" father (Gerson 1993; Hamer 2001). An important product of the Roosevelt administration that recorded this distinction was the hundreds of thousands of photographs taken for the Farm Security Administration (FSA). While imagined as an inclusive record of images of the hardships caused by the dust bowl and the Great Depression, those perceived as the undeserving poor do not appear. The photographers generally did not depict the urban ghettos, mobile male labor referred to as "hobos" at the time, orphans and the homeless. Of primary interest were intact families struggling against invisible conditions over which they had no control. The notion of the "deserving poor" has haunted every poverty program since, easily seen in today's headlines calling for drug testing of Supplemental Nutrition Assistance Program (SNAP) recipients, or specifying the kinds of food that can be bought with welfare money.

Men's ability to be the breadwinner of the family had consequences for women fulfilling their obligations as mothers. Women married to wage earners with good jobs, pay and benefits were able to fulfill their role as "good mothers" because they had the privilege to become full-time mothers and wives. However, not all women were the wives or daughters of husbands or fathers earning a "family-wage," and the majority of these less advantaged women were non-white and immigrants. Married women frequently contributed economically to the family by reducing family expenditures and producing essential commodities. Poor working mothers lacked the luxury of engaging in full-time motherhood and were consequently considered inferior caretakers. Single mothers entering the labor force were usually limited to "women's work," which was poorly paid, and had access to state assistance for their children, but usually under punitive conditions. It is frequently assumed that public policies affect individuals, families and communities in similar ways. A closer look at the plight of mothers of color points to the ways systems of oppression interacted to limit opportunities, while politicians and society judged them by the same criteria used to assess mothers who had received race, class and citizenship privileges.

One way to unravel systems of domination is to recognize an unequal distribution of opportunities combined with everyone still being held to the same standard. Intersectional analysis revealed the frequency with which states denied assistance and labor protections to Black mothers while assisting white mothers in similar situations. A different narrative was used to frame social policy aimed at Black mothers. Daniel Moynihan, a sociologist serving as the Assistant Secretary of Labor, wrote the most damning statement against Black mothers, *The Negro Family: The Case for National Action* (known as the Moynihan Report), in 1965. Moynihan identified Black single-mother families as contributing to the high rates of poverty. His critics argued that he blamed the victim in an effort to divert responsibility away from social structure factors to the behaviors and cultural patterns of the poor (Ryan 1976). While these women as workers cared for the children of privileged white families, politicians treated them as inferior mothers who contributed to the development of bad moral character in their own children. Black mothers' high rates of labor-force participation resulted in Black families being labeled as deviant because they were used as an indicator of a matriarchal family structure, which was in opposition to the patriarchal family structure embraced by the state. Instead of recognizing that poverty was high among most female-headed households because of their low wages and lack of access to welfare, social science researchers compared and contrasted these families with white families headed by white males receiving white wages, and concluded that Black mothers, particularly single heads of households, were the source of poverty. Since Jim Crow, these attitudes have supported arguments to cut federal assistance programs as a strategy to promote marriage and working fathers. Rather than addressing employment discrimination and increasing access to social benefits, eliminating programs such as Aid to Families with Dependent Children (AFDC) was a means to discourage divorce and children being born out of wedlock in Black families. Similar arguments emerged in Herrnstein and Murray's (1994) book *The Bell Curve: Intelligence and Class Structure in American Life*. They supported the belief that welfare creates "dependency," and proponents call for reducing assistance to these poor families. Welfare regulations requiring mothers to work, many times without providing job training, education, childcare or access to a living wage, serve to worsen the plight of poor Black mothers. Systems of race, class and gender oppression intersect to maintain inequality in the labor market for Black mothers, which creates obstacles for them as they try to comply with the prevailing ideology of motherhood and engage in intensive or competitive mothering.

Clearly marriage, labor, immigration and welfare laws helped to construct social systems and beliefs that privileged white affluent heterosexual parents who were US citizens. These same beliefs then become stereotypes used to justify discrimination. Welfare policies benefited white families much more than families of color or immigrant families. Keeping a focus on the intersections of systems of power illuminates the ways in which seemingly race–gender–class–sexuality-neutral policies have completely different consequences for different groups of people. An intersectional lens is crucial in analyzing state–market–family relations.

Discussion questions

1 What intersectional dynamics of race, gender, class and other systems of domination are evident in disparities in healthcare, and how are these connected to formal institutions and policies?
2 How does analyzing state–market–family relations through an intersectional perspective contribute to the sociological imagination, connecting private troubles to public issues?

Summary

The message that I want you to take from this chapter – and from this book – is that intersectionality is a sociological concept for unraveling the complexities of systems of power. In other words, by avoiding only looking at racism, sexism, classism or other "-isms" apart from one another, we focus on the intersection of these various forms of oppression as they actually exist in our daily lives. We have many social identities that position us in different places at different times in relation to dominance or subordination. There is not an essence of race or any other social identity because each identity exists simultaneously with others; and therefore, they change the way we experience each. However, analyzing the complexity can be overwhelming when we think of all the possible combinations in different times and locations.

In the examples of parenting and childhood, lived experiences differ because circumstances related to power relations place persons in dominant or subordinate positions. Single working mothers employed in high-paying jobs, or with flex time, have more resources to assist with childcare and can fulfill gender expectations involving volunteer activities that elementary schools might expect. Poor working parents juggling two jobs or long hours with no sick leave will not be able to fulfill expectations, and risk being judged by teachers as uncommitted parents who don't value education. Non-Christian parents may not want to participate in holiday-related school activities during Christmas or Easter time. Undocumented parents may feel hesitant about participating because of their immigration status. Applying the Rubik's cube metaphor, visualize the rotation of various combinations of social identities, exposing the source of privilege – that is, the advantages, benefits and options one group has in this context. Similarly, observe the oppression, or the disadvantages, harms and restrictions other groups may experience (Weber 2010). The privileges or barriers group members experience change as specific systems of inequality interact.

Understanding the dynamics of social inequality is essential in our pursuit of social justice. The link between scholarship and social justice becomes apparent when we turn to the history of conceptualizing intersectionality in the next chapter. From its early recognition of the interconnectedness of systems of power, we find its roots in activism and scholarship developed from social justice concerns about social inequality. Now that we've seen how we can begin to identify intersectionality in social life, the next chapter will offer an overview of the development of intersectionality that points to both a scholarly and activist tradition.

2

Where Does Intersectionality Come From?

For a moment, it might help to make clear what intersectionality is *not*. Critical race feminist scholars have cautioned against the dangers of interpreting intersectionality as diversity (Davis 1996; Bannerji 2000; Mohanty 2003; Alexander 2005; Ahmed 2012). Over the last decades, many sites in society have called for multiculturalism and diversity. While the celebration and application of "diversity" popularized in the 1980s and found in corporate initiatives and school curricula did attempt to provide a space for different voices, this multiculturalism was not aimed at eliminating social inequality. Calls for representational inclusion were responded to with a "Benetton model" of diversity (referring to the advertising campaigns of the Benetton clothing company) with the goal of commercial value (Lury 2004; Moor 2007), or the incorporation of people of color in the media within hegemonic frameworks perpetuating stereotypes and racist tropes (Gray 2005). Here, people are simply an array of races and cultures, experiencing various levels of disability, standing apart from the power relations that are the important meaning attached to these differences. Institutional diversity practices and language uncover the "manufacturing of cohesion" (Alexander 2005) or "multiversity diversity" (Hill 2004), which does not address inequality. Celebrating difference for the sake of inclusion does not dismantle the everyday practices of privilege or oppression. Intersectionality is not concerned with "diversity" or "multiculturalism" but with power relationships, specifically the ways in which difference embeds domination and oppression. White, male, heterosexual and citizenship privileges are not personal but are institutional arrangements that provide non-disabled persons classified as white, male and heterosexual greater access to power and resources that are not similarly available to people of color, women, LGBTQ individuals or non-citizens.

Intersectional scholarship can be traced to early inquiries and concern over social inequalities, arising from social activism. As activists attempted to explain the different material conditions or economic circumstances within specific groups, fellow activists felt marginalized because their experiences were not included. These marginalized activists challenged others to capture their circumstances, which led to intersectional theorizing about inequalities. Conceptualizing class, caste and status were among the top endeavors of these scholar-activists. However, class alone did not explain different experiences of men and women of the same class. Racialized laws restricting voting, marriage or labor opportunities did not explain the different experiences of men and women of color. In other words, one-dimensional conceptualizations of individuals or groups did not capture the complexity of people's lived experiences. These approaches failed to identify issues that were inclusive of all women, all the working class or all people of color. Conceptualizations of race were needed that did not erase the experiences of women of color, immigrants of color, gays and lesbians of color. Social hierarchies are not one-dimensional, and power relations in families, communities and nations cannot be explained without examining how and why certain social identities are subordinated to others and interact with each other in different ways. This chapter traces the conceptualization of intersectionality as emerging from an activist tradition – a tradition linked to a lived experience of activism that aimed to generate solutions serving to eliminate oppression. I will first consider how the term "intersectionality" came about.

Coining the Term

Academics disagree over the emergence of intersectionality as a conceptual framework and organizing tool (Ferguson 2012). Most frequently, legal scholar Kimberlé Crenshaw is credited for coining the term "intersectionality" in her 1989 article "Demarginalizing the intersection of race and sex: A Black feminist critique of antidiscrimination doctrine, feminist theory and antiracist politics." Crenshaw's (1989, 1991) widely cited legal writings on intersectionality emerged from the inability to capture the experiences of Black women in anti-discrimination law. When going to court as plaintiffs in discrimination cases, Black women were unable to prove gender discrimination because not all women were discriminated against, and they were unable to prove race discrimination because not all Black people were discriminated against. Courts failed to recognize Black women's accounts about experiencing race and sex discrimination simultaneously. Instead, their injuries were marginalized by forcing them to claim either gender or race discrimination, and refusing to recognize how sexism and racism operated simultaneously. In her law review article on anti-discrimination, Crenshaw used an example of a traffic accident to illustrate race and gender as having their own lane in the street:

> Consider an analogy to traffic in an intersection, coming and going in all four directions. Discrimination, like traffic through an intersection, may flow in one direction, and it may flow in another. If an accident happens in an intersection, it can be caused by cars traveling from any number of directions and, sometimes, from all of them. Similarly, if a Black woman is harmed because she is in the intersection, her injury could result from sex discrimination or race discrimination. (1989: 149)

Her analogy demonstrates that if Black women are discriminated against because of experiences from *both* gender and race discrimination, the law does not recognize their experience. Crenshaw's use of intersectionality articulated the inadequacy of anti-discrimination law as a tool for addressing injuries to women of color.

I will address in this chapter how other Black feminist scholars and activists theorized the problem by assuming that gender and race functioned as mutually exclusive categories, which erased the experiences of women of color. Crenshaw's term gained popularity for starting to untangle how racism and patriarchy interact; the interaction had often gone unnoticed in contemporary feminist and anti-racist discourses (Crenshaw 1989, 1991). Intersectionality calls attention to additional invisibilities in feminism, anti-racism and class politics. A significant aspect in conceptualizing the oppression faced by women of color is the recognition that "the intersectional experience is greater than the sum of racism and sexism, any analysis that does not take intersectionality into account cannot sufficiently address the particular manner in which Black women are subordinated" (Crenshaw 1989: 153). Furthermore, as Crenshaw argued, the concept "[e]nables us to recognize the fact that perceived group membership can make people vulnerable to various forms of bias, yet because we are simultaneously members of many groups, our complex identities can shape the specific way we each experience that bias" (AAPF 2013: 3).

I now turn to the sociological roots of intersectionality, which are firmly planted in the mid-1800s and early 1900s, in struggles for women's and African American rights in the US. Historical analysis reveals that race, gender, class and sexuality were central to understanding the social inequality that existed for over a century (Guy-Sheftall 1986; Dill & Zambrana 2009). Ann DuCille (1993: 31) rightly noted that "like most black Americans, with issues of race identity and social equality, black female artists and intellectuals writing at the turn of the century recognized that for them and their sisters the race question did not exist separate and distinct from the woman question and vice versa." The quest for an intersectional paradigm was simply stated as early as Sojourner Truth's 1851 address to the Women's Convention in Akron, Ohio: "Ain't I a woman?"

Early Conceptualizations of Intersectionality

Several prominent Black women stand out in referencing multiple identities in the fight for women's rights and for civil rights for African Americans. Most noted were Maria Stewart, Sojourner Truth, Anna Julia Cooper and Mary Church Terrell. Maria Stewart was one of the first African American women to lecture on the unique position of Black women facing racism and sexism. Born in Hartford, Connecticut, in 1803, she became a domestic servant when her parents died and after leaving service, she obtained a religious education, which was evident in her lecturing on anti-slavery and women's rights. Stewart "called on black women to develop their highest intellectual capacities, to enter all spheres of the life of the mind, and to participate in all activities within the community" (Richardson 1987: xiii–xiv). As a writer and activist, she also considered Black women's class oppression and advocated for establishing cooperative economies to gain economic independence (Gines 2011). Unlike Stewart, Sojourner Truth was born a slave and, after 26 years, she managed to escape with her daughter, leaving three children behind. She eventually won a court case and gained freedom for her son (Painter 1996). A few years older than Stewart, Sojourner Truth (1999 [1851]) is better known because of her famous "Ain't I a woman?" speech that highlighted the invisibility of Black women in the discussion of women's oppression:

> That man over there says that women need to be helped into carriages and lifted over ditches, and to have the best place everywhere. Nobody ever helps me into carriages, or over mud-puddles, or gives me any best place! And ain't I a woman? Look at me! Look at my arm! I could have ploughed and planted, and gathered into barns, and no man could head me! And ain't I a woman? I could work as much and eat as much

as a man – when I could get it – and bear the lash as well! And ain't I a woman? I have borne thirteen children, and seen them most all sold off to slavery, and when I cried out with my mother's grief, none but Jesus heard me! And ain't I a woman?

In 1858, Anna Julia Cooper, born enslaved, became one of the first African American women to earn a doctoral degree. In her book, *A Voice from the South*, Anna Julia Cooper wrote:

> The colored woman of to-day occupies, one may say, a unique position in this country. In a period itself transitional and unsettled, her status seems one of the least ascertainable and definitive of all the forces which make for our civilization. She is confronted by both a woman question and a race problem, and is as yet an unknown or unacknowledged factor in both. (1990 [1834]: 134)

Cooper taught and eventually became a school principal in M Street School, and later the President at Frelinghuysen University in Washington, DC. She founded the Colored Women's League of Washington and was a strong leader for racial justice and women's rights. Mary Church Terrell, known for her activism for civil rights and suffrage, was born in 1863 to former slaves. She was a founding member of the National Association for the Advancement of Colored People (NAACP), the first President of the National Association of Colored Women, and founder of the National Association of College Women, now known as the National Association of University Women. In her 1898 address before the National American Women's Suffrage Association, Terrell referenced the intersecting systems of oppression: "Not only are colored women with ambition and aspiration handicapped on account of their sex, but they are almost everywhere baffled and mocked because of their race. Not only because they are women, but because they are colored women" (Marable & Mullings 2009: 166).

The writings of these four Black women activists and intellectuals are significant in that they show how the roots of intersectionality lie embedded in the lived experiences of marginalized groups' struggle for social justice. As Maria Stewart, Sojourner Truth, Anna Julia Cooper and Mary Church Terrell fought to end racism, economic inequalities and abuses of women's rights, they made visible the inadequacy of platforms set forth by white women suffragists or civil rights leaders. Groups who fall outside the dominant groups most visibly perceive intersectionality; these groups recognize how "major" contenders in power relationships and oppression did not capture the intersecting systems of domination. Early Black feminists engaged in activism to gain rights for women and for all African Americans, their work capturing the intersection of race and gender.

While the theoretical foundation of intersectionality is clearly located in eighteenth-century Black feminist writings, many scholars also acknowledge W. E. B. Du Bois's inclusion of interconnecting systems of oppression, namely race, class and nation, in his writings (Hancock 2005; Dill & Kohlman 2012). For example, Patricia Hill Collins (2000: 42) credited Du Bois with the "[i]mplicit use of intersectional paradigms of race, class, and nation in explaining Black political economy. Du Bois conceptualized race, class, and nation not primarily as personal identity categories but rather as social hierarchies that shaped African American access to status, property, and power." In addressing social problems plaguing the Black community, Du Bois examined racist ideologies and practices as structures of capitalism. He recognized and investigated the power that the US imposed on its colonies through international policy, invasion, and colonization. He described the color line as: "[t]he relation of the darker to the lighter races of men in Asia and Africa, in America and the islands of the sea." Du Bois conceptualized class, race and nation as interlocking systems, which reinforced each other to oppress African Americans. Bonnie Thornton Dill and Ruth E. Zambrana argue that Du Bois created a new "cultural social analysis" in examining the connection between race and class in labor debates (Dill & Zambrana 2009). To be clear, as used in their book, a system comprises social structures interrelated by functions. Structures are socially created, and extremely persistent. Examples might include feudal and slave states. They lasted hundreds of years but were eventually dismantled and replaced. The functions that maintain and connect social structures, then, are relationships like sexism, racism and class warfare.

Du Bois's inclusion of women has been highly contested by some Black feminists but Collins pointed out that he did write about women's struggles in family, community and labor, even though he did not specifically identify gender as a system of power. More recently, Aldon Morris (2015: 220) has joined the debate over Du Bois's contribution to intersectionality, drawing on the following quote to illustrate that he did recognize the interaction of systems of oppression and acknowledge the importance of gender: "What is today the message of these black women to America and to the world? The uplift of women is, next to the problem of the color line and the peace movement, our greatest modern cause. When, now, two of these movements – woman and color – combine in one, the combination has deep meaning." Like the early feminists who also wrote and spoke during the same time, W. E. B. Du Bois's research and writing were deeply embedded in the scholar-activist tradition.

Feminists in the 1970s, 1980s and 1990s

The next significant period in the development of intersectionality arose with the activism and writing of Black feminists in the 1970s and expanded over the next three decades. The social movements in the 1970s organized around specific issues of racial or gender equality, thus familiar issues arose as women of color found their realities erased. Black men's experience represented racial oppression while white women's experience represented gender oppression. Again, Black feminists challenged one-dimensional conceptualizations of race or gender, and theorized the interactions of structures of social inequality operating under capitalism. Black feminists in the 1970s and 1980s called attention to the need to address all forms of oppression, and their writings illustrated the strong link between activism in the Black community and systems of social inequality.

Examining this period of writing, I'll turn to Frances Beale, the co-founder of the Black Women's Liberation Committee of the Student Nonviolent Coordinating Committee (SNCC), who wrote one of the defining documents of Black feminism, "Double jeopardy: to be Black and female" (Ross 2006). Originally published as a pamphlet, the essay demonstrated the link between the intellectual paradigm of "intersectionality" and the concrete practice of social activism. The pamphlet was later revised and published in Toni Cade's (1970) edited collection *The Black Woman: An Anthology.* Beale's essay is an early illustration of Black feminist writings that presents race, class and gender as interlocking systems and addresses the necessity for an intersectional approach in the struggle against racism and capitalist exploitation. Beale argued that racism and capitalism produced and maintained problems in the Black family and community. In her analysis of economic exploitation, she never loses sight of the intersections of race, class and gender. She connected the capitalist exclusion of Black men from the labor force with hiring Black women at low wages in reproductive jobs with poor working conditions (e.g., as domestics, nannies and nurses). The functional consequence created circumstances denying Blacks the resources to achieve manhood and womanhood as defined under US capitalism (i.e., working breadwinner men and home-making caregiving women). Nevertheless, African Americans internalized these mainstream gendered ideologies, causing tensions and frustrations between Black men and women. Beale challenged Black men to gain racial equality and liberation, but without male privilege that subordinated Black women. She advocated productive lives for Black women, and the development of academic and technical skills and talents for both men and women.

Beale chastised white feminists for treating the women's movement as monolithic. Her writings and speeches further elaborate why feminists must adopt anti-imperialism and anti-racist ideologies to understand their plight – but also their privilege – as white women. Beale is one of many noted Black feminist activists participating in the Civil Rights and Feminist Movements to confront social justice issues concerning Black women, and Third World and working people.

Another noted contribution during the late 1970s was the Combahee River Collective, who took their name from the place where Harriet Tubman planned an action to free more than 750 slaves. The Collective is significant for including sexual orientation in Black feminism. As a Black feminist lesbian organization in Boston, they were active in a number of social justice campaigns, including the desegregation of Boston schools, protests against police brutality in Black communities, and against violence against women. Their activism as feminists and lesbians did not advocate for separatism but was committed to inclusive coalition-building with progressive Black men. After numerous retreats aimed at articulating the tenets of Black feminism, in 1977 they issued *The Combahee River Collective Statement: Black Feminist Organizing in the Seventies and Eighties*:

> The most general statement of our politics at the present time would be that we are actively committed to struggling against racial, sexual, heterosexual, and class oppression, and see as our particular task the development of integrated analysis and practice based upon the fact that the major systems of oppression are interlocking. The synthesis of these oppressions creates the conditions of our lives. As Black women we see Black feminism as the logical political movement to combat the manifold and simultaneous oppressions that all women of color face. (Marable & Mullings 2009: 501)

The statement is an important contribution to further theorizing intersectionality in the multiple identities people experience as interlocking systems of oppressions, which include not only race, class and gender but also sexuality. Their statement has been depicted as "one of the strongest, earliest, and most often reprinted manifestos of feminist identity politics in the United States" (Grant 2000: 184), as well as "a bedrock foundation of black feminist theory" (Bowen 2000: 118). The *Combahee River Collective Statement* presented a multi-dimensional analysis of race, class, gender and sexuality with several important characteristics: simultaneous oppressions, multiple interlocking structures, the rejection of ranking functions, and acknowledging that these oppressions are created and maintained by capitalism, imperialism and patriarchy.

Black feminist coalitions made common cause with other groups of women of color to generate further critiques of mainstream feminist practice. The intellectual critiques helped to further articulate their activist goals of inclusion while the writing continued to develop the analysis of multi-dimensions of inequality. In other words, scholarly theory and social justice practices emerged as a praxis, a term used effectively by Paulo Freire (1973), whose book *Pedagogy of the Oppressed* was widely read at this time. An important feminist anthology arising out of such coalitions is *This Bridge Called My Back: Writings by Radical Women of Color*, edited by Cherríe Moraga and Gloria E. Anzaldúa (1981). Many credit the chapters with providing intellectual foundations for third-wave feminism, which linked feminism, race, class and sexuality. In one of the frequently cited essays from the anthology, "Across the kitchen table: A sister-to-sister dialogue," Barbara and Beverly Smith (1981: 61) highlighted the interconnectedness of systems of oppression, in opposition to exclusionary and one-dimensional approaches of only considering patriarchy: "The reason racism is a feminist issue is easily explained by the inherent definition of feminism. Feminism is the political theory and practice to free all women: women of color, working-class women, poor women, physically challenged women, lesbians, old women, as well as white economically privileged heterosexual women. *Anything less than this is not feminism, but merely female self-aggrandizement.*" Like other Black feminists, Smith and Smith insisted that, without an inclusive approach to gender, there could not be a feminist agenda.

Another example of the growing popularity of intersectional critiques of white feminism appeared in Angela Davis' (1981) book *Women, Race and Class*. She recounted the history of Black and white women's fight for social equality and highlighted white feminists' failure to uphold a political agenda inclusive of women of color. Davis challenged the strongly held belief that women only recently started to work outside the home and were then denied employment opportunities on the basis of femininity. As slaves, Black women labored side-by-side with Black men and were submitted to the same punishments of flogging and mutilations. Rather than protecting them as mothers, as they did white women, slave owners classified Black women as breeders and sold their children as livestock. Unlike Black men, they "were victims of sexual abuse and other barbarous mistreatment that could only be inflicted on women" (Davis 1981: 6). The chapter on "Racism, birth control and reproductive rights" offered a compelling example of the dangers in conceptualizing and organizing around gender as a one-dimensional system of oppression.

Voluntary motherhood had emerged as an important woman's issue but considering only gender, the solution white feminists proposed was birth control and access to abortions. When the leading birth-control activist, Margaret Sanger, began the crusade for birth control in the 1900s, she worked with the Socialist Party. After her break with working-class activists, anti-Black and anti-immigrant rhetoric influenced her campaign, moving it closer to the eugenics movement. Women listed unfit for motherhood under compulsory sterilization law included women of color and immigrant women. Sterilization was the only means of birth control provided for many Native American, Mexican American, Puerto Rican and Black women when abortion rights activists resumed campaigning in the 1970s. Davis (1981: 219) noted: "By the 1970s over 35 percent of Puerto Rican women of childbearing age had been surgically sterilized." Reproductive rights are indeed a feminist issue but easily framed by a racist agenda unless we recognize the dangers of eugenics and the centrality of policies inclusive of race, class and gender.

During the early 1980s, another Black feminist who pushed thinking beyond one-dimensional frameworks of difference was Audre Lorde. In her essay, "Age, race, class and sex: women redefining difference," Lorde (1984: 116) called attention to the European tendency to postulate simple dichotomies such as "dominant/subordinate, good/bad, up/down, superior/inferior," which, in the process, function to establish a "mythical norm":

> In america, this norm is usually defined as white, thin, male, young, heterosexual, Christian, and financially secure. It is with this mythical norm that the trappings of power reside within society. Those of us who stand outside that power often identify one way in which we are different, and we assume that to be the primary cause of all oppression, forgetting other distortions around difference, some of which we ourselves may be practicing. By and large within the women's movement today, white women focus upon their oppression as women and ignore differences of race, sexual preference, class and age. There is a pretense to a homogeneity of experience covered by the word *sisterhood* that does not in fact exist.

The "mythical norm" defines human differences outside the norm as deviant. Lorde (1984: 116) challenged white women "to see Black women as women and different from themselves" and to recognize the range of women's issues these differences present. She further explained that Black women share oppressions with Black men but they are different. In the same way, Black women share oppressions with white women, but they are different. Without recognizing how Black women share oppressions differently, white women can become tools of patriarchal power. Again, situated in activism for social equality and justice, Lorde argued that: "we must recognize differences among women who are our equals, neither inferior nor superior, and devise ways to use each other's differences to enrich our visions and joint struggles" (1984: 122). Lorde, like Davis, the Smiths and Beale, was instrumental in bringing together the idea that all forms of oppression differ and are significant in understanding social inequality.

Discussion questions

1   How do the development and emergence of intersectional perspectives from activism help to ground the conceptualization of "intersectionality" in lived experiences?
2   How were Black women activists in the late 1800s and early 1900s central in conceptualizing the intersection of systems of domination?
3   What important theoretical contributions did Black feminists in the 1970s and 1980s make to our understanding of intersectionality?

Women of Color Sociologists' Theorizing of Dynamics of Power

I can now turn to more contemporary and specifically sociological writings about the intersection of power relations. In our specific discipline, scholars of color examined their own positions at the crossroads of race, class and gender. Failing to find a sociological tradition, they turned to the growing research in the field of sociology of gender and found the analysis incomplete. A wave of sociological research on Black (e.g., Dill 1980; Rollins 1985; King 1988; Collins 1990; Brewer 1993), Latina (e.g., Baca Zinn 1980; Segura 1989; Romero 1992) and Asian American (e.g., Glenn 1986; Abraham 1995; Chow et al. 1996) women called attention to the absence of their experiences in the expanding fields of both race and gender. These studies highlighted the significance of race, ethnicity, class and gender in conceptualizing their experiences and demonstrated that understandings of gender inequality that begin from the lived experiences of white, middle-class heterosexual women do "not apply to Black women and therefore could not account for their subordination" (Glenn 1999: 3). These scholars of color argued that women of color's experiences cannot be comprehended or understood by separating race and gender or by adding one to the other. Only by recognizing the interconnectedness of gender and race can we understand how systems of oppression interact and reinforce each other.

A major contribution by this generation was the theme of intersecting systems of oppression and the need to address multiple forms of domination as reoccurring themes. A most notable essay addressing this point is Deborah King's article "Multiple jeopardy," cited above. She began by remarking on Black women's connection to shared experiences of all women and to Black men. She recalled Fannie Lou Hamer's reference to interlocking systems of oppression in a 1971 speech made to the NAACP: "You know I work for the liberation of all people because when I liberate myself, I'm liberating other people...her [the white woman's] freedom is shackled in chains to mine, and she realizes for the first time that she is not free until I am free" (1988: 43). King draws from the tradition of African American feminism to emphasize that the elimination of sexism requires dismantling racism because white supremacy does not exist separate from patriarchy. She summarized the constant theme of interlocking systems of oppression: "The necessity of addressing all oppressions is one of the hallmarks of black feminist thought" (1988: 43). A significant component of King's conceptualization is identifying multiple jeopardies and consciousness, which challenged the dominant sociological practice of using a race–sex analogy (e.g., that the caste-like status of Blacks and women can be treated as similar) to discuss women's experiences and political mobilizations. While the analogy may have been useful for white feminist theorizing of women's oppression, the analogy erased the dual discriminations of racism and sexism in Black women's experiences and failed to recognize the dynamics of multiple forms of discrimination. These systems of domination are not experienced as fixed or absolute conditions, but are "dependent on the sociohistorical context and social phenomenon under consideration" (King 1988: 49). Consequently, the attempt to account for multiple jeopardy by adding the two (racism + sexism) to equal the Black women's experiences merely reproduced the one-dimensional approach to understanding social issues and privileges from the position of white males. Turning to an analysis of political movements, King further elaborated the concept multiple jeopardy by showing the limitations of "monist" approaches, or a one-dimensional perspective on liberation, and highlighted the tensions and contradictions that create a distinct Black women's ideology. It is through this multiple jeopardy "that black women define and sustain a multiple consciousness." She concludes that "Although the complexities and ambiguities that merge a consciousness of race, class, and gender oppressions make the emergence and praxis of multivalent ideology problematical, they also make such a task more necessary if we are to work toward our liberation as blacks, as the economically exploited, and as women" (King 1988: 72). King's work is significant in addressing the multi-layered analysis required to conceptualize the complexity of multiplicative social relations dominated by the state, economy and culture.

A crucial step forward in the sociological theorizing of intersectionality is Patricia Hill Collins' work on Black feminist thought. She brought together the knowledge that Black women produced, making it evident that conceptualizing Black women's lived experiences required analyzing intersecting oppressions and power relations. Collins conceptualized race, class, gender, nation and sexuality as standing alone "as well as as part of each of these distinctive systems of oppression" (Collins 2000: 134). Similarly to King, Collins did not accept additive approaches to explaining domination and argued for "a fundamental paradigmatic shift" that treats "these distinctive systems of oppression as being part of one overarching structure of domination" (1990: 222). Collins rejected previous arguments that sexism and racism are part of capitalism. Instead, Collins' concept of the matrix of domination intended to capture the fluidity of intersectionality by visualizing multiple layers of domination, which people experience at three levels: the personal, group or community, and in social institutions. The personal level accounts for our unique biography, which includes emotions and values influenced and shaped by individual experiences. The group and community level captures the cultural context of shared experiences and collective memory. Social institutions, such as the law, education, church or the media, account for the systematic level.

Collins argued that excluded groups confront different dimensions of the matrix in various social, political and economic contexts. Depending on the context, individuals may sometimes encounter privileges and other times face subordination; thus, a person is both "a member of multiple dominant groups, *and* a member of the multiple subordinate groups" (Collins 1990: 230). For example, an intersectional perspective on gender is more complex than simply focusing on differences between men and women. If only the wage gap between women and men employed full-time in 2015 is considered, then we find an overall 20% wage gap. In middle-skill occupations, women earn only 66% of what men do. Comparing "the average hourly wages of white men with the same education, experience, metro status, and region of residence" to Black men and women offers an intersectional perspective. Black men make 22.0% less and Black women make 34.2% less than white men do. However, Black women earn 11.7% less than their white female counterparts do (Wilson & Rodgers 2016). Understanding oppression in context is important for researchers to identify the unearned privileges that some do not have in certain settings and the limited opportunities found in others. The intersecting and fluid structure of domination requires social justice activism to engage on all three multiple layers of domination: individual, group and social institutions.

Collins identified two dimensions of the connected relationships among systems of oppression: intersectionality and the matrix of domination.

> Intersectionality refers to particular forms of intersecting oppressions, for example, intersections of race and gender, or of sexuality and nation. Intersectional paradigms remind us that oppression cannot be reduced to one fundamental type, and that oppressions work together in producing injustice. In contrast, the matrix of domination refers to how these intersecting oppressions are organized. Regardless of the particular intersections involved, structural disciplinary, hegemonic, and interpersonal domains of power reappear across quite different forms of oppression. (Collins 2000: 18)

The matrix of domination accounts for the historical development of oppression found in segregated schools, neighborhoods and hospitals. These, and other, social institutions establish and maintain practices that discriminate. Keep in mind that social institutions can change their practices and the form of regulation used to dominate. Using intersectional paradigms not only explains oppression but also provides the understanding to reorganize social relations of domination and develop resistance.

Discussion questions

1 How did the racial analogy used by white feminists for theorizing women's oppression erase Black women's experiences and fail to recognize the dynamics of multiple forms of discrimination?
2 Why did Black feminist scholars reject additive approaches?
3 How can we be members both of dominant groups and of subordinate groups?

Social Constructionism

Social constructionism is concerned with understanding the way in which meaning is attached to an object or event. The focus is on uncovering how individuals and groups construct their perceived, taken-for-granted social reality; how we come to define "man," "woman," "Black," "immigrant," etc. As women of color scholars were theorizing multiple consciousnesses, the matrix of domination and intersecting systems of oppression, race scholars were conceptualizing the social construction of race, and gender scholars were conceptualizing the social construction of gender. Examining the social construction of race and gender begins to identify the social processes and social structures that make race and gender appear inevitable, and predetermined.

In their classic work *Racial Formation in the United States*, Omi and Winant (1986) theorize race as a socially constructed identity shaped by social, economic and political circumstances. This thesis was later presented in Ian Haney López' (1996) analysis of legal constructions of whiteness. Examining legal cases, Haney López demonstrated not only the legal restrictions based on race having to do with such activities as marriage, citizenship, voting, and serving on juries, but also the fluidity of racial constructions of whiteness. Similarly, with gender, as early as Simone de Beauvoir's (1973: 301) *The Second Sex*, gender scholars theorized how "one is not born a woman, but becomes one." Feminist scholars examined the socially constructed meanings of gender in daily interactions and socialization. Feminist sociologists further developed the idea of gender as a social construction by theorizing the way that social status is gendered (Lorber 1994), and how institutions are gendered (Acker 1990).

Building on the social constructionists' work in race and gender scholarship, Evelyn Nakano Glenn (1999: 9) argued for the development of an integrative framework to bring together: "[r]elational concepts whose construction involves both *representational and social structural process* in which power is a constitutive element." Glenn referred to relational concepts such as the construction of oppositions, such as man/woman and Black/White. Here, the emphasis is on establishing stark differences in which variations in each category are non-existent. Racial formation, gendered social status and gendered institutions are concepts that highlight the institutionalization and cultural representation of race and gender in social structures. For example, chapter 1's discussion of parenting demonstrated that occupational segregation in the early 1930s limited workers of color to specific jobs. Today, domestic service is considered work for poor immigrant women while employers depict them as ideal because of their cultural attributes of mothering (Romero 1992, 2011a). Race and gender "differences" are established and maintained through social structural arrangements. In the case of undocumented immigrant Latinas, laws prohibiting them from getting some jobs without documents limit them to jobs in the underground economy, such as cleaning houses and caretaking. Another illustration of representational and social structural process is the racial–gender disparity reported in foreclosures after the 2007–8 housing bubble crash. The common cultural explanation was that people with poor credit records and little experience managing money had received mortgages. However, researchers found that, after adjusting for loan amounts and the income of the borrowers, Blacks were 2.3 times more likely, and Latinos twice as likely, to get high-cost mortgages compared to Whites. In many cases, the only lenders operating in communities of color were mortgage companies offering nothing but subprime loans (Bajaj & Fessenden 2007). In comparison to men with similar financial characteristics, 30 percent more women were provided with risky mortgages. Single Black women were 256 times more likely to have a risky subprime loan than white men in similar financial situations (Baker 2014a). The concrete example of predatory lending shows how organized power is throughout race and gender structures.

The consequences of defining citizenship using the home/work dichotomy which placed women in the home and men in the labor force are revealed in the citizenship distinction made in social benefits: men receive unemployment benefits, old-age insurance and disability, whereas women receive "welfare." Glenn demonstrated the intersection of race and gender in the labor, political and legal systems. Generally, gender scholars conceptualized women's unpaid work maintaining the household, raising children and caring for the sick and elderly as reproductive labor. Race scholars focused almost exclusively on men, and conceptualized workers of color in dual-wage markets, dead-end jobs and marginalized positions as unskilled labor. Applying an integrative framework, Glenn presented the missing piece of women of color's reproductive labor in employers' homes and later as low-wage workers like nurse's aides, kitchen and hotel workers, and hospital janitors.

Race analysis of citizenship focused on the exclusion from citizenship rights stemming from the US history of slavery, conquest and colonization, which denied full citizenship rights to indigenous peoples, Mexicans, Chinese, Filipinos, Puerto Ricans and other racialized nationalities and ethnicities. Slavery, conquest and colonization were vital in the construction of the racial category of "white" in the US. These historical processes socially constructed whiteness as a place of privilege in society. No longer ignoring or simply accepting this as the norm, researchers have examined the social structures maintaining being white as a position of privilege and studied the everyday practices reinforcing white privilege. Similar to other social identities, whiteness intersects with class, sexuality, age and other differences. Examining the wage gap among workers, one immediately recognizes that poor Whites do not have the same privilege as upper-class Whites, and poor white women do not make as much as poor white men. Social movements gradually resulted in gaining more equity in citizenship rights for men of color and white women. However, when receiving social benefits, such as social and health services, women of color are considered dependents rather than as entitled to services. The framing of racialized–gendered citizenship is significant in examining the way that women of color experience inferior rights. The inclusion of citizenship "as system of equality and as a major axis of inequality" is one of Glenn's major contributions to theorizing intersectionality (1999: 22).

In expanding the conceptualization of intersectionality, research used lived experiences as the framework for capturing the simultaneous interaction of structures of power. In doing so, other feminist concepts addressing questions about the gendered production of knowledge emerged. The next section introduces concepts emerging from inquiries into lived experiences, which recognize differences and are closely related to intersectionality. These concepts further expand our understanding of intersectionality and its significance in theorizing about social inequality.

Discussion questions

1   What examples of how the law socially constructs race and gender categories can you give?
2   Think through some examples of the institutionalization and cultural representations of race and gender in social structures.

Situating Knowledges

In addition to the ideas of multiple jeopardy, multiple consciousness, and matrix of domination, closely related themes in conceptualizing intersectionality include positionality, situated knowledges and standpoint theory. These feminist concepts emphasize the need to analyze women's lived experiences to understand the social relationships and social world that construct their perspectives and social positions, such as race, class, gender, sexuality and citizenship. The inequalities experienced from these social positions not only result in differences in standpoints but are also reflected in knowledge produced, which is based on the facts, information and skills acquired from our everyday experiences and education. Understanding of the social world comes from these various standpoints, which means all knowledge is socially situated.

Positionality is critical in the relationship between inequalities, power, and the production of knowledge. Since the adoption of the Heisenberg principle, researchers have to recognize that they themselves are part of the research. As Jean-Paul Sartre (1963 [1960]: 32n.) wrote: "The only theory of knowledge which can be valid today is one which is founded on that of microphysics: the experimenter is a part of the experimental system." Therefore, it is essential to consider the researcher's status in relation to research participants. Social science has a long tradition of studying the powerless and normalizing unequal relationships between the researcher and the participant. The primary concern is how "the other" is represented by researchers who traditionally do not share the same axis of oppression but rather have race, class and gender privilege. Identifying the researcher in written representations of culture and people is now the norm among ethnographers (e.g., Van Maanen 1998; Rosaldo 1989).

Clearly, this is a methodological issue concerning feminists and scholars of color who blazed the trail and began to confront a body of literature produced about their subjectivities based on western knowledge produced by white, European, middle-class and predominantly male researchers. Following the tradition of critical scholarship (e.g., Marx, the Frankfurt School), feminists and scholars of color challenged the positivist notion of "objectivity" and argued that this framing of scientific methodologies concealed power in research relationships. Rather than being "objective," feminists demonstrated how this research produced a masculinist science and consisted of a partial perspective on the social world (Haraway 1988). A prime example is studying the plight of single-women heads of households from the perspective of middle-class men. Feminists analyzed this "objective" approach by revealing the research process by which persons in privileged positions reproduced knowledge based on their perspective, which served to legitimate their privilege in the society. In the case of single-women heads of households, a closer examination of the lived experiences of mothers reveals sources of poverty to be low wages and lack of benefits in traditional female occupations, expensive and inadequate childcare services, and the position of women as recipients of punitive welfare services rather than as having entitlements as first-class citizens (Chaudry 2004). Critiques of western male knowledge exposed the power structure that reproduced and maintained domination. By calling attention to the relationship between epistemology and domination, situated knowledges reveal and identify researchers' standpoints. Patricia Hill Collins defined the knowledge obtained from resistance and controlled by marginalized groups as subjected knowledge.

"Standpoint" and "standpoint theory" are concrete examples of intersectionality in action. It is what intersectionality means in practice for us as sociologists – not only for our research subjects. The most prominent standpoint theorists in sociology are Dorothy Smith and Patricia Hill Collins. Smith began developing the notion of standpoint theory early in her career as she experienced a discrepancy between her lived experiences as a mother, academic and sociologist in a male-dominated world, and the existence – as well as non-existence – of sociological theorizing of the social world she encountered (1987). Early in her work, Smith argued that what we know about the social world depends on our location, and as sociologists we need to recognize our "point of entry" as we conduct our investigation, reflect upon it and problematize it. As a researcher, the

> only route to a faithful telling that does not privilege the perspectives arising in the sites of her sociological project and her participation in a sociological discourse is to commit herself to an inquiry that is ontologically faithful, faithful to the presence and activity of her subjects and faithful to the actualities of the world that arises for her, for them, for all of us, in the ongoing co-ordering of our actual practices. (Smith 1987: 143)

This view ran counter to mainstream sociology that aimed for the "scientific" and the "objective," but which she accurately critiqued as follows: "Its method, conceptual schemes and theories had been based on and built up within the male social universe" (Smith 1990: 23). Reflecting on the incongruities between the social worlds of home and university that she encountered daily, she experienced "two subjectivities" that maintained "two modes of knowing, experiencing, and acting – one located in the body and in the space that it occupies and moves into, the other passing beyond it" (Smith 1987: 82).

Collins also highlighted the researcher's position or standpoint in society in the production of knowledge, which she referred to as standpoint epistemology. She asserts that "specialized thought challenging notions of Black female inferiority is unlikely to be generated from within White-male-controlled academic settings because both the kind of questions and the answers to them would necessarily reflect a basic lack of familiarity with Black women's realities" (2000: 254). Collins presented a standpoint that incorporates all of these interlocking status positions, such as race, class, gender, nationality and sexuality. This "matrix of domination" includes not only sites of oppression but also ones that can serve as sites of resistance. As mentioned earlier, Collins' matrix includes the following three levels in which individuals simultaneously experience subordination and resistance: "the level of personal biography; the group or community level of the cultural context created by race, class and gender; and the systemic level of social institutions" (Collins 1990: 227). While Collins acknowledged that standpoints are not static, she asserted that "these ties between what one does and what one thinks illustrated by *individual* Black women can also characterize Black women's experiences and ideas as a *group*" (2000: 24). Individual Black women sharing class and sexual identity are likely to confront the same circumstances when interacting with the police, school administrators or doctors. She explained that this group standpoint occurs when individuals encounter similar forms of discrimination (i.e., substandard housing, neglected neighborhoods and schools). Instead of acknowledging institutional discrimination, these experiences are justified based on the individual's own characteristics, e.g. their "intelligence, work habits, and sexuality" (2000: 25). By sharing these similar power relations or "angles of vision," individual experiences become group-based, leading to similar interpretations of reality (1990: 249).

To further explain the unique position of Black women's experiences, Collins introduced the concept of "outsider-within," which captures how they are simultaneously included and excluded in "social locations or border spaces marking the boundaries between groups of unequal power" (Collins 2000: 300). An ideal example of the "outsider-within" is the domestic worker who is certainly not a family member in the employer's household but is privy to their personal lives. I used a similar social location in my own research analyzing the narrative of a maid's daughter who lived in the employer's home with her mother. As the daughter of a Mexican immigrant, she spent summers with her poor working-class relatives in Mexico and many weekends with her godparents in the Latino-dominated low-income neighborhoods in Los Angeles. However, most of her time growing up was alongside the sons and daughters of the elite living in gated communities. She was in a unique position to experience the contradictions of gaining the American dream through hard work or the myth of meritocracy. Watching the elite obtain unearned opportunities from inheritance, college entrance as legacies, and special privileges from police investigating car accidents, drunken-driving cases or drugs, she juxtaposed these experiences with those of poor immigrants and their children in Los Angeles. The maid's daughter was simultaneously included and excluded in her mother's employers' lives: her social position in their home, country club or private schools was determined by them. At any time, she might be relegated to the same space in the kitchen as her mother. She was always aware of the ways in which these unequal power dynamics shaped her relationships with the employers and their children, as well as the Mexican maids, nannies and landscapers that worked in the gated community (Romero 2011a).

Discussion questions

1   Examine the different standpoints that explain the range of interpretations citizens have of President Trump's leaked comments when he was a host for *Access Hollywood* or other comments he has made about women.

2   Research and explore how organizing on the grounds of intersectionality has used standpoint perspectives to build coalitions.

Main Points

The history of intersectionality is highly debated. Nevertheless, challenges to one-dimensional views of personhood and to scientific objectivity have roots in a number of gender and racial interdisciplinary projects.
However, activism and the pursuit of social justice have fueled these projects (i.e., Beale 1970; Davis 1981; Crenshaw 1989; Collins 1990, 2000;
Bhavnani & Talcott 2012). The primary aims of intersectionality, as an
intellectual and activist project, are to challenge and change research
and institutional practices that have objectified and marginalized groups
(frequently referred to as "others"), denied subordinated groups a voice,
and privileged certain perspectives over disadvantaged groups through
social processes that legitimate the status quo. Intersectionality is a vital
concept in understanding and dismantling the inequality perpetuated by
social, political and economic power structures (Abraham 1995, 2015;
Purkayastha 2010).

Selecting images that portray key aspects of intersectionality is likely
to continue as critical scholars and activists apply the notion of intersectional inequalities to their analysis, theory or method. Embedded
in social justice and politically engaged agendas, these intellectual and
activist projects do share general principles:

- multiple identities are experienced simultaneously and are holistic
  (Brewer 1993);
- these identities are socially constructed and interact to shape multiple
  dimensions of personhood (Brewer 1993; Nash 2008);
- these multiple dimensions are always present, but one or more
  may become more salient in different social settings (Weber 2004;
  Anderson & Collins 2006);
- intersectionality is a lens for reframing the discourse surrounding
  people of color, women and other marginalized individuals based on
  their lived experiences (Weber 2004; Anderson & Collins 2006);
- intersectionality is a tool for creating new systems of knowledge for
  greater understanding of domination and resistance (Beale 1970;
  Crenshaw 1989; Brewer 1993; Collins 2000; Dill & Zambrana 2009;
  Weber 2010);
- identities are linked to existing systems of power and are manifested
  in relationships of dominance and subordination at both macro and
  micro levels (Collins 2000; Weber 2010);

- intersectionality examines the interconnectiveness of marginalized identities to produce an understanding of the overall structure of oppression and opportunities (King 1988; Baca Zinn & Dill 1996);
- intersectionality is not an additive approach to difference but rather recognizes that identities are experienced simultaneously (King 1988; Brewer 1993; Glenn 1999; Collins 2000);
- intersectionality seeks to understand how the embodiment of each identity helps to collectively create the individual (Yuval-Davis 2006); and
- identities are "contextually rooted in history and geography" (King 1988; Glenn 1999; Weber 2010: 129).

Why Intersectionality Matters

Diversity and multicultural discourse are focused on individual characteristics of race and racist attitudes rather than a structural understanding of a nation's history of slavery, imperialism, immigration, labor laws and civil rights legislation (Bannerji 2000). Emphasis on diversity obscures the reproduction and maintenance of inequality and domination, which allows people to believe they are a tolerant and accommodating people, whereas intersectional approaches address social structure: the historical, political, social and economic context of power relations that have significant influence on people's life chances. The phrases "I don't care if they are green, purple or yellow, it doesn't matter to me" or "I don't see color" deny that racial discrimination exists, also reflecting the failure to see the significance of social inequality and oppression that difference represents. The color-blind perspective assumes that treating everyone the same will eliminate racism. It also ignores the structural position of "white privilege." However, privilege does not disappear by us ignoring its existence, and ignorance will not result in social equality. Too often educators and reformers view diversity as an opportunity to interact with persons of different racial, ethnic, class, gender and sexual identities to experience that we are all the same, and thus argue that these interactions promote social harmony. In contrast, the aims of intersectional analysis are to understand how privilege and domination function in creating and maintaining differences and to begin to create systems of equality. Intersectionality is interested in exposing the unearned privileges certain groups receive by simply being socially assigned or identified as white, male, heterosexual, or a citizen, or being non-disabled. Another aim is to begin to examine the institutionalization of privilege and to analyze how it exists as invisible, common-sense, natural, and even as an earned achievement when it is not.

Most importantly, intersectionality is a challenge to one-dimensional approaches to race, class, gender, sexuality and citizenship, and instead requires us to acknowledge systems of oppression. Standpoints or position-taking contextualize social identities and structure the space of lived experiences of race, gender and class privilege and oppression. Only by recognizing that mono-dimensional approaches to schools, family, media, the law and other social institutions preserve the practices that maintain social inequality can we begin to identify and resist the privilege embedded in everyday interaction. All of these categories of privilege in the US are socially constructed and can be explained through the history of oppression and resistance.

We now turn to examining everyday life using intersectionality. The next chapter illustrates intersectional experiences on college campuses, and the way they intersect with systems of social inequality.

3

Intersectionality in Everyday Campus Life

In the fall of 1981, I began my first tenure-track position in a midwestern university in the US. One of the first formal functions of the school year was the faculty assembly, followed by a reception to welcome the new faculty. The University President's first comment was a self-congratulatory announcement about last year's recruitment efforts, which resulted in a 300 percent increase in affirmative action hires of minority faculty. When he asked us to stand to be identified, I looked around and saw only two other faculty of color standing. I then realized that the 300 percent increase sounded much better than the reality. A second comment took place by the same President at the reception. After a brief introduction that included my saying that I had taught at the University of Texas at El Paso the previous year, he told me that he had not encountered many Mexican women before but he did recall seeing them as prostitutes in Tijuana while stationed in San Diego during military service. He proceeded to remark on the progress that "my people" had made and welcomed me to the university. Shocked, embarrassed and unable to respond, I attributed his racist, sexist and classist remark to his ignorance and complete lack of familiarity with a diverse faculty.

At the beginning of my career, I wanted to think that my first experiences at the faculty assembly and reception were isolated events. However, over the last decades this ceremony welcoming me to academia has become very symbolic of the types of incidents that reoccur when one does not possess the social identities, networks and routine experiences that are the expected norm for student, professor, administrator and staff.

More than a decade later, an undergraduate student told me about a similar encounter with an alumnus from a private college she attended. This 18-year-old first-generation Mexican American college student brought her 5-year-old sister to a college event. A white male alumnus attending the event asked her if the child was her daughter. This same alumnus would never ask such a question of a white middle-class male or female student accompanied by a younger sibling. As she recounted the story, she acknowledged that, had she been a lighter-skinned Mexican American from an upper-middle-class background, she might not have had the same experience.

This chapter explores intersectionality and everyday life. As students and professors, we are generally familiar with the routines and rituals of college life. We may assume that everyone's experiences are similar. Using an intersectional framework to explore everyday life on campus shifts the emphasis away from diversity and multiculturalism and turns attention to power relations. Some campuses have hired racially diverse office staff, some in managerial positions, but, for the most part, office staff members continue to be white, and almost all women with the exception of a growing number of male computer technicians. The "student standard" is still assumed to be young, white, middle-class, non-disabled heterosexual women and men; and, in some disciplines, particularly the sciences, women, African American and Latino students continue to be an oddity. Older working students with families do not fit the norm perpetuated in college images on pamphlets and websites of young 18- to 21-year-old single men and women. Yet approximately 17.6 million nontraditional-age students are starting or returning to college (US Dept. of Education 2010). They are likely to be mistaken for staff instead of students. As college has become more expensive, many more students are workers and employed more than 10–15 hours a week (Perna 2010). Working students confront difficulty in maneuvering campus life when administrative and faculty office hours do not include evenings or weekends.

Faculty members who are not white heterosexual males from middle-class backgrounds encounter expectations that do not reflect their identities. Although half of all college students are women, less than 15 percent of presidents at doctoral degree-granting institutions are. "As of 2014, women hold 31% of the full professor positions at degree-granting postsecondary institutions" (Johnson 2016: 5). Women faculty in male-dominated fields and faculty of color frequently report encountering students who mistake them for administrative staff or academic advisors. In describing why she researched engineering culture, Karen Tonso wrote:

After fifteen years as an engineer, I left the only career I ever really wanted as a survival strategy. In casting about for a meaningful way of life, I gravitated toward high school math teaching, the second-career choice of many former engineers, where I studied explanations for women's underrepresentation in math and science careers. I took considerable umbrage with the predominant arguments, which cast the dilemma in terms of what was wrong with women. (2001: 174)

Not fitting the norm, LGBTQ faculty, particularly those from working-class backgrounds, encounter exclusionary social events assuming heterosexual partners, and hostile social and teaching environments in departments with traditional curricula (LaSala et al. 2008). I have heard several accounts from my Latino male colleagues involving uncomfortable incidents with white staff who assumed they were janitors. Both Black women and men faculty face the constant harassment of university police who question their presence on campus. While I was working on debates on racial profiling on campuses in 2015, two incidents involving faculty at Vassar College and at Arizona State University emerged. Two Vassar College professors described discriminatory treatment by police when they were assumed to be suspects until they showed faculty IDs. At Arizona State, a Black woman professor was body-slammed and forced to the ground and arrested for an incident involving jaywalking. As many of my colleagues wrote in the book *Presumed Incompetent*, fighting for legitimacy in the academy is a common experience for women faculty of color. Grounds maintenance and janitorial workers frequently come from the poor and the working class, and, depending on the campus location, are usually workers of color (Halpern 2003). In the past, janitorial jobs on campus included benefits and opportunities to send the janitors' children to college. Now many universities contract these jobs to a third party. This transition to outsourcing jobs results in janitors working invisibly at night for minimum wage, and the elimination of benefits and opportunities to send their children to college (Margolis & Soldatenko 2016). These are a few examples of the ways in which institutional practices exclude certain groups through everyday routines and interactions.

Everyday practices underpinning racism, genderism, classism and other -isms are present in the use of campus space, which indicates value placed on various disciplines and the people who teach and take these classes. For instance, several researchers include the use of physical space as part of the hidden curriculum in higher education (Margolis et al. 2001) that conveys messages of marginalization. Marina Gair and Guy Mullins (2001) used visual imagery to reveal the hidden curriculum concealed in plain sight on campus. Analyzing images of "classroom structures, architecture, fraternity and sorority gatherings, and representations of school pride" captured class, gender and racial exclusion (Gair & Mullins 2001: 22). As one of the faculty interviewed reflected, on the messages conveyed in the physical environment:

> Looking at the building you are to have a certain attitude towards education and towards that institution that's embodied in that building. When you walk through the doors – through the arched door with the gothic work on the wood, and the stone work, and the windows and all of that – you are to feel a certain something. The way in which you structure an institution tells you about the desires and agendas of that institution. (Gair & Mullins 2001: 27–8)

Similarly, in her study of differences in professionalization, Carrie Castello (2001: 45) compares law students to students earning a graduate degree in social welfare and notes the significance that space has:

> [P]hysical settings do not function as socializing agents *sua sponte*; they are things. The people who design, ornament, and maintain them are the true sources of socializing messages, and the settings are merely the means by which these messages are propagated. Yet physical structures persist and continue to affect the people who inhabit them long after those who designed and built them have passed from the scene.

Undergraduate and graduate students majoring in professions that are likely to bring them into contact with communities of color, single mothers, and the poor working class are usually housed in the least attractive building and equipped with the oldest technology. Students socialized into high-paying professions, such as those offered by law and business schools, are housed in architecturally inviting and intellectually inspiring buildings.

To examine intersectionality in everyday life, this chapter investigates the privileges and domination embedded in social relationships. Institutional arrangements create different educational experiences on the basis of race, class, gender, sexuality and age. By focusing on the various interactions taking place on campuses I will call attention to institutional practices that establish, maintain and reproduce power relations in higher education. Using the familiar environment of campus, this journey through everyday life at college aims to make visible the many daily microaggressions and unearned privileges that normally go unnoticed. Writing about microaggressions encountered on college campuses, Derald Sue (2010: 5) defined these as "brief and commonplace daily verbal, behavioral, and environmental indignities, whether intentional or unintentional, that communicate hostile, derogatory, or negative racial, gender, sexual-orientation, and religious slights and insults to the target person or group." Examining microaggressions is a helpful strategy for uncovering power, privilege, and oppression through everyday life. These slight putdowns directed toward a person's race, gender, sexual orientation, age or other identities, or impairment, serve to exclude groups who are socially marginalized and to reinforce privileged identities. While the President who made racist–sexist comments to me may not have been intentionally racist, sexist and classist, he did not make similar comments to new white male or female faculty because he viewed them as familiar – as like him. They were welcomed as normal members of the university and not as related to European hookers or sex workers in a foreign country. Their presence as new faculty members could have been success stories from poor white communities, but that is generally invisible. The microaggression experienced by the undergraduate Latina student alienated her from other classmates. As she told me the story, I heard the message she received: "This university space is still for white middle-class people!" I heard the lack of confidence entering her thoughts, resulting from the assumption that she was an unwed teenage mother. Students, faculty and staff with marginalized identities experience microaggression as an everyday part of campus life.

Exploring the familiar university environment and the activities of everyday life, such as attending classes, engaging with fellow students, faculty and administrators, enables rethinking of situated experiences. Using ethnographic case studies situated in universities makes visible both privileges – advantages, benefits, options, opportunities – and oppression – disadvantages, hindrances, harms and restrictions. Students may not relate to every aspect of the journey I describe but do reflect on the different lived experiences that are intersectional but go unnoticed. Along with personal narrative and reflections, I draw on sociological research framed by an intersectional lens to examine social identities and interaction in institutional practices that shape our activities of teaching, studying, and working at colleges and universities.

Discussion questions

1   How do microaggressions maintain social inequality on campus?
2   This chapter will explore sociological research based in the US. Research the following education campaigns to explore how intersectionality can help to improve equality and social justice on campuses globally: the #FeesMustFall movement in South Africa;

#iTooamOxford in the UK; and the Gandhi Must Fall campaign in Ghana.

Everyday Life Experiences of Black Deaf Women Students

Nationally, only 30 percent of deaf students complete their undergraduate degree (Barnartt 2006; Williamson 2007). As well as facing the challenges of navigating an educational system established with hearing students as the norm, Black deaf women are also marginalized by race, gender, and frequently by class. The absence of deaf faculty and staff of color increases the isolation these students experience from not having access to role models sharing similar identities. A 1993 survey of professionals employed in deaf education programs in the United States found only 10.4 percent were professionals of color and, of those, only 11.7 percent were deaf (Andrews & Jordon 1993). Research shows that an increased number of faculty and staff of color, including persons of color who are deaf and women of color, establishes a sense of belonging for these students and "inspires self-confidence" (Parasnis & Fischer 2005). However, most African American deaf students identified race and ethnicity as more important than deafness in mentors (Parasnis & Fischer 2005: 57). Similar to hearing students of color, deaf students of color experiencing racial discrimination and conflict on campus were less satisfied with the educational environment, which may explain their lower retention rates.

This section draws on Reshawna Chapple's (2012) dissertation research on the college experiences of Black deaf women, which offers an intersectional perspective on the multiple facets of their identities. An ethnographic study, her research also included focus groups and interviews with 25 undergraduate students attending a campus with nine colleges, one of which offered specific services to students who are deaf or have partial hearing loss. The campus was only 6 percent African American and surrounded by a predominantly white community in upstate New York. In focus groups and interviews with students, Chapple asked the students about their gender, race, class and deaf identities, and the significance of each in their daily lives on campus. For many, living on campus was a completely different environment from living with their families and friends, and in the neighborhoods that they were familiar navigating. Many of these students of color came from urban areas with large communities of color. The campus climate was quite different from their high school experiences and did not reflect the culture of their home communities.

As Chapple explored the campus, she observed that college services for deaf students were located apart from the rest of the campus. This physical distance created and represented the social distance between hearing and non-hearing students. While deaf students moved around the entire campus taking classes throughout the day, hearing students avoided areas of the college offering special services. The campus layout was the immediate imagery of exclusion deaf students experienced. In addition to the physical separation of hearing and non-hearing student services, Chapple observed a further separation by race that appeared to be self-imposed by both deaf and hearing students. Consequently, the Black deaf students did not interact with either the white deaf or the Black or white hearing students. She found a similar pattern among the white deaf students. Wearing hearing aids or a cochlear implant easily identified deaf students, and hearing students avoided contact with them.

> Right now the minorities are separate from white people. And deaf is separate from hearing. Also, there is a problem if you are deaf and you sign that is a problem. There is no sense of community.
>
> When I am on the campus I noticed that hearing people don't try to communicate with us. As deaf people we are proud to be deaf and we are proud to use sign language but if we wave at a hearing person they don't wave back or they refuse to date deaf people because they can't communicate with us but they can if they try. They can write notes or text or try to learn sign but they won't do it.

The most common explanation given for the segregation was establishing "comfort" – that is, each group was able to avoid awkward interactions and misunderstandings. As one student explained:

> I talked to a hearing friend yesterday and he said that the [Black] deaf people, separate ourselves from [Black] hearing people and we stay with [Black] deaf people. I tried to explain to him that we don't try to separate ourselves from hearing people we are just trying to be around people we feel comfortable with. For example if a deaf girl goes up to a hearing guy she likes, he rejects her just because she is deaf. So most deaf girls don't approach hearing guys because they feel that the hearing guy won't like her because she is deaf…even if she really likes him.

Black deaf female students felt disconnected and socially isolated from the larger student body, which sometimes included white deaf students. However, students did not initiate all segregation practiced on campus. Students described incidents in which faculty generated the segregation within their class. In organizing group work in their classes, faculty commonly placed all the Black students, all the Black deaf students, or all the deaf students in the same group: "In a hearing class, deaf people are automatically grouped together. Is it for easy communication accessibility? I don't know. But at the same time that kind of comment reflects negatively on the students. Some of the Black students asked, 'Why can't all the Black students just work together also?' It's like the same type of discrimination." The faculty rationalized the practice on the basis that they segregated with shared commonalities and the groupings facilitated communication. While some students embraced the comfort in these segregated group formations, others viewed the placements by race or abilities as a lost opportunity for diverse exchanges that they normally did not have on campus. Separating a deaf student might be ability grouping but the message was the inferiority of deaf students.

Sports were another area of exclusion. A common example of exclusion of the deaf was the college's major sport event, which was hockey – a sport that most students of color had no experience playing or watching, and most were not familiar with the rules of the game. The focus on hockey instead of football was strange to many of the students of color, both hearing and deaf. There were limited opportunities to play sports, particularly for female students. Some found themselves having to join men's teams if they wanted to play. Several students described incidents in which hearing persons assumed that deafness also affected their other abilities. As a deaf basketball player, one interviewee felt she had to prove to her team that her deafness did not pose any disadvantages for her athletic abilities. Like other female students joining a basketball team, she failed to adhere to feminine norms of dress, mannerism and muscular physique. All too often, she found that assumptions were made about their sexuality solely based on wearing sweatpants, T-shirts, and basketball shoes to class.

The number of instructors who do not know sign language or understand deaf culture exacerbates the exclusion of deaf students. The university conveys a strong message of the insignificance of sign language by not requiring faculty to know or to use it. Hearing students are not encouraged to learn about deaf culture or learn sign language. Deaf students encounter some difficulty communicating with staff in dining halls and bookstores because the latter do not know sign language and are in a rush to serve the next customer. Feelings of isolation affected some of the students academically. A student majoring in engineering described all her classmates as white, male and hearing. When they offered assistance, they tended to treat her as completely helpless when she used sign language. Since interpreters were only available in classes, deaf students had difficulty communicating during office hours with faculty who did not know sign language. The frustration of not communicating adequately sometimes resulted in students not seeking out additional help when classwork and assignments were not clear. Students may not seek out advisors, find mentors or use support services for similar reasons. Students reported that faculty and hearing students frequently questioned their helping each other as forms of cheating, even though they were unclear about the information communicated from one student to another. Chapple found that deaf students who were oral did not always support the other deaf students' needs:

> The other students in my tutoring session complained. They said I did not need an interpreter because the tutor can sign. The other students with me in tutoring are deaf too but they are oral. They speak. I told them I need an interpreter to understand what they are saying in the session. They told me the interpreter slows things up and makes me look stupid.

Hearing students sometimes complained to classmates that the assistance provided by interpreters gave deaf students an advantage of not having to struggle through giving an oral presentation to the class and attributed some of the presentation content to the interpreter. Hearing students or deaf students who are oral complain about the pace during tutoring sessions when they must rely on an interpreter.

Given the few Black college students and an even smaller Black deaf student population, race and deafness were the most marginalizing aspects of their identities. In describing their everyday life on campus as Black deaf women, the students began by discussing one of their many identities and soon moved to including others. In describing microaggressions, they did not identify acts specifically as racism, sexism, classism or audism because their identities were intersecting and the situational fluidity was constantly changing. For example, a student who identifies as Black, Puerto Rican and White addressed the challenges she faced on and off campus:

> Being a lesbian on campus is difficult. It is the hardest thing about going to school here. I am confronted all the time, harassed and questioned. I'm a Black, deaf, lesbian and every day I am confronted about who I am! People actually get right up in my face and ask me questions about being gay....I still think that being gay on campus is very hard. But, race is a problem too. You know? Some people are just rude. I remember when I was younger and we went on vacation to DC. A woman came up to me, grabbed me and asked if I had been

kidnapped by my parents. My mom is mixed but she looks White and my dad is Black.

This student described experiences that highlight the ways that she did not "fit" in and was expected to explain what others viewed as abnormal. Students questioned her identity as a lesbian, which they refused to accept from a Black deaf woman. Similarly, the woman in DC socially constructed race as a very fixed identity, as well as assuming that all family members share the same skin color and other physical traits. Chapple's interviews elicited numerous accounts of incidents involving the students being questioned about their racial background. Many of these accounts about race included colorism.

However, the campus did offer a rare college environment that included a larger population of deaf students and access to interpreters, tutors and note-takers. There were also more Black deaf students than on other campuses. One student described her transition from high school to this college campus as follows:

My deaf school was small and there are so many deaf people here. At the deaf school, I knew everyone there. But here there are 300 new faces every year. It is cool because I get to meet new people and learn different signs from all around the country. I'm from Pennsylvania and I notice the signs are different. It's interesting but it's nice and I have been here for three years and it's been good.

Nevertheless, with only 6 percent African American students, the campus was far from diverse. To counter the isolation, students aggressively sought out others who were willing to be friends or to join study groups. At the same time, meeting new friends and breaking out of cliques aided in avoiding petty disagreements, competition, peer pressure and gossip.

Moving toward eliminating systems of domination based on race, class, gender, audism, and sexuality can begin by changing institutional practices that privilege white, middle-class, male heterosexual and hearing students. In her focus groups and interviews, Chapple asked students about recommendations to improve their educational experiences. Students advocated for programming that was inclusive, which would encourage Black and white, hearing and deaf students to engage in one environment to learn new skills, particularly how to work in diverse groups. Many of the job opportunities and training programs geared toward hearing students of color did not include deaf students of color. These students advocated for activities that addressed all of their identities, not just being deaf. They wanted to talk about race, class, gender and sexuality. Too often, activities targeting deaf LGBTQ students or

Black deaf students were restricted to dancing and entertainment rather than education or training; the activities did not include hearing students with similar needs. Improving many of these one-to-one interactions among students, between students and faculty, and between students and staff involves restructuring the campus and placing value on learning sign language, and hearing students taking classes or attending events about Deaf culture. Physically integrating the colleges would increase everyday exchanges and opportunities to learn from each other. Employing faculty, administrators and staff that know sign language is a strong message that this is a valued language. Hearing students learning sign language would increase their marketability and expand their ability to work with diverse populations later in the labor force. An intersectional approach provides solutions to the issues that deaf Black women students face by understanding them as the embodiment of classed, racialized, gendered, sexualized and differently abled bodies (Barnartt 2006).

The following section explores the intersectionality of everyday life on campus based on the experiences of janitors employed in a research university.

Interactions with Low-Wage Employees

As in many institutional settings, universities have an army of workers who usually wear uniforms, move throughout campus, and are invisible to students, faculty and administrators. Yet, without these workers, there would be a great deal of interruption to university life and other work. The intense cleaning and sprucing up on campuses at the beginning of the semesters and before graduation ceremonies is significant in recruiting and retaining students (Reynolds 2007). Like similar labor involving cleaning, janitors' work is devalued – not only by pay and by the lack of equivalent benefits to other university employees: they are stigmatized by their work of cleaning up after others. Janitors are likely to live in substandard housing and live from paycheck to paycheck. Interactions reflect this stigma, as "[p]rofessionals and managers do not mingle much with service or industrial workers and if they have conversations, they are short, and the subject matter is trivial because they simply do not inhabit the same worlds" (Aronowitz 2003: 31–2).

Class and race differences between these workers and the other employees, as well as the student body, are quite distinct and place them in different worlds. Janitors are among the poor working class who are predominantly of color, and in many locations also immigrant, whereas faculty and administrators are predominantly white from middle- and upper-middle-class backgrounds. During economic hardship, custodians are the first to have their budgets cut, which means fewer custodians and more work for each employee. The contract building-cleaning industry has embraced Taylorism and has moved away from assigning workers an area to clean to assigning specific tasks. The result has been "work intensification" and "rigidity in the gender division of labour" (Aguiar 2001: 240). Janitors and custodians are among the top occupations for developing musculoskeletal disorders, such as back injury, repetitive stress disorder and carpal tunnel syndrome (Flores & Deal 2003). As David Owen describes the functional properties of whiteness: "[b]eing located in a social position by whiteness is not merely a location of difference, but it is also a location of economic, political, social and cultural advantage relative to those located defined by non-whiteness" (2007: 206).

On many campuses today, the janitorial crews are moved farther into the university shadows as they are replaced by contracted labor. On my own campus, this move occurred about a decade ago. Arizona State is an extremely large university with, at the time, about 65,000 students. We knew the middle-age Latina woman who cleaned our offices and the overall building. She was included as staff when the department gave the Christmas bonus. More importantly, the university provided these workers with health insurance and other benefits. One of the most prized benefits was the tuition waiver offered to their children, many of whom were among the first-generation graduates every year. However, as the university moved further toward corporatization and neoliberalism, divisions grew between faculty, staff, janitors and administrators, and any alliances were ground away. The entire custodial staff was fired and so were the more skilled workers in buildings and grounds: plumbers, electricians and carpenters. The work was contracted out and some workers were "offered" their old jobs at a lower rate of pay and benefits.

To lessen faculty protests against the budget cuts resulting in firing janitors, the transition to a third-party vendor occurred in the summer and their schedules changed to night shifts, which made them invisible to faculty and students. Their workdays ended before 6.00 a.m. and they never started work until all classes had ended, ensuring they remained invisible. Their existence in the everyday life on campus is relevant, and indeed essential, in maintaining race, class and gender privilege (Halpern 2003). Interestingly, the shift to low-wage contract companies made the campus less safe. Many of the new custodians were transients. Faculty no longer knew who was cleaning their office, and we were advised to lock our desk drawers and not leave "small electronics" like cell phones, computer tablets and MP3 players where they were visible.

Drawing on Becky Petitt's (2008) dissertation on low-wage workers at a research university, we can examine an intersectional approach to the everyday lives of custodial workers. She began her dissertation by pointing out the significance of race, class and gender oppression and noting the contradiction in the university's mission to "serve society and the larger community." By maintaining wages so low that workers fall into the category of the working poor, the university fails to fulfill this mission. Her point is further made by juxtaposing the observation of a largely oppressed labor force on campus, consisting of low-wage workers who engage in grueling physical labor to keep buildings clean, against the privileges of faculty and administrators with ergonomically engineered offices, enjoying numerous catered lunches during the year, along with salaries six to ten times more than those of these workers. Petitt (2008: iv) argues that these conditions function to reinforce the janitors' marginalized positions and place them first in line "to feel the impact of major institutional shifts, such as increases in student and faculty bodies, and large-scale economic recovery initiatives." While denied a living wage, these women pay the same for parking permits as the highly paid faculty and administrators. Constant surveillance and the practice of moving workers around to other locations on campus without notice maintain a culture of fear. Expected to clean human and animal waste even when the mess is a result of a prank reinforces their subordination. Administrators respond to their organizing efforts to increase pay and benefits with threats of outsourcing custodial services.

This study of women custodial workers conducted at a research university in the Southwest included white, Black and Latina women. As in most research universities, the student enrollment, faculty and administrators were predominantly white and the custodians predominantly Black and Latina. This racial division has a long tradition in universities but here there is a particular history. The first janitor hired was a former Black slave and his fifth-generation great-great-granddaughter is a custodian at the same university today. Petitt shared the following conversation she had with her: "I want something better for my kids. I hope I'm the last to clean out here. Back then, my people used to call State University the 'plantation.' Ain't much changed since then. No, Lord (shaking her head side to side). I don't want this for my kids." At the beginning of the university's history, the color line was enforced by requiring all Black and Latino workers to carry a "Certificate of Identification" to justify their presence on campus. The certificate read:

This certificate will be carried by the party whose name appears hereon and will be produced when directed...No householder, department, contractor, or individual will employ any Negro or Mexican in any capacity whatsoever on this campus unless they have this certificate...And I understand that failure to produce this certificate when directed to do so by inspectors of the college will cause detention and possible arrest. (Petitt 2008: 188)

Visual images of the legacies of this history appear in the continued appearance of confederate flags and decals on residential hall windows and student vehicles, the occasional noose on campus, and hate speech on bathroom walls. Workers shared rumors about the continued presence of a secret White supremacist organization. The university is now more diverse than ever in its 130-year history but most of the diversity is among the lowest-paid employees. Similar to the Black deaf undergraduate female students whom Chapple interviewed, the women custodians were unclear whether the microaggressions they experienced were gender-, race- or class-based. As one Black woman custodian explained to Petitt (2008: 157):

> I don't know if it was because of being Black, or maybe she thought it (using the same restroom) wasn't clean. I don't know. Probably because I'm Black.
> These White folks out here, I'm telling you. Like on the elevator ...they don't want you there with them – they snarl up at you...or act like you're not even there. And they won't speak. Sometimes, I'll say, "good morning," or if it's afternoon, I'll say, "Good afternoon," and they turn their head, stick their little pointy noise in the air.

Another Black woman custodian was clear about the issue of race: "White people just give you them mean looks" (Petitt 2008: 273). However, the level of racism that the women of color custodians encountered ranged from racist comments, verbal abuse, acts devaluing their work, KKK paraphernalia and cleaning up after "ghetto parties" that depicted Blacks as gangsters, rappers and over-weight women, to hanging a Black doll with a noose in the custodial supply cabinet.

Women of color employed as custodians also confronted racism from their co-workers. Several of these women noted that the white women custodians were disrespectful to their supervisors of color and, when they did not get their way in disputes, they occasionally sought the support of other white employees. As one Black woman custodian explained the behavior of her Black supervisor:

> She won't say nothing to them (white employees), just let them walk all over her. But let that be me, she'll write me up and get me in trouble so fast...She scared of losing her job. Like, she think the Black people will just take it, but she's scared those other people will go to the office on her, especially the White people, she scared of them.

There were also comments between white and Black workers:

> And this one time this White lady that worked with us – you know what she told me one day? She say, "Clara, I braided my little girl's hair last night, and she looked just like a little nigger. Just like a little jigaboo." And I went and told my supervisor she said that and that me and the other Black ladies had got mad about her saying that because that was racist. (Petitt 2008: 282)

Mexican women custodians were more likely to be targeted for both limited English proficiency and speaking Spanish in the presence of English-only speakers. Attempts to eliminate monolingual Spanish-speakers from employment involved conducting English-only interviews and discouraging workers by segregating Spanish-speakers from the rest of the crew assigned to the night shift. Even though Spanish-speakers dominated the custodial staff, there appeared to be no attempt to hire bilingual supervisors or advance bilingual workers into supervisory positions.

Women dominated the custodian workforce and men dominated grounds maintenance at the university:

> The people in the physical plant and area maintenance [predominantly male workgroups] are making like seventeen dollars an hour – not supervisors: regular workers – and they just ride around in their trucks. Now, I know they probably fix stuff, but for the most part, they just ride around in the truck. And I'm like, "Well come on, give us some of that money," you know. (Petitt 2008: 283)

It did not escape the notice of many of the women that their work involved hard physical labor and the men spent a portion of their workday driving around transporting equipment and did not perform work that was more strenuous; and yet grounds maintenance staff were paid much more than the custodians were.

In addition to the wage differentials in the occupational segregation of these women workers, they also experienced a hostile sexual environment, particularly those assigned to residence halls. Sexual harassment included cleaning rooms in the residential halls covered with pornography, and male students exposing themselves to women custodians. The university responded to the racist and sexist photos and posters by issuing an "Offensive Printed Material" policy, which mandated that students remove the images prior to the days when custodians enter the area to clean. Petitt's (2008: 273) summation identified the message behind addressing a hostile work environment while maintaining white male privilege: "Put offensive material away while they are around, but once they leave, you may safely display racist, sexist, hate-filled material. Backroom bigotry is permissible." Such a policy not only protects race and gender privilege but also ensures the reproduction of racism, sexism and classism.

Keeping invisible the work that women custodians do for faculty, staff and students, accomplished by refusing to acknowledge their presence, was significant in maintaining privilege. One interviewee explained that this behavior made her work more difficult:

> just like if they have a trash can up under their desk, you know, and it's hard to get to, they act like they don't want to move so you can get it...I got one lady in my...buildin' that...when so you can get to the trash, she kind of in my, you know, she'll just sit there and she sees I'm trying to get her trash, you know, [but] she won't try to move. She'll make me have to reach over her. (Petitt 2008: 109)

Faculty and students are unlikely to spend much time thinking about the person who has to pick up the trash from the bathroom, classroom and office floor, such as left-over food, food wrappers, spilled coffee, ketchup, tobacco spit in a cup, newspapers or the rolled-up papers that missed the rim of the trash baskets. Policies also make them invisible by only allowing them to take a break or take an emergency phone call outside the presence of others, usually in the custodian closet since former break areas have been reclaimed for other uses. One administrator sympathetic to the plight of these workers recognized the invisibility of these women:

> Most of the low-wage earners are people of color and women, and most of their supervisors or administrators are White men...Their voices are relatively muted. This sense of invisibility combined with the kind of work they do present them in a valueless way.
>
> We take them for granted. We know that this work is done, but we have no idea who does it and clearly no personal relationships with these individuals. The lights stay on, and the place stays clean; services are delivered: but it's taken for granted....They don't have a staff senate that represents their interests, and they won't come forward as individuals because they're afraid of losing their jobs. They are expendable, and they have no power as a group. (Petitt 2008: 286–7)

The workload has increased dramatically due to the increasing number of faculty hired and undergraduate students enrolled, but custodians work with a reduced staff and a larger area to clean during their shift; wages have stagnated or decreased due to inflation. Labor becomes more difficult with the expanded workload and deteriorating equipment.

Institutional practices keep these women invisible, which renders the elimination of their jobs in times of economic constraints acceptable.

Petitt's dissertation resonated with me because I saw similar patterns at my own university. Since my arrival at Arizona State University (ASU), I observed the student body grow drastically, including the development of two new campuses. However, the number of faculty did not grow at the same rate. As economic conditions worsened, and the state legislation cut funding to higher education, tuition rates increased, staff were cut, and custodial services were outsourced. As with the blue-collar custodial workers, many office workers were let go. Computers and the internet made many "pink-collar" workers redundant – some of the workload was shifted to students who were expected to register, pay tuition and keep track of their schedules on-line. Faculty experienced an increased workload, as grading, scheduling classes and interactions with students also went "on-line." Academic departments merged to eliminate business managers and academic and administrative assistants. However, at the same time new buildings appeared, sculptures were erected to provide shade, the student recreation center expanded to twice its original size, and several new luxury dorms were built. As Walmart moved into the bottom floor of one of the dorms, countless eateries and Starbucks became part of the ASU landscape. Class differences were always apparent on campus, particularly the distinction between students forced to juggle work schedules with classes and those who have the financial means to be full-time students without working, but these changes make them even more apparent. The marked differences between students are most evident in the availability of valet parking and residence halls assigned according to the student's major – many of which include an option of paying for maid service. The transition from student to customer is not formally recognized, although the university President calls students "our product" in his commencement address. Advertising the university has increased one-hundredfold, and the innovations aimed at recruiting wealthy students appear to dominate expenditure decisions over the last decade. Wealthy international students who pay full tuition are counted as part of the "diversity" on campus. While the university brands diversity, particularly inclusion and community engagement, the highly paid administrators are white males with a few women and men of color in diversity-initiative positions that are isolated from the overall university governance.

Discussion questions

1   How does an intersectional analysis explain the experiences of Black deaf women students and women of color janitors differently from

a one-dimensional analysis? How can you apply the Rubik's cube analogy to these situations?

2   Campuses can interpret and make use of the term "diversity" in different ways, and some examples have been given in this section. How does an intersectional analysis challenge some of these uses of "diversity" and ensure that diversity requirements are appropriately used as a tool for social justice?

Summary

As Chapple's and Petitt's research demonstrates, intersectional understanding of everyday life on college campuses unravels the ways in which our social identities shape our experiences in the classroom, faculty offices and maneuvering our daily activities. Both studies highlight the microaggressions that maintain race, class, gender, sexuality and other structures of power. Students, faculty and workers who are positioned on various points of the axis of power are likely to experience an intersection of racism, sexism and classism. Microaggressions are not necessarily intended to insult or hurt others but they function to maintain inequality. These occur as comments, glances or other body movements expressing discomfort or disdain or simply refusing to acknowledge one's presence. Faculty may use teaching strategies they find convenient or useful but which serve to treat some students as inferior. Hierarchies might be indicated by the architectural design or age of the buildings that house disciplines with wealthy and white students, compared with those with high enrollments of the working class and students of color. Meaningful inclusion and diversity cannot exist without addressing social inequality.

The transformation of academia from a monocultural elitist environment inhabited by upper- and upper-middle-class white males has been an ongoing process. The GI Bill marked a significant opening to working-class white males, and the 1960s saw the gradual inclusion of women and racial ethnic minorities. However, the most recent trend represented by Hopwood v. Texas (2003) restricts the use of race as a factor in achieving a diverse student body. Armed with a social justice agenda, a conscious race, class, gender, ethnic and sexuality agenda in teaching, research and service has the potential for changing the university into a more inclusive environment and shifting power relations between communities.

I now turn to examining the intersectionality of social identities by examining gender. The next chapter illustrates gendered experiences as race- and class-based, as well as intersected with other systems of social inequality.

4

Intersectionality and Social Identities: Examining Gender

Diane Sawyer's interview with Bruce Jenner, the former Olympic gold medalist and member of the Kardashian family, was the most watched television special in 15 years of ABC's *20-20* news program, drawing 16.8 million viewers. At the time of Jenner's interview about his transition from male to female, he asked to be referred to with the pronoun "he" (Stell 2015). Less than two months later, the pronoun requested was "she" for her appearance in a white satin corset with her hair flowing on her bare shoulders on the cover of *Vanity Fair*, with the headline, "Call me Caitlyn." She began her Twitter account with the tweet: "I'm so happy after such a long struggle to be living my true self. Welcome to the world Caitlyn. Can't wait for you to get to know her/me" (Somaiya 2015). Jon Stewart, the host of *The Daily Show* (2015), argued the public's acceptance of Caitlyn as a woman was evident by the sexist media coverage, which treated her like a woman by focusing entirely on her appearance. "You see, Caitlyn, when you were a man we could talk about your athleticism, your business acumen – but – now you're woman and it's your looks is the only thing we care about." Or as Ronda Garelick (2015) wrote in her *New York Times* opinion piece, "It [*Vanity Fair* cover] is a commercial spectacle on an enormous scale, revealing some disturbing truths about what we value and admire in women."

However, questions circulated about her new identity as a woman. For many, her choice to appear on the cover of *Vanity Fair* as a hyper-sexual image of a 65-year-old upper-class white woman did not seem consistent with personal freedom and self-expression or struggling to be her true self. This appearance runs counter to women's experience as they get older and become invisible. Jenner created further discomfort among feminists with her essentialist description of woman as a fixed category rather than a socially constructed identity. She spoke of "being born with the wrong body" and having a woman's brain or a female soul rather than the feminist view: that gender identity is a social construction (Burkett 2015). Decades of feminist research demonstrate the significance of socialization in developing gendered identities. In contrast, the notion of gendered brains suggests that male and female identities are monolithic and nature is more important than nurture – in other words, "gender" is a "fact of nature" rather than the product of socialization. Other feminists questioned Jenner's motives in light of the financial gain involved with this public coming-out followed by a reality show, *I Am Cait*. Still, the overwhelming media coverage, blogs and tweets considered her a role model for transgender youth who encounter hate, ignorance and violence (Kristof 2015).

Caitlyn's coming out as a trans person did give some in the transgender community pause to think about the meaning of her image in advancing transgender issues, because her experience is far from the norm (Grinberg 2015). This perspective was one that Laverne Cox (2015), the openly transgender actor in *Orange Is the New Black*, reflected upon in thinking about the motives behind her own photo shoots. She wrote that her photos functioned: "to serve up various forms of glamour, power, sexiness, body affirming, and racially empowering images of the various sides of my black, trans womanhood....I also hope that it is my talent, my intelligence, my heart and spirit that most captivate, inspire, move and encourage folks to think more critically about the world around them." She pointed out that not all trans people have the financial means, the genes or the desire to "embody certain cisnormative beauty standards"; "It is important to note that these standards are also informed by race, class and ability among other intersections." Cox argued that there was a need for a wide range of media representations that capture many different trans narratives. She acknowledged her own privilege and called for support for trans persons who lack healthcare or are unemployed, homeless or are at risk because of their gender and/or sexual orientation, immigration status and economic circumstances. Cox, like other transgender activists, celebrated the transgender visibility resulting from Caitlyn's publicity, but she urged the public to realize that her experience is far from the reality that most transgender people face (Grinberg 2015).

In an interview with CNN, Lourdes Ashley Hunter, the director of the Trans Women of Color Collective, noted that "Caitlyn's coming out is relatable to mainstream American society because she is white, Republican, rich and famous" (Grinberg 2015). Commenting on the uniqueness of *Vanity Fair*'s publication of Caitlyn on the cover, Kylar W. Broadus (2015), the director of the Transgender Civil Rights Project, released the following statement:

> The realities that transgender people experience in America is [sic] truly alarming. Transgender people are twice as likely to be unemployed and four times more likely to live in poverty when compared to the general population – and these disparities are much greater for transgender Black and Latina women. And for transgender people who are able to find a job, ninety percent of them experience harassment, discrimination or mistreatment at the workplace.

Many activists commented on the contradiction in mainstream media embracing Caitlyn's coming out, while trans people face extreme violence and discrimination (Haberman 2015). Too often, the violence against LGBTQ people is homogenized without recognizing poor trans people of color are most vulnerable (Meyer 2012), particularly youth of color (Singh 2012).

Transgender narratives of the social construction of women's gender identity are contested territory (Emmons & Marcus 2015) with feminists like Elinor Burkett (2015), who argue that the social identity of woman is a process shaped by social circumstances. She explained her argument in her opinion piece published in the *New York Times*:

> Ms. Jenner's experience included a hefty dose of male privilege few women could possibly imagine. While young "Bruiser," as Bruce Jenner was called as a child, was being cheered on toward a university athletic scholarship, few female athletes could dare hope for such largess since universities offered little funding for women's sports. When Mr. Jenner looked for a job to support himself during his training for the 1976 Olympics, he didn't have to turn to the meager "Help Wanted – Female" ads in the newspapers, and he could get by on the $9,000 he earned annually, unlike young women whose median pay was little more than half that of men. Tall and strong, he never had to figure out how to walk streets safely at night. (Burkett 2015)

This description of gender experiences can be further complicated by intersecting gender identities with race, ethnicity, class and sexuality; and, as the controversy surrounding Caitlyn Jenner highlights, trans women's identities are also complicated by these same intersections (Beyer 2015).

I begin this chapter on gender identities and intersectionality with Caitlyn's experience as a transgender woman to highlight the way that gender identity is a social construction that appears in many forms and is interactive with systems of oppression and privilege. In Caitlyn's case, her gender identity as a transgender woman included an emphasized feminine sexual appearance or hegemonic femininity, which not only points to the significance she places on the physical appearance of her body and style in her gender identity as a woman, but reflects her race and class privilege. She carefully avoids discussion of sexuality, which would distract from her performance of hegemonic femininity. While Caitlyn's presentation as a woman made transgender identity visible, hiring a showbiz publicist, Alan Nierob, to handle the process enabled careful control over the images of her new gender identity (Littleton 2015), and ensured a successful enactment of traditional normative femininity. Her 20-20 interview and media coverage in *Vanity Fair* illustrate the process of producing a hegemonic feminine identity through a narrative of memories, experiences, and interpretations (Lawler 2014).

Caitlyn recalled how, as a young boy, he secretly wore dresses and later his third wife's daughter, Kim Kardashian, caught him in a dress. However, Cox's Tumblr feed reminds us that transgender identity does not necessarily follow cisgender normative standards, which refers to having the gender identity to match the sex assigned at birth. Many women responded to Caitlyn's choice of hypersexualized representations of her womanhood as objectifying women. Feminists argued that these "cultural practices and ideology [are] associated with femininity that reflects a gendered power structure in which women are subordinate to men, and in turn, some women attain a higher status ... resulting in social devaluation of other women" (Cole & Zucker 2007: 1). Overwhelmingly, the media embrace of her new gender identity demonstrates the power and status she received by embodying hegemonic femininity. Feminists challenged these normative standards because race, class, sexuality, religion and bodily status marginalize many women. A closer look at the intersectionality of gender with race, class and sexuality emphasizes the connection between social identities and power, and the manifestation of privilege, opportunities and subordination.

In sociology, intersectional approaches to social identities expand our knowledge and understandings of gender, race, class and sexuality as lived experiences. These approaches require sociologists to "examine gender concretely in context" and as historically "produced, reproduced, and transformed in different situations over time" (Scott 1999: 6). This chapter elaborates how gender identity takes on more than a singular, homogeneous category of femininity or masculinity. The range of gender identities are manifested with multiple dimensions of identity – including racial, ethnic, class, sexual and age – which position individuals in different locations of power. Exploring gender identity through intersectionality includes the connection to other identities that organize social relations in a complex socio-structure of larger power relationships in society – again, think of the Rubik's cube. Identities are not independent or separate from the processes of inequality: "The goal of most intersectional research is to address ways in which intersecting identities often create conflict between and within groups in an effort to create a richer and more thought out transgressive politics and/or a dynamic understanding of the social world" (Battle & Ashley 208: 3). Tasks critical to intersectional approaches to gender include: identifying gender regimes, recognizing the policing of gender boundaries, and assessing the cost for transgressing boundaries (Reardon 2012). We see this conflict in the case of Caitlyn, who chose a hegemonic femininity that embraced her race and class privilege. Understanding the everyday practices that evoke, shape and articulate identities and categorize them as marginalized or ideal will contribute to the deconstruction of essentialisms and move toward developing empowering articulations of individual and collective identity (Hall 1992). Narratives of poor transgender youth of color challenge the assumption of a hypersexualized presentation of womanhood as natural or of certain aspects as fundamental and absolute in gender identity. This chapter examines the intersectionality of gender identities and their relations to domination and privilege.

Intersectionality and the Construction of Femininity and Womanhood

For most of its history, culture in the United States has treated gender identity as binary, fixed, natural and determined at birth (however, this is not the case with all cultures, including Native Americans). Essentialist approaches to gender identity that define differences, variations or transgressions as deviant and unnatural stem from Abrahamic religious traditions. For the more well-to-do social classes, an essentialist gender approach has relegated women to care-taking and domestic activities, on the basis that they are supposedly naturally inclined to such labor and women are better at these skills than men. Traditional views of womanhood have essentially denied women full participation in government and public life. Laws, religion, the economy and culture are institutions that establish and maintain the superiority of men over women. Common law introduced by English colonists placed women under the legal control of their husbands or fathers. A woman could not own property or sign contracts, rarely controlled her own earnings, and had no legal standing separate from her husband. Rape was a property crime against her husband or father. Based on white upper- and middle-class values, the idea of femininity was linked to a piety, purity, submission and domesticity requiring a devotion to enriching home and family. Abrahamic religions – Christianity, Judaism and Islam – restricted leadership roles to men, and only recently revisited religious documents to reconsider the significance of women. Five characteristics generally accepted as constructing femininity are: beauty, demeanor, marriage and family arrangements, heterosexuality and whiteness (Collins 2004). How did these ideas come about and why do they remain dominant themes? To answer these questions, I will examine social institutions, historical processes, and social practices that construct and maintain femininity.

Historical Intersections: Domesticity under Slavery, Conquest, and Colonialism

As discussed in chapter 2, Evelyn Nakano Glenn's (1999: 9) use of an integrative framework is helpful in identifying "important points of congruence between the concept of racial formation and the concept of socially constructed gender." US history constructed femininity, as well as masculinity, through its history of slavery, conquest and colonialism. Social structure and cultural representation are key concepts in the interpretative framework of gender and race. Social structure arranges privileges, opportunities and subordination around specific combinations of gender and racial identities. The economy structures the labor market into class, gender and racial segregation, allocating different monetary rewards to different positions. Upwardly mobile positions were traditionally "White-only" or "men-only" jobs. Race and class residential segregation had negative consequences for the education, health and well-being of families of color. Government classification of who the deserving poor were resulted in providing benefits to white mothers, which improved their families' life chances. Simultaneously, migrant farm workers and domestics were ineligible for most benefits. As noted in the first chapter, institutions such as education, economy and religion imposed power relations based on race, class, gender and sexuality that even today influence everyday activity such as parenting.

Central to an integrative framework are relational concepts. In other words, we understand gendered concepts through their relation to another concept. In the case of femininity, white middle- and upper-class women's relationship to Black women on the plantation informed the processes that constructed the Black woman slave as a breeder rather than a mother, or as a seductress rather than a rape victim, and as the master's property rather than a Black man's daughter or wife. Similarly, indigenous women were devalued on reservations and in boarding schools and urbanization programs, while white middle-class women engaged in missionary work. Colonial relations in Puerto Rico, Hawaii and the Philippines established whiteness against the "other" living in occupied territory, and relegated women of color to the lowest ranks in society unless they were of royal ancestry – and then, at times, incorporated them into the government hierarchy as *compradors* to subjugate their own people. In many of these historical processes, religion and education contributed to defining and maintaining privilege and opportunity based on class, race and gender.

The ideal type of femininity required privileges which were denied to women who were poor, immigrant, Black, American Indian and Mexican. Excluded from the privileges and protections of domesticity, women of color could not obtain class and race privileges through birth or marriage because their fathers and husbands did not have the right to own property in many cases; and many men of color were relegated to the lowest-paying jobs. Instead, Black women, and many Mexican and Indian women, toiled alongside their husbands, fathers and sons in fields or worked as domestics, laundresses and cooks (Glenn 2004). Instead of gaining the full privileges of marriage, women of color entered the labor force to contribute necessities for their family (Dill 1988). Employers did not assume they were weak, fragile or in need of protection. Nor did they consider them first as mothers who needed to provide care for their children. Divisions in employment, referred to as occupational segregation, further structured poor and women of color's chances of attaining the social class necessary to maintain the ideal form of femininity.

A good place to start an integrative analysis is the culture of domesticity or cult of true womanhood, which was the normative standard for women during the eighteenth and nineteenth centuries in the US and Great Britain. Social roles were based on two premises: (1) that the standards for women were universal (but could only be lived up to by upper- and upper-middle-class families); and (2) that the social world is divided into a private and a public sphere. The *private* sphere is the home and was assigned to women of means as their natural calling; the home was contrasted with the *public* sphere of men in business and politics. Femininity in the US was tied to the cult of domesticity, and thus to social-class-based gender enactments of "being a lady." Along with being submissive to her husband and father, she was expected to be domestic, pious and pure, as well as weak and dependent. The making of a lady required leisure time and wealth to groom a specific type of appearance, to learn the mannerisms and style of the elite, upper-class and white etiquette, while engaging in activities suited to her position in life. One of these roles was to provide charity aimed at the poor. Constructed by powerful beliefs and reinforced by social structures of class, race and sexuality, this form of femininity was only for wealthy, white, heterosexual women who had access to the privileges that placed them in a position of power over other women and some men.

As the wives and daughters of wealthy white men, these women held power over poor and immigrant women, especially women of color employed in the kitchens and home, doing the cooking, laundry, housework and childcare. In effect, they were labor supervisors in the private sphere, as their men were in the public sphere. It is interesting that these aristocratic roles are so popular in the twenty-first century in television series like *Downton Abbey*. While Victorian and Edwardian England had a different, less racialized, social structure, US audiences seem fascinated by the ways the "Lady of the Manor" and the Dowager Countess asserted their power as managers of the home. They are portrayed as "powers behind the throne." The cult of domesticity viewed women's place as in the home, but the "lady" was called to the " 'higher' tasks and to supervision" of her servants, who were relegated to the drudgery of the physical labor (Dudden 1983: 155). The "lady" of the house was also in charge of the "help's" religious and moral training, or of educating poor, immigrant women and women of color to become respectable. Engaging in volunteer work and participating in "good works" in low-income neighborhoods reinforced their superiority over all other women. Several US dramas have introduced the color line and issues of race into the roles of "lady of the house," for example *Imitation of Life* (1959), *Driving Miss Daisy* (1989) and *The Help* (2011). In each case, this role of the upper-class female is held as an epitome of womanhood.

While the cult of domesticity assured elite, upper-class, white women protection from the drudgery of dirty and dangerous work, it also limited their physical movement, aspirations and talents. They were dependent on their husbands or fathers. However, "historically, 'the lady' was an ideological tool useful for controlling all women, but it affected poor women and/or women of color differently. Those women were controlled by exclusion" (Meyers 2004: 36). Excluded from the protections of working and living in safe environments, working-class women held factory jobs working long hours, under deplorable conditions, and lived in crowded housing. Women of color and poor immigrants serving and caring for their employers also faced long hours. In addition, their living conditions lacked privacy, and even outside, their movements remained under the employer's watch. They gained none of the privileges of "true womanhood" and were denied access to the circumstances required for this type of femininity. Yet they were constantly evaluated by their failure to meet the criteria of being a lady.

It is important to remember that there was significant push-back by working-class women. For example, Mother Jones said, "No matter what the fight, don't be ladylike! God Almighty made women and the

Rockefeller gang of thieves made the ladies." Sojourner Truth's famous speech "Ain't I a woman?" included a scathing critique of domesticity and the way this ideology denied her experience as a hard-working woman. Sojourner Truth based her gender identity on her realities of being a Black woman born into slavery, sold, beaten and mistreated, who eventually escaped slavery and became a preacher and abolitionist.

For the poor and women of color, the experience of being a woman is much broader than prescribed by the cult of domesticity. Judged against normative white upper-middle-class standards of womanhood, neither Mother Jones nor Sojourner Truth ever experienced the privileges of domesticity but both confronted the disadvantages of gender, race and class. Poor women wore the scars of their identity as a Black woman or as a working-class woman. However, unlike the "ladies," they were outspoken and political. Eventually, women of the upper class came to realize that they were in a gilded prison, as even one of the privileged daughters in *Downton Abbey* demonstrated for women's rights.

In her essay "Double jeopardy: To be Black and female," Beale (1970: 91) provided a clear analysis of imperialism, racism and capitalism in the US definition of femininity. Writing the first draft in 1969, she identified the ideal model, consisting of being "estranged from all real work, spending idle hours primping and preening, obsessed with conspicuous consumption, and limiting life functions to a simple sex role." Beale argued that Black women could not engage in such activity because they must seek employment to provide shelter, food and clothing for their families. Moreover, she wrote that seeking the feminine existence should not be a goal to strive for, because bourgeois women live their lives through their husbands and are reduced to a biological function and a "parasitic existence." For Black women to limit their contributions to having children ignored the vibrant history of strong Black women leaders. Beale defined Black women's place in a technologically advanced society like the US to be as "teachers, doctors, nurses, electronics experts, chemists, biologists, physicists, political scientists" (1970: 93), rather than as unpaid care workers.

Current Structures and Media Representations

Intersectionality is tricky and attempts to portray it in popular culture are even trickier. The intersections of race, class and gender were contentious social issues in the 1970s and 1980s: civil rights demands had moved from the South to the North – in housing, schooling and the work-place, they had produced race riots. School bussing and court-enforced integration led to violence in some northern cities. Through the decade of the 1970s, women pushed hard for an equal rights amendment to the constitution, but lost in the early 1980s. Beginning in the decade of the 1970s, the decline of the American working class began to be seen as a significant and long-term problem. These tangible and in some ways intractable social problems were played out in political life and on the streets. Television and popular culture played an important but not always helpful role.

Intersectionality is clearly visible in attempts to portray Black families and women as the same as white middle- to upper-middle-class families, except in blackface. However, even while attempting to confront racism, *The Jeffersons* (1975–85) and *The Bill Cosby Show* (1984–1992) continued to reproduce strong elements of the cult of domesticity, mirroring the stereotypes of white women in TV series. *The Jeffersons* was a spin-off of *All in the Family* (1971–9), but whereas the main protagonist of *All in the Family* was white and working class, *The Jeffersons* focused on a Black middle-class family, aiming to reduce the threat to Whites from the rising Black middle class – George Jefferson ran a string of dry-cleaning shops, a stereotypically immigrant path to mobility (Chinese laundries being the archetype). The producer, Norman Lear, a white liberal and founder of People for the American Way, was normalizing race, class and gender stereotypes in order to confront the social changes of the time. The white working class was nervous about losing place and privilege to people of color, so the rising Black middle class portrayed was not a threat, nor was the Women's Movement.

Decades later, researchers continue to report that Black women fail to meet feminine standards set by white upper-class women, and instead are depicted in the media as unattractive, aggressive, and incompetent mothers (Cole & Zucker 2007). In other contemporary contexts, they are assumed to be asexual and nurturing or domineering and emasculating (West 2004). The asexual and nurturing set of characteristics is the "Mammy" role, which has been around throughout the history of Hollywood films. Recent film depictions of Mammy are *The Help* (2011), *Madea Goes to Jail* (2009) and *Big Momma's House* (2000). For some, the *Oprah Winfrey Show* was a contemporary example of the quintessential Mammy as she cried with her mostly white female audience. "Since the Oprah Winfrey Show's inception, the fan base has described its relationship to Winfrey much as white society did to the mammy" (Stanley 2007: 41).

The alternative stereotype of African American women as hypersexual, domineering and emasculating makes up the characteristics of the "Sapphire" stereotype; unlike the Mammy, Sapphire dominates men and usurps their roles. Spike Lee's first film, *She's Gotta Have It* (1986), attempts to create a strong female character, Nola Darling, who claimed the male prerogative of promiscuity with three partners, but ends up unhappy and alone. In *Madea Goes to Jail*, the main character is portrayed as having anger management problems, which degrades strong African American women as the "Angry Black Woman." Shonda Rhimes, television producer and writer, created leading roles intended to depict strong Black women in *Scandal*, *Grey's Anatomy* and *How to Get Away with Murder*. However, a *New Times* critic reduced them to just angry Black women (Stanley 2014) rather than complex characters. The trope of the Angry Black Woman is so common that conservatives frequently framed the former first lady, Michelle Obama, as the Angry Black Woman – when she was anything but.

In the mid twentieth century, when middle-class white women entered offices as clerks, secretaries and other "pink-collar" positions, many women of color continued to toil in agriculture and domestic service. Poor white women and women of color dominated the dirty jobs in factories, sweatshops, poultry farms and canneries (Glenn 2004). As increasing numbers of Black women achieved class privileges, Black femininity did not always embrace the submissive and fragile characteristics imposed on white women. Instead, they were more likely to incorporate independence, intelligence and engagement in race consciousness activities in the larger community (Carlson 1992: 62). Comparing and contrasting these different gender constructions of femininity demonstrate that there are important gender, race and class intersections that have deep historical roots.

These oppositional categories are overgeneralizations to accentuate differences. For example, encountering women engaged in activities normally considered men's roles, such as the few Mexican women running businesses, riding horses bareback or smoking, generated depictions of seductive and loose women in the newly acquired territories after the Mexican–American War. The elite classes in the occupied territory perceived white women as a gentler sex, delicate and refined. The dichotomies established during this early history included Whites constructed against Blacks, or Anglos constructed against Mexicans. Subordinated groups were characterized by negative traits, such as being immoral, lazy or hypersexual. US soldiers invading Asian countries during World War II, and the Korean and Vietnam wars, imagined Asian women as "hyperfeminine: passive, weak, quiet, slavishly dutiful, submissive, sexually exotic, and available to white men" (Pyke & Johnson 2003: 36). It is remarkable that these imagined characteristics survived even when confronted by female Asian warriors. However, these stereotypes are controlling images that serve "not to reflect or represent a reality but to function as a disguise, or mystification, of objective social relations" (Carby 1987: 22). These controlling images of women of color seep into and present racialized gender expectations in such places as work, with colleagues and supervisors; in school, with teachers and classmates; and in clinics and hospitals, with nurses and doctors. An employer denying Black women promotions because he considers them irresponsible and aggressive is an example of the effect of controlling images. In schools, this might take the form of assuming Black and Latina adolescent girls to be promiscuous because they wear make-up (or think of the assumptions made about the Mexican American undergraduate and her 5-year-old sister from the preceding chapter). Healthcare workers may assume Black, Latina and indigenous women will abuse pain medicine and require them to undergo pain management supervision when given a prescription after surgery.

Colorism

The intersectionality of race, ethnicity, class and nation are vital to understanding the ways in which colorism constructs gender. Black, Mexican, Indian and other dark Latinas and Asians are more likely to be depicted as unattractive and failing to attain the norms of female whiteness, and frequently have been represented as aggressive, sexually promiscuous and bad mothers. Unfortunately, even within their own cultures, lighter skin tone, "good hair" and western features are perceived as prettier. The legacy of slavery, conquest and colonialism defined whiteness as civilized, virtuous and beautiful; whereas non-Whites were considered barbaric, savage and physically ugly. Ideologies of white supremacy include the hierarchies of color or colorism in which is found a structure of privilege for individuals, particularly women of color, who have European physical characteristics. Women of color who are more likely to adhere to the white woman's appearance, and more likely to have some European ancestry, are characterized as attractive and exotic. Today, selecting lighter-skinned women over darker-skinned women in acting, modeling and television news anchors is a common practice. Preference for lighter skin color also incorporates hair texture and the size of lips, eyes, nose, and overall appearance. Related to racism but having a distinct position to institutional power, colorism operates differently at the local, regional, ethnic and national levels and is understood through the context of class, gender or national markers. To capture the significance of colorism to social identities, Angela Harris (2009) calls our attention to the economies of color linked to production, exchange and consumption. Colorism has functioned in the Black community dating back to slavery when mulattos were given advantages such as "desirable skilled and domestic positions, better food and clothing, and manumission and educational opportunities" that placed them in a better position to become the social and economic elite in the African American community after the Civil War (Keith 2009: 27). Privileging of color continues and shapes their community of scholars, business owners and politicians, to such a point that color has become symbolic of one's class position (Hughes & Hertel 1990; Keith & Herring 1991).

In her study of women using skin-lightening products in the Philippines, Joanne Rondilla (2009) links colorism to Spanish and American colonialism as well as the emergence of a Chinese and Spanish mestizo middle class. Analyzing ads in the Philippines and the US, along with interviews with Asian Americans and Asian immigrants, the study highlights the significance of regional, national and ethnic levels. Advertisements promote "a very specific kind of beauty consisting of extremely pale skin, straight jet-black hair, and large, double-lidded, almond-shaped eyes" (2009: 64). While many in the US attribute light skin to European influences, Rondilla notes that light skin is a marker of higher class between the Chinese. Dark skin among Asian immigrants denotes class because of working outside. However, in the US, tanning in the summer is related to the leisure class and vacationing. Rondilla illustrates the use of Asian European models who blend the desired Asian traits with European notions of beauty to create "a distinct and unique identity" that is globalized (2009: 69). Examining the interaction between intersecting race, ethnicity, class and nation systems of inequality is critical to understanding colorism in the construction of gender.

Discussion questions

1   How does an intersectional perspective provide a more comprehensive understanding of the privileges and disadvantages of acting like a "lady?"
2   Using an intersectional framework, explain the privileges and disadvantages popular women athletes experience. Use the Rubik's cube as an analytical tool to discuss different sports, such as tennis, track and gymnastics.

Gender and Intersectionalities of Sexuality

At this point, I want to broaden the examination of gender and intersectionality by examining sexuality. Alternative gender performances emerge at the intersection of gender and sexuality; race and class will also be considered. In her study of gay identities and motherhood among Black women, Mignon Moore (2011) identified three gender identity representations in Black lesbian communities: "femme," "gender-blender" and "transgressive." Gender performance involves a selection of appearance, such as clothing, dress and hairstyles; and behavior, so that walking, gesturing and speaking take on specific meanings in the presence of other Black lesbians. Once the women select a style for public and private gender performances, they usually adhere to it. This presentation is not only an expression of gender identity but also a reflection of class, ethnicity and other group memberships. Moore explained the intersectionality of class, sexuality and gender as follows: "Middle-class lesbians avoid transgressive gender presentation because it interferes with their attempts to erect moral and symbolic boundaries that signify their class status and facilitate their assimilation into larger society. Working-class lesbians embrace nonfeminine gender display and use it as an act of resistance to social norms" (Moore 2011: 70).

Although femmes presented gender in feminine dress, hairstyles and accessories, they were not passive or submissive and had no problem being assertive. Since Black women have a different experience of femininity from white women, femmes do not perceive it as linked to a patriarchy framework that defines women as weak, dependent or frail. Gender-blenders emphasize neither femininity nor masculinity. Instead, they mix both gendered styles to create a different presentation. Transgressive women presented a non-feminine or masculine gender style. Moore (2011: 75) described this style as an incorporation of "Black social and cultural markers and Black aesthetic style with Black masculinity on their bodies – to display multiple identities while openly acknowledging their gay identity."

Generally, research shows that gender and sexual identities of lesbians of color are frequently uniquely different from those of white lesbians. Sabrina Alimahomed's (2010) ethnographic study offered an examination of some unique features. Collecting data on queer-identified Latinas and Asian/Pacific Islander women in Los Angeles and San Francisco, Alimahomed found that white lesbians primarily focused solely on their gay identity. Lesbians of color did not necessarily choose to privilege one identity over the other and did not only identify as gay but rather had an intersectional identity. The lesbians of color Alimahomed interviewed recognized other identities that shaped their gender and sexual identities as well as the different social contexts involved in negotiating aspects of their identities. For instance, an interviewee explained that her Koreanness informed the meaning of being butch, which was distinct from performing white butch. These women encountered rigid definitions of gender identity from white women who rejected the notion that queerness does not have to be a western lesbian identity. However, not conforming to western lesbian gendered norms made them invisible in queer events and social spaces, while being a lesbian sometimes made them invisible as a Latina or Asian in other situations. Multiple identities of women of color lesbians "erased the authority" of their lived experiences (Alimahomed 2010: 161), which can be potentially harmful when seeking educational, health and social services. Reflecting on the Rubik's cube as an analytical device, one can shift the systems of inequality in various settings to observe the salience of one identity over the other, as well as the interaction of multi-identities operating when seeking healthcare or applying for family assistance for bilingual children or a monolingual Chinese-speaking elderly mother.

Geographically, it is fruitful to examine further complexities at the intersection of gender and sexuality identity with race, class and ethnicity. For instance, in the case of Puerto Rican lesbians' gender performance, family and community pressure is more significant on the island than on the mainland. Marysol Asencio (2009) found that many migrant Puerto Rican lesbians in her study engaged in femme gender performance, particularly in social settings that included their families or their community. In Puerto Rico, these women felt enormous pressure to conform to feminine ideals and contrasted their lack of freedom with that experienced by males within their families, the community and the larger society. Retaining strong family and community ties, and keeping employment, required these lesbians to maintain a feminine performance in public. While siblings and parents might be aware of their sexual orientation, as long as they performed feminine, families did not inquire about their sexuality. As adolescents, many of these lesbians escaped parental and community scrutiny by appearing to lack interest in having a boyfriend. However, as they became older, the expectation of marriage and children defined the absence of a boyfriend as no longer gender-conforming behavior. Some middle-class lesbians who pursued higher education were able to maintain an adolescent behavior of showing lack of interest in men because they were studious and serious women. Puerto Rican lesbians reported relocation to the States allowed for more integration of sexuality and gender identities in public spaces.

Rural and urban geographies also change the norms of gender performance, by marking female masculinity differently. In her research on white rural lesbians, Emily Kazyak (2012) found that female masculinity was more normative than transgressive. Consequently, these lesbians' gender performance as strong and hard workers, wearing practical clothes, linked them to the country rather than the city – which was no different from heterosexual women. They experienced a sense of belonging and acceptance in their communities. Research on white lesbians living in rural America suggests that geography plays an important role in understanding gender identity and gender representation. While, in urban areas, masculine appearance and mannerism are markers of lesbian identity, these same masculine gender practices in dress, work and mannerisms were common for women in traditionally non-female jobs, regardless of sexuality.

Women who are white, upper- or middle-class, heterosexual, non-disabled and US citizens possess the attributes required to obtain the ideal appearance, and to fulfill normative gender roles. Women are likely to engage in hegemonic femininity for power and status, as demonstrated in the choices Caitlyn Jenner made. The gender traits of upper- and middle-class white women being held as the norm for all women functions to maintain inequality and persuade "subordinated people that ideologies favorable to the ruling group are natural or common sense" (Cole & Zucker 2007: 1). Interestingly, families and communities of color that enforce norms of colorism, including rejecting potential marriage partners with dark skin or keeping their female children out of the sun in fear their skin will darken, face a conundrum. Working-class women who enter working-class-male-dominated occupations outside, such as construction, mining or firefighting, cannot escape the sunshine, thus are constantly having their gendered identity policed.

Discussion question

1   How does an intersectional framework further our understanding of gender performance among lesbians?

Intersectionality and Masculinity

Just as the femininities of women of color and of immigrant and working-class women are marginalized social identities, not all men experience the same male privilege in our patriarchal society. Judaism, Christianity, Islam and other religious traditions sanction patriarchy as the natural order and offer patriarchal authority to high-ranking religious and political figures. History records the procession of clerics and kings the world over who held the most powerful positions and retained the most wealth. Victor Seidler (1988: 272) summarized the tradition as follows: "Within a patriarchal society our understanding of the nature of political authority has been tied up with our sense of the position of the father within the family." Patriarchal societies tend to link masculinity with rationality, discipline, morality, independence and self-sufficiency, which serve to identify men from outside their social circle of power as weaker, less rational, immoral and dependent. The Anglo-Saxon history of colonialism further served to characterize non-European men as barbaric or more childlike, and in some cases, perceived them as less human. As Michael Kimmel (1996: 5) explained, "In large part, it's other men who are important to American men; American men define their masculinity not so much in relation to women, but in relation to each other. Masculinity is largely a homosocial enactment."

This comparison to other men is evident in exploring the intersectional axis of disability and masculinity. The masculine characteristics of independence and strength are in conflict with being a disabled man. As Coston & Kimmel (2012: 101) wrote: "Disabled men do not meet the unquestioned and idealized standards of appearance, behavior, and emotion for men. The values of capitalist societies based on male dominance are dedicated to warrior values, and a frantic able-bodiedness represented through aggressive sports and risk-taking activities, which do not make room for those with disabilities." Disabled men may distance themselves from hegemonic masculine images, reformulate these ideals to accommodate their physical or mental abilities, or completely reject these ideals (Gerschick & Miller 1994). These processes are dynamic and not mutually exclusive in everyday practice and in different social contexts (Gerschick 1998). Gender identity is not completely shaped by disability – needless to say, it includes the intersections of class, race and sexuality. More recently, researchers have considered the different impact that the various types of impairment have on gender identity, the effect of the time the impairment occurred, and the changes during different life phases. An example is an undocumented Latino day laborer in San Francisco, who, after serious job injuries, became disabled and was no longer able to meet his family and community gender expectations, which include working and sending home remittances. Many disabled male workers acknowledged that their parents, children and wives consider them failures (Walter et al. 2004). An intersectional understanding of disability and gender identity is the only approach that captures various power relations in specific contexts and life phases and moves "beyond a static understanding of disability and of masculinity" (Shuttleworth et al. 2012: 186).

I want to explore the intersectionality of gender, race and class in more detail, focusing on masculinity, to illustrate the social dynamics of multiple identities interacting within society's hierarchies. The next subsection highlights the institutional structures establishing opportunities and privileges for some groups of men, and constraints and barriers for others. The law and policing are areas that point to the different consequences in responding to the intersection of masculinity and race. Then,

I turn to two other activities – sports and employment – which construct and socialize different types of masculinity based on race and class.

Gender Intersecting with Race and Class

Central to masculine gender identity today were the early race and class legal restrictions that denied citizenship rights to non-white men, and denied the rights that were granted to white men with property to men without property (López 1996). The law marginalized men who did not conform to heterosexual masculinity or lacked the ability to demonstrate their independence. Examples are the laws that structurally marginalized Asian immigrant men through racist policies including immigration laws, land exclusionary laws, exploitation of labor, residential exclusion, and violence (Takaki 1993). One can trace popular-culture depictions of Asian men as effeminate to the exclusion of Chinese women and miscegenation laws, which forced the establishment of all-bachelor Chinese communities and their frequent employment in labor considered as "women's work."

In today's media-obsessed world, East Asian men have three different stereotyped roles where western-perceived race and gender display intersect: (1) Fu Manchu, the inscrutable evil villain; (2) clever nerds who are perceived as effeminate; or (3) hyper-masculine action "good guy" figures skilled in arcane martial arts to battle crime. Compare Fu Manchu with George Takei with Bruce Lee. The original evil genius, Dr. Fu Manchu was popular before World War II when the Japanese became the "Yellow Peril." He was a brilliant masculine villain. In *The Insidious Dr. Fu Manchu*, the author, Sax Rohmer (1965 [1913]), described him thus: "Imagine a person, tall, lean and feline, high-shouldered, with a brow like Shakespeare and a face like Satan...one giant intellect, with all the resources of science past and present....Imagine that awful being, and you have a mental picture of Dr. Fu-Manchu, the yellow peril incarnate in one man."

Bruce Lee, like the other martial arts stars Jet Li and Jackie Chan, was hyper-masculine, capable of amazing physical feats and, unlike Fu Manchu, who was always thwarted, the Asian Kung Fu was undefeatable. George Takei, who began his acting career as Lt. Sulu on *Star Trek*, was selected in the multicultural environment of the Star Ship *Enterprise* to represent all Asians as the staff physicist. In that role, Sulu follows Charlie Chan (played by Anglos in "yellowface") and a long line of Asian houseboys who served quietly in the background – mostly silent but super-smart. George Takei has become one of the most beloved internet sensations since he came out as a gay man with progressive politics, but he refused to allow *Star Trek* to do a new episode with a gay Sulu because it would be historically inaccurate. At the time of the original series, gay men had not "been liberated."

The intersection of perceived Black characteristics with masculinity is portrayed distinctly differently from these portrayals of Asians; consider *Moonlight* (2016), *Fences* (2016) or *Straight Outta Compton* (2015). Hyper-masculine athletes and on-screen personalities like Richard Roundtree, Samuel L. Jackson or Wesley Snipes work in two directions, reflecting the deep ambivalence in US culture. On the one hand is the villain like Jackson reciting a made-up Bible quote before shooting a bunch of white boys too punk for the drug trade. Physically imposing, merciless and prone to violence – the Black man is a dangerous animal. They grow up in tough neighborhoods like Detroit or Baltimore – setting for *The Wire* (2002–9) – where one has to fight like a man to survive. (This is obviously emphasized by punk Black boys like Urkel in *Family Matters*, or Carlton on *The Fresh Prince of Bel-Air* (1990–6), whose upper-class Black masculinity is presented as not authentic in contrast to Will Smith's street smarts.) Even in Blaxploitation films, they are violent, large and hyper-masculine.

Along with perpetuating international images of Black men as dangerous and hypersexual, US popular culture contributed to negative images of Latino men. Like Black men, Latino men's masculinity is similarly cast as hypermasculinity – "the exaggerated exhibition of physical strength and personal aggression" (Harris 2000: 785). Popular culture characterizes Latino men's masculinities as static, defined by a "cult of exaggerated masculinity" that includes control over women, and other men (Chant & Craske 2003), referred to as *machismo*. A classic stereotype is the revolutionary social bandit based on mainstream culture, which reduced the Mexican–American War and the history of resistance and struggle against the dispossession of land and oppression to the image of a violent, barbarous and ferocious Mexican *bandido*. Latino male images have saturated the silver screen with images of gang members, drug dealers, wife abusers, prisoners and other violent characters (Romero 2001).

Latinos do not have to be physically imposing and are usually in a gang or "drug cartel." As in *Scarface* (1983) or *No Country for Old Men* (2007), Latinos are capable of pitiless torture and murder. Danny Trejo and Robert LaSardo were the archetypal Mexican bad guys in more than a hundred westerns and drug-cartel movies. However, some of these recent films are meant to be read against the grain, which is to say the stereotype is meant to appear ridiculous. Robert Rodriguez' *El Mariachi* (1992) series was firmly in this genre. Danny Trejo becomes "Machete" in crime comedies like *Machete Kills* (2010) and *Machete Kills Again*

(2013). There is also a deconstruction going on, as *Once Upon a Time in Mexico* (2003) and *Pulp Fiction* (1994) feature apparent intersections of racialized violence that are intended to be mocked. In other words, the stereotyped intersection of masculinity, race, ethnicity and violence has been revealed in fictional media.

In real life, nothing much has changed. A closer look at current legal restrictions and law enforcement practices that construct Black and Latino masculinity in opposition to hegemonic white masculinity further illustrates the intersectionality of race and gender. "News" media constantly repeat stereotyped images of Black men as hypersexual, dangerous, thugs, and criminals. The "stigma attached to their skin color, age, gender, appearance, and general style of presentation" results in the Black male being identified with criminality, incivility, toughness and danger (Anderson 1990: 163). Women and Whites lock car doors, cross the street, hold on to or hide their belongings when encountering Black men, an everyday reminder that US society fears their bodies.

The police use of lethal force in confronting a Black man suspect is so much a part of the daily news that parents with Black sons are irresponsible if they do not teach young boys how to stay out of harm's way. Responsible parenting for Blacks and racialized Latinos means having that difficult conversation with their sons about the way society views them as dangerous and parents emphasize everyday practices that might reduce irrational white fears (Bell et al. 1998; Greene 1992). The *New York Times* devoted an entire multi-media series to this discussion (Gandbhir & Foster 2015). Black and Latino parents correctly fear for their sons' safety in police encounters (Fine & Weis 1998; Dottolo & Stewart 2008) particularly when they are driving. As Katheryn Russell (2009 [1998]: 61–2) explained:

> They are subject to vehicle stops for a variety of reasons, some legal, some not:
>
> 1   Driving a luxury automobile
> 2   Driving an old car
> 3   Driving a car with other Black men
> 4   Driving a car with a White woman
> 5   Driving early in the morning
> 6   Driving late at night
> 7   Driving a rented automobile
> 8   Driving too fast
> 9   Driving too slow
> 10 Driving in a low-income neighborhood known for its drug traffic
> 11 Driving in a White neighborhood
> 12 Driving in an area where there have been recent burglaries

13 Fitting the profile of a drug courier
14 Violating the vehicle code (e.g., failure to signal, excessive speed, exposed tail light).

These incidents are so common, we know them as DWB (Driving While Black or Driving While Brown).

Contrast the above difficult conversation to white middle-class parents instructing their sons about their rights to remain silent and resist warrantless searches. Their conversation is unlikely to emphasize how to appear less threatening but rather how to assert their rights, not to speak to the police without a lawyer, and not to be intimated into giving evidence. Here the focus is on their white, male and class privilege, which is a very different type of conversation.

Police use of racial profiling of male youth of color, dressed in attire defined as "urban" (e.g. baggy pants, T-shirt, baseball cap worn backwards, hooded sweatshirt) demonstrates the intersectional profile of race, gender and class (Meeks 2000; Wilson et al. 2004; Young 2004). Police do not suspect white suburban males dressed in similar clothing and listening to rap music. Police racial bias was the focus of the hoodie movement, which sparked the debate over race and justice. After the shooting death of Trayvon Martin, the media blamed wearing a hoodie as responsible for George Zimmerman's use of lethal force. Zimmerman was a neighborhood watch coordinator in the gated community where Martin was living. Although Martin was unarmed, Zimmerman claimed self-defense under Florida's Stand Your Ground statute, which resulted in his release. Protesters wore hoodies to demonstrate that fashion choices are not criminal. Among the most prominent protesters were Miami Heat basketball players who posed for a group photo wearing black hoodies, and Representative Bobby Rush (Democrat from Illinois) who addressed the House of Representatives on Capitol Hill wearing a hoodie. Police surveillance of male youth of color generates the belief that they are engaged in drugs and gangs, which not only places them in harm's way of the law but also results in them being perceived as unsuitable as co-workers, neighbors or acquaintances (Wilson et al. 2004).

Victor Rios' (2009: 151) research on the criminalization of Latino and Black youth attended to the consequences of punitive criminal justice treatment that is reinforced through constant surveillance of youth activities and "stigma imposed by schools, community centers and families." The school-to-prison pipeline operates in the context of high unemployment and few, if any, alternative opportunities. Rios examined structural practices – stopping, recording, policing, incarceration and probation – that result in youth developing gendered practices of hyper-masculinity *that are shaped by* the exchanges youth have with the police, probation officers, and personnel in detention facilities. Rios examined the intersection of race and class in the development of specific forms of masculinity shaped through repeated interactions with the criminal justice system. In these encounters, being a "real man" requires meeting gendered expectations to receive and maintain respect. The consequences of being disrespected, of not conforming to gendered norms of being tough and willing to fight, hinder the chances of survival on the streets and during incarceration.

In considering privilege, men of color's negatively perceived "hypermasculinity" is replaced by a mainstream white "hegemonic masculinity." Bethany Coston and Michael Kimmel (2012) addressed the role expectation of men as white, heterosexual and non-disabled. Notions associated with a "real man" include wealth, bravery, physical strength, emotional stability, and the ability to be rational. White heterosexual upper-middle- and upper-class men are in hegemonic positions of power and decision-making in economic and political institutions. Civilized, proper breeding and refinement are the traditional traits characterizing upper-class masculinity. Similar to the ideal womanhood of domesticity, meeting the standards of an ideal man's masculinity is difficult, if not impossible, particularly for men marginalized by race, class, sexuality status or disability. Even though "men of more disadvantaged backgrounds (for example, minority, working-class, gay) reap certain privileges...they lack hegemonic masculinity because the masculinity that they deploy cannot often be exchanged for the most dominant forms of power and capital" (Ocampo 2012: 451).

Men of color may use male privilege in interpersonal interaction within their families and communities; however, the privilege is unlikely to extend to spaces dominated by heterosexual middle-class white males. The meaning of "hegemony" is the presumption of dominance, the invisible power of ruling ideas that shape expectations generally shared by members of the society. Hegemony leads people to see Black and Latino youth as a danger, and a white man in a suit as just the opposite – even if a fountain pen is more likely to rob you than a switchblade.

Masculinity and Sports

Competitive sports are central to male socialization in the US and continue to be important sites for developing skill, physical power and aggression (Grindstaff and West 2011). This is evident by the parenting activity that fathers engage in when participating in sports with their children. Recent scholarship on masculinity identified two types emerging from fathers' involvement with their children's sports: "'*Orthodox*' masculine traits include risk-taking, competitiveness, tolerance of pain, and injury; '*inclusive*' masculinity is a nurturing practice of manhood in which fathers are 'supportive of their children regardless of their performance, acting on the belief that this reinforcement is important for their self-esteem and confidence'" (Gottzén & Kremer-Sadlik 2012: 640). Inclusive characteristics are becoming more common among fathers of the white, middle-class male athletes and students observed on college soccer and rugby teams (Anderson 2009; Adams 2011).

The types of sports supported in different communities are largely class- and race-based, and are closely related to opportunities available in schools or those that parents can afford. Middle-class men have options to enter professional employment or to move into managing sports rather than pursuing long-term athletic careers. Working-class men and men of color tend to pursue athletic careers to gain access to education or seek celebrity athletes' fame and wealth (Messner 1992). Professional sports are among the most sex-segregated institutions in terms of who plays, who owns teams, who coaches, and who reaps the greatest financial rewards (Walker 2005). Media coverage of professional sports is shaped at the intersection of race and gender identity when white male athletes are described by their skill, effort and determination, whereas similar talents embodied by Black male athletes are described as *natural* and sometimes compared to animalistic characteristics. Sports commentators repeat conventional racial stereotypes (Eastman & Billings 2001). By overachieving in specific sports, Black athletes are recognized as superior to white athletes; however, African Americans are underrepresented in managerial, coaching, administrative and related sporting occupations.

Basketball is a quintessential American sport, played and watched by millions. It is also a court where racial identity is played out. The role expectations for Black and white Americans is brilliantly expressed in the film *White Men Can't Jump* (1992). The basis for the film is a con game played out on the informal courts where games are bet on. Wesley Snipes and Woody Harrelson run a scam based on the perception that white guys cannot play B ball as well as Blacks. Snipes, the Black player, offers to play but is a man short. When Harrelson offers to fill in the stakes go higher because everyone thinks he can't play because he is white and they don't know he is an expert. The film only works by playing on the Black/white role expectations Americans hold about race, masculinity and the game.

Stanley Thangaraj (2010, 2012, 2013, 2015) researched masculinity formation among South Asian American basketball players in Atlanta. Historical background is important in identifying structures of oppression and opportunities. The first South Asian immigrants arrived in the late 1800s and early 1900s as agricultural workers and were racialized as

"Hindoos" even though most were Muslim and Sikh. Like many terms used for immigrants of color, "Hindoos" was imbued with negative gender, race, sexual and social-class meanings. The South Asian American men Stanley Thangaraj researched were the children of immigrants who entered the US a century later to work in science- and health-related professions. The occupations re-created the stereotype of South Asians as nerdy. However, since 9/11, South Asian men now confront the opposite stigma of being "Muslim-looking," which, unlike the "model minority," now triggers excessive hate. In fact, the first target of racist violence post-9/11 was a Sikh man who ran a gas station and convenience store in my neighborhood in Arizona. He was shot and killed for wearing the Sikh turban that marks South Asians as forever-foreign (Thangaraj 2015), despite the fact that they were not involved in the attack on the World Trade Center.

Enter second- and third-generation South Asian boys growing up in Atlanta, Georgia. In this context, South Asian American basketball players had to construct masculinity in relation to African American, Asian American, and white masculinity. Growing up in the South, surrounded by the White–Black binary of race, Black aesthetics become class indicators and marked working-class masculinity for South Asian youth who lacked cultural capital to achieve the model-minority standard (Thangaraj 2010). Being racialized as "foreigners" placed the boys outside the boundaries of hegemonic masculinity "in relation to white, middle-class, heterosexual normativity" (Thangaraj 2015: 7). Creating an "Asian Ballers League" became an important "means by which South Asian American men socialized, navigated, and expressed their identities in 21st-century America" (Thangaraj 2015: 3). They constructed their own racialized masculinity and sense of belonging by embracing the popular American sport. Demonstrating skill on the basketball court challenged the portrayal of Asians as nerdy. Racialized muscular bodies that achieve skilled basketball maneuvers serve to present "themselves as strong, able-bodied, aggressive, respectable, and heterosexual men" (2015: 4). In the ethnically exclusive circuit of the Asian Ballers League, South Asian men's call to "man up" was a collective reshaping of racialized masculinity in the context of an American sporting identity. Yet their class differences, resulting from the different social, political and economic circumstances of their families' migration to the US, create different resources available to "man up" as basketball players and as worker/professionals.

The case of South Asian men in Atlanta playing in the Asian Ballers League demonstrates the nuances of intersectional analysis. The presumed class, set by the "model-minority" stereotype, further complicates their racialized masculinity. In other words, South Asian men are presumed to be nerds or computer geeks, but not all are – some are working-class and risk failing to meet American notions of sport and masculinity. By creating their own league, they complicate the Black/ White binary implicit in American sport discourse. The intersectional viewpoint is visible in another film that also takes place in the Deep South, *Mississippi Masala* (1991). In Greenwood, Mississippi, a South-Indian woman, expelled from the Uganda of Idi Amin, falls in love with Demetrius, played by Denzel Washington. Even though they have similar skin tones, both families are terribly upset by the relationship. The issues of his working-class status, race and social background are set against her ethnicity and refugee status and the presumption of upward mobility for an Asian American, making for a fascinating example of how race, class, gender, ethnicity and role expectations can play out.

Now I'll explore practices and norms of masculinity in employment. Using an intersectional paradigm, I consider social positions of race, ethnicity and citizenship status in constructing masculine identity in traditional male occupations.

Masculinity and Employment

Areas of employment and labor are important sites for the construction of gender identity, particularly in affirming, challenging and negotiating masculinity (Kimmel 2000; Padavic & Reskin 2002; Messerschmitt 2004). Construction, coal mining, policing and firefighting were working-class male-dominated occupations. As union jobs, these occupations provided workers with decent pay, benefits and job security. The histories of unionization among these trades document the fight to keep men of color out – aimed at holding on to white male privilege (Roediger 1999). One structural mechanism was "father and son unions," where boys followed their fathers into the occupation and the labor union – essentially closing the shop to men of color and sorting occupations by ethnicity. This is how, in big Eastern cities like New York, there were Irish police and firefighters; there were German and Irish butchers in Back of the Yards, Chicago. Most unions, including the powerful American Federation of Labor (AFL), did not admit Blacks or women. However, in 1925, Black sleeping-car porters organized the first African American Union. It was a strong brotherhood on the US rails when there was a passenger service. While the social construction of masculinity would seem to favor working-class men for their physical strength, the occupational hierarchy placed them in vulnerable and precarious employment. They are perceived as "dumb brutes" or "working stiffs" with a career that was meaningful but limited. Unlike white middle-class fathers who hope to serve as role models for their sons, working-class fathers sometimes wanted more for their sons and frequently viewed themselves as negative role models (Coston & Kimmel 2012). In an oral history of western coal miners, one old Welsh miner said he'd scoop manure in hell before he saw his son go into the mines.

A memorable illustration of this point appears in Studs Terkel's (1974) opening interview in *Working: People Talk About What They Do All Day and How They Feel About What They Do*. Terkel interviewed Mike LeFevre, a steel-mill worker, who told a story of hard work, tiredness, and being treated with little respect. After showing where injuries had left black and blue marks on his arms and legs, he says, "You know what I hear from more than one guy at work. 'If my kid wants to work in a factory, I am going to kick the hell out of him,' I want my kid to be an effete snob. Yeah, mm-hmm. (Laughs.) I want him to be able to quote Walt Whitman, to be proud of it" (Terkel 1974: xxxii). He described his dream of a 20-hour working week that would allow him time to be with his family and to go to college. This tension between a working-class life and an intellectual life is a theme throughout the interview: "If my kid ever goes to college, I just want him to have a little respect, to realize that his dad is one of those somebodies" (Terkel 1974: xxxv). Lefevre described an interaction with a college student who expressed surprise that he read books instead of just the sports page in the newspaper like the other workers. He criticized the student as "a nineteen-year-old effete snob" (Terkel 1974: xxxvii). Terkel called Mike's attention to the contradiction that he wants his own son to be an effete snob. Mike acknowledges the contradiction and explains that he does not want his son to work like him but dreams of a world in which college kids and steelworkers talk and interact respectfully toward each other. Mike describes his dream:

> Where a workingman could not be ashamed of Walt Whitman and where a college professor could not be ashamed he painted his house over the weekend.
> If a carpenter built a cabin for poets, I think the least the poets owe the carpenter is just three or four one-liners on the wall. A little plaque: Though we labor with our minds, this place we can relax in was built by someone who can work with his hands. And his work is as noble as ours. I think the poet owes something to the guy who builds the cabin for him. (Terkel 1974: xxxvii)

In the 1997 film *Good Will Hunting* the character played by Matt Damon is an individual representation of the tension between those who work with their hands and those who sit at desks and work with their minds. While an unrecognized mathematical genius, Damon's idea of masculinity requires fighting, drinking and hanging in a male-dominated culture. At first, he resists Robin Williams' attempts at "therapy," but eventually comes to recognize alternative definitions of masculinity. The drama is a compelling "psychological reductionism" in focusing on the single character of Will Hunting, when this tension between masculine and non-masculine work is a big social structural chasm.

Richard Sennett and Jonathan Cobb (1973) referred to this loss of human dignity and inability to gain self-respect as the hidden injuries of class. Over the past several decades, white lower-middle-class and working-class males have experienced downward social mobility in both income and lifestyle. Factory jobs are being moved offshore where labor is cheaper; coal and metal mining are still being done in the US, but have become highly mechanized, requiring a much smaller workforce. Where miners used to be a powerful part of the labor movement, fighting for safety as well as wages and hours, much of the industry is now non-union. Construction jobs have also been mechanized – they cannot be offshored like manufacturing – but divisions of labor have reduced what used to be highly skilled jobs – such as those of plumbers, electricians, and carpenters – to jobs that unskilled labor can do. Declining employment in well-paid union jobs, previously dominated by white working-class males, has resulted in a perceived loss of white male privilege.

Much has been written about the role of white working-class men and women in the election of Donald Trump. Probably because Trump's opponent was a woman, gender as much as race and social class intersected in the 2016 election more than ever before in recent politics. Trump positioned himself as a hyper-masculine male in such a way that accusations of sexual harassment and groping women actually played in his favor as a "man's man" engaging in "locker room talk." Race was also important, probably because the US president for the past eight years was an African American. Before the election, an article in the New Yorker put Trump's appeal this way: "The base of the [Republican] Party, the middle-aged white working class, has suffered at least as much as any demographic group because of globalization, low-wage immigrant labor, and free trade. Trump sensed the rage that flared from this pain and made it the fuel of his campaign.... And Trump has replaced it with something more dangerous: white identity politics" (Packer 2016).

In NBC's (2016) exit polling 63 percent of white voters without college degrees in the "rust belt" states of Pennsylvania, Ohio, Michigan and Wisconsin voted for Trump. An intersectional analysis of social class, gender and ethnicity revealed a major shift of identity politics. Where previously Whites had been seen as "the norm" in US society, part of Trump's success was due to his appeal to these voters as another aggrieved ethnic group, much like Blacks or Latinos. In such times of crisis, white male workers scapegoat the "other" as the cause of the problem of declining jobs in these sectors of the economy – women, gays, immigrants or workers of color (Fine et al. 1997; Rodino-Colocino 2012). David Embrick and colleagues (2007: 757) found working-class men discriminated against gays and lesbians and in the process "constructed and maintained a form of White male solidarity, a collective practice directed toward women, People of Color, and non-heterosexuals that maintains racism, sexism, and homophobia in the local, national, and global context." Marginalizing and devaluing masculinities of gays and men of color is one strategy to bolster properties of hegemonic masculinity that white working-class men *do* possess (Connell 2005). Cultures of hyper-masculinity, sometimes accompanied with gender and race discrimination, are responses to the lack of job security and declining union power. This point is evident in Kris Paap's (2006) research among construction workers who perpetuate sexist and racist behavior and whose attitudes to safety bolster a sense of being "man enough" for the job – but serve to put workers in harm's way.

Working-class masculinity among male immigrants working as construction workers and landscapers illustrates the intersection of race, gender, class and immigration on this topic. Reliance on stereotyping Mexican masculinity as *machismo* ignores the significance of intersectionality, social structure and social interaction. For instance, in their study of construction workers in Las Vegas, Leticia Saucedo and Maria Morales (2010) examined gender identity as central to defining male immigrants' work experiences. When construction arrangements changed from hourly employment to independent contracting, women workers were more likely to complain than were immigrant men, and were critical of employers for not providing safety equipment or adequate tools to increase their efficiency. These workers, on the other hand, took personal responsibility for their own safety. Immigrant male workers took pride in their ability to endure, to be tough – to be manly. Narratives of masculinities promoted risk and ambition, and framed the worker as an entrepreneur. Employers viewed them as stepping forward and improving working conditions on their own. Consequently, masculine narratives perpetuated gender-based barriers by squeezing women out of construction work. However, their hyper-masculine narratives also served to place them at higher risk. As white working-class workers experience declining wages and fewer benefits, employers gain from the perpetuation of working-class masculinities in low-wage jobs. Immigrant workers' employment options are limited. The working-class immigrant masculinity enables them to endure risks to fulfill their patriarchal obligations as responsible family providers. The Occupational Safety and Health Administration report that the leading causes of deaths in construction in 2014 were falls (39.9 percent), electrocution (8.2 percent), being struck by an object (8.1 percent) and being caught-in-between objects (4.3 percent). Latino workers accounted for 804 of these injuries, more than 15 deaths a week, or 2 Latino workers killed every single day in 2014 (NIOSH and ASSE 2015).

Hernan Ramirez' (2011: 97) study of *jardineros*, or Mexican immigrant gardeners, in Los Angeles, examines working-class masculinity as experienced in the context of "racialized nativism and citizenship hierarchy in the United States." After decades of out-migration, certain communities in Mexico develop a "culture of migration" that serves as a transition to manhood (Davis 1990). Once in the US, they devote their time to hard work, developing physical strength and calloused hands, which signifies masculinity, and is the path to acceptance among the other Mexican male immigrants. "*Jardinero* masculinity is centrally concerned with physically hard manual labor and embodied toughness, and it unfolds in a specific working-class occupational and regional context" (Ramirez 2011: 98). " 'Manly' dirty work is how they can justify their presence in a hostile environment" and being away from their loved ones (Ramirez 2011: 106). Landscaping is dangerous work, as is evident from the use of loud, gasoline-powered leaf blowers worn on their backs, and the use of lawn mowers and weeders. Although employers provide gloves, facemasks and protective goggles, *jardineros* do not use protective equipment. Like the immigrant construction workers whom Saucedo and Morales wrote about, these *jardineros* placed themselves in danger by accepting personal responsibility, which reinforced a tough working-class masculinity. However, unlike white US male citizens engaged in manual labor, they encountered women homeowners' complaints and supervision delivered with disrespect. Similar to women of color employed as domestics for white women (Rollins 1985; Romero 1992), they retained their dignity by finding non-confrontational strategies in order not to lose their jobs. *Jardineros* "occupy a place near the bottom of the social and economic ladder, where they are subjected to personal threats to their pride and restrictions on their authority, as well as limits to their ability to support and protect their families" (Ramirez 2011: 108). Understanding *jardineros'* masculinity requires an intersectionality framework to understand "an ongoing 'doing' of a version of masculinity that is closely tied to their status as marginalized, working-class, immigrant men of color" (Ramirez 2011: 111).

However, not all working-class masculinity or cultures of hyper-masculinity include race discrimination. Mathew Desmond (2007) illustrates that in his study of firefighters that included a mixed-race crew of Native American, Latino, Black and white men from rural working-class backgrounds. Desmond linked hyper-masculinity with the organizational structure of the forest service. He argued that the firefighters' shared "country-masculinity" prepared them with skills acquired while growing up on farms and in small towns; consequently, they embrace the risk-taking of wildland firefighting together. In this rural-life context, "country-masculinity" means being comfortable in the woods and the related activities of fishing, hunting, hiking, camping and just being outdoors. Their definitions of the "other" are people who prefer working and being indoors – in other words, city folk and environmentalists who threaten US forest firefighting practices. Resort hotels and campsites for city visitors decrease the forest area and change the small-town environment. Cities and urban areas represent crime and violence, as well as living next to strangers. The independence and love of the outdoors contained in country-masculinity provide the perfect bond for engaging in the hard work and risk-taking involved in wildland firefighting. Like mining and deep-sea fishing, firefighting is a tough "macho" occupation. Deaths and injuries are to be expected as part of the job and are the result of "human error" despite rigorous safety regulations. Desmond's analysis of firefighters' masculinity demonstrates the significance of class and geography (rural) in a shared country-masculinity that cuts across racial and ethnic differences.

Intersectional approaches to the practices of masculinity in the male-dominated jobs of firefighting, construction and landscaping point to the ways in which the occupations not only are gendered but are class-based, racialized, and further subordinated by citizenship status. Where they rely on forms of hyper-masculinity, these jobs also serve to reproduce existing systems and power relations.

Discussion questions

1 How does an intersectional framework analysis explain the disparities in policing in different communities?
2 How does the competitive world of golf tournaments reward masculinity intersected with race, class and age differently from professional football?
3 How do vulnerable male workers use hyper-masculinity to succeed in a competitive job market?

Masculinity and Sexuality

Another lens for looking at alternative gender performances involves examining the intersectionality of gender and sexuality, here through the analysis of race and class. During the twentieth century, popular media presented gay men as feminized and unable to succeed in traditional male occupations like sports (Anderson 2005; Anderson & McCormack 2010a) or the military. While social attitudes are gradually changing as more gay athletes and military personnel come out of the closet, in large part they remain stereotyped in unmasculine occupations such as those of hair stylists, interior decorators or professional dancers (Coston & Kimmel 2012). However, gender identities are much more fluid in the gay community and include both hegemonic and hyper-masculinity. Masculine sexual identities are only one axis of gay, bisexual and transgender experiences – race, class and disability are among others. Research on gays of color uses intersectionality to illustrate the fluidity of other identities and the contexts in which certain identities become more salient than others. Intersectional understandings of race, class, gender and sexuality illuminate the various power relations operating in spaces dominated by gays and those dominated by communities of color.

For instance, Lisa Bowleg (2013) examined the intersections of gender, race and sexual identity in her analysis of Black gay and bisexual men's life narratives. Their narratives highlighted the interconnectedness of their identities: while certain social locations acknowledge their male privilege, in other situations they were subjugated as Black men or as gays. Unlike race or gender identity, sexual identity can be invisible. Consequently, Black identity is more central in experiences of racial discrimination because LGBTQ discrimination can be avoided by "passing" in ways that race generally cannot. Similarly, rather than being embraced by the LGBTQ community, Black gay and bisexual men recounted experiences of racism among white gay and bisexual men who accepted their sexual identity but engaged in racial microagressions. Those practices served as reminders that their Black identity was not accepted. Other researchers report that Black gay men consider gay culture in the US "too white," dominated by white middle-class men (Anderson & McCormack 2010b). This may also shed light on why 20 percent of gay citizens voted for Donald Trump, even though he disagreed with gay marriage (Lang 2016). In a related analysis of Black and gay male athletes in US sports, Eric Anderson and Mark McCormack (2010b) observed that gay men are constructed as white, and Black men are constructed as heterosexual. Gay culture is assumed to be a white space and Black men's race identity overshadows their sexual identity. Quoting the Black gay cultural activist and poet Essex Hemphill, Bowleg highlighted the salience of the intersection of race and gender for Black gay and bisexual men: "I can be gay in only a few cities in this country [the US], but I'm Black everywhere I go" (2013: 764). The sexual identity of Black gays is likely to be salient only in predominantly African American communities.

Black gay men are not the only gay men of color to view gay culture as too white. Latino gays report experiencing racism, as well as classism, in mainstream gay communities (Diaz 1997; Cantú 1999; Guzmán 2006). Like many other gays of color, Latino gays may decide not to come out of the closet in order to maintain ties with their ethnic and racial community (Moore 2010). However, in the case of Latino gays who are financially independent or maintain their position as breadwinner, they report an acceptance of their sexuality and their partner at family gatherings (Carrillo 1999). Expressions of gay Latino masculinities are not static but related to class and migration. For example, working-class Mexican men may dress in ranchero-style clothing to dance in Latino gay clubs in Southern California or baggy clothing with a shaved head in urban settings (Rodríguez 2006; Almaguer 2007; González 2007). In his ethnographic study of gay Latino men in Los Angeles, Anthony Ocampo (2012) examined the ways they negotiated masculine boundaries and their strategies for "doing" masculinity. His analysis did not lose sight of the fact that they are racialized men in the US and socialized in immigrant families and neighborhoods. Therefore, their strategies for "performing" masculinity reflect both their gender socialization in immigrant families and communities, and their interaction with mainstream gay culture. Race and class shape gender performance, which in this case requires avoiding a feminine or affluent appearance, and is in opposition to their perceptions of white gay men. This opposition was demonstrated when venues catering to Latino and African American gay men were changed into white spaces by placing clothing restrictions against "too urban" clothing or changing the music: "respondents' understandings of the relationship between 'appropriate' gender presentation and public spaces reflected not only differences in cultural tastes between Latino and White gay men, but also illustrated how Latino gay men negotiate their gender presentation and racialization simultaneously" (Ocampo 2012: 458).

Unlike for African American and Latino males, popular culture does not stereotype Asian American men as hyper-masculine but as effeminate and non-masculine, regardless of their sexuality. Therefore, Asian American gay men face different stereotypes concerning their racialized gender identity, as explored previously in accounts of South Asian American members of the Asian Ballers League in Atlanta. Richard Fung (1991) argues that gay pornography erases the desires of Asian gays, who are stigmatized as effeminate. Racial domination in the gay pornography industry objectifies Asian gays as subordinated to white gay men. Some Asian American gays engage in hyper-masculine gender presentations to counter their stigmatized gender in the gay community. For example, Chong-suk Han's (2009) ethnography of Seattle's Asian and gay communities examined Asian gay men's gender presentation as a means to manage stigma on two fronts: sexual preference in the Asian community, and race in the gay community. Asian gay men present a hyper-masculine gender identity in gay communities in opposition to the feminine stereotype imposed on them. However, this gender performance had limited success in acquiring white gay partners, who many perceived as more desirable. In interracial couples, the white partner is dominant in these gay relationships. An alternative strategy among gay Asian men was using the racialized gender stereotype to their advantage and competing with white gay men in drag performances and presenting themselves "to gain recognition and notoriety" (Han 2009: 107). Other researchers (e.g., Wilson & Yoshikawa 2004) concluded that some Asian gay men respond to racialized gender discrimination in gay communities by avoiding situations that are hostile to any gay men of color regardless of ethnicity. The ethnographic studies cited above used intersectional analysis to see how sexuality and gender performances were negotiated in Black, Latino and Asian communities. They were able to capture nuances and subtleties of social interaction that previous one-dimensional approaches missed.

Discussion question

1   What social inequalities in LGBTQ communities become visible when one uses an intersectional framework?

Summary

It is not surprising that many feminist scholars consider intersectionality to be the major contribution to theorizing gender identity. Without considering age, class, race, ableness, and sexual orientation as social identities, gender exists as an empty signifier. Only by acknowledging the overlapping systems of oppression and privilege can one understand gender privilege or oppression. Returning to Caitlyn Jenner, her race, class and ableness were essential in her ability to construct a heteronormative feminine persona and gain public support and acceptance for her gender identity as a trans person. An intersectional approach is essential to capture nuances embedded in news coverage, letters to editors and opinion pieces related to Caitlyn's presentation of her new gender identity. Without knowing the different historical contexts of gender privilege and oppression experienced by white and Black women, Laverne Cox's and Caitlyn Jenner's choices of a hyper-feminine gender identity appear similar. However, as Cox's comments revealed, the purpose for her photo shoot was to create "racially empowering images of the various sides of my black, trans womanhood." Gender privileges of femininity have traditionally been denied to Black women in the US, which is not the case for white women.

Male-dominated sports and occupations supervise, discipline and police gender practices. However, this is true for women as well. Kareem Abdul-Jabbar (2015) drew attention to the racial inequality in the endorsement cost of not meeting certain female ideals of beauty. Even though Serena Williams beat Maria Sharapova in the two Grand Slam tournaments where they met in 2015 (Williams going on to win three of the four Grand Slam titles that year), Williams only earned $12 million from endorsements, less than half of the $29 million Sharapova earned. Women athletes have always had to struggle with performing hetero-normative femininity but women of color are expected to reproduce an ideal that never included them. Thus, in 2014, the Russian Tennis Federation President, Shamil Tarpischev, referred to Venus and Serena Williams as the "Williams Brothers." Attention to Black women not fitting the white ideal of femininity emerged in the 2015 summer coverage of Wimbledon that involved body-shaming Serena Williams. Even though she had just won her 21st Grand Slam singles title and the 4th in a row, *New York Times* sports writer Ben Rothenberg (2015) titled his article, "Tennis's top women balance body image with ambition," concluding that Serena was non-feminine because she is muscular. Citing numerous coaches of other tennis players, he implied that Serena wins only because of her physique, which he argued places others who wish to stay looking like women at a disadvantage (Williams 2015).

One white player, Radwanska, claimed, "any gain in muscle could hurt her trademark speed and finesse," and "she also acknowledged that how she looked mattered to her." Other players recognized that strengthening their muscles contributed to being a better athlete. While some readers expressed outrage over the policing of women athlete's bodies, few could deny the racism. In Serena Williams' case, this has been an experience throughout her career. Her friend and fellow tennis player Caroline Wozniacki imitated Serena in Brazil in 2012 to illustrate the lack of awareness of racism and sexism. She stuffed towels into her bra and shorts creating larger breasts and bottom to perform an impression of Serena. There is also blatant racism exhibited by floods of hate speech on Twitter after every win by Serena.

Controlling images of Black women's bodies is a constant in US sports. However, Black women experience similar rejection in other activities, including skating and ballet. Misty Copeland made history as the first African American women to be principal dancer for the American Ballet Theater. Previously a ballet academy had rejected her when she was 13 because she didn't have the right body type. In a commercial for Under Armour, she recalled what she had heard that day, "Dear candidate, thank you for your application to our ballet academy. Unfortunately, you have not been accepted. You lack the right feet, Achilles tendons, turnout, torso length and bust. You have the wrong body for ballet. And at 13, you are too old to be considered." Yet 13 years later, she is principal dancer! Too often, Ms. Copeland encountered the stereotype of a Black woman being too muscular, too tall, too big, or lacking the flexibility to succeed.

For centuries, Black women and other women of color were denied entrance into certain activities because their physical presence of womanhood did not fit the white western ideal. In mass media and theater, they have often been cast as servants or in bit parts. When Michelle Obama appeared in a sleeveless dress, revealing muscular arms, "conservatives" attacked her relentlessly for revealing too much flesh for a first lady. On numerous occasions, she has been compared to a gorilla. Meanwhile, Mrs. Trump's photographs as a nude model were a mark of true beauty. "This seems to indicate that the conservative voters were only criticizing Mrs. Obama not because it isn't 'First Lady-like' or because it goes against their conservative, religious views, but simply because she is a Democrat and maybe even because she's African American and that in itself is not suitable" (Acuesta 2016). The particular way that Michelle's gender is racialized becomes invisible without looking at the ways in which systems of gendered and racial oppression intersect in the experiences of women and men of color.

I presented examples drawn from research and popular culture in this chapter to illustrate how gender identity is not fixed but socially constructed. This social construction occurred historically within certain socio-economic contexts, meaning that it can change in different settings. Racism, sexuality and sexism are not fixed but malleable. The ideal heteronormative femininity among middle-class Christian girls in New Orleans is not the same as for middle-class Muslim girls in Iran. Examples also demonstrate how, when social settings and circumstances are changed, there is a shift in one's social identity – for instance, race becomes more salient in some settings than sexuality, and vice versa. As a Mexican American woman academic from a working-class background, while listening to my heterosexual female colleagues discuss their college days in a sorority and summers at Martha's Vineyard, I felt my class and race differences more than gender. My economic circumstances framed summer breaks as opportunities for full-time employment, usually in jobs dominated by other women workers. Alternately, when in meetings with male Latino professors, it was the experience of gender that made me feel out of place – the only woman in the group. Like these colleagues, my experiences in college were class- and race-based ones. I joined political campaigns and organizations aimed at fighting for social equality. In those groups social class, or at least class solidarity, may be readily assumed, while gender and race were variously identified and may have seemed sites for conflict. These multiple identities – gender, race and class – are experienced simultaneously but differentially.

When intersectional relations are not examined, identities appear universal, as gender was in feminist theorizing in the 1960s and 1970s. Frequently, the absence of intersectionality results in confusion and blurring of social identities, which fails to capture lived experiences, such as those of immigrant male construction workers or landscapers. All too often, gender and sexual identities are confused and treated as one, particularly in everyday conversation. Being gay or lesbian is not the same as being cismale or cisfemale. Gay men do not all have the same gender identity, as described in Ocampo's ethnographic study of Latino men in Los Angeles or in Han's ethnography of Seattle's Asian and gay communities. What is feminine to an upper-class lesbian living in Manhattan is not likely to be the norm of femininity for a poor working-class heterosexual immigrant woman living in Los Angeles. Straights, lesbians, bisexuals and trans people do not all have the same gender identity. To understand lived experiences, one needs to examine the interconnectiveness of each marginalized or privileged identity. One can be privileged in one social setting and discriminated against in another. As the cases in this chapter have shown, an intersectional approach to gender identity provides tools to reveal existing systems of power manifested in social relationships of dominance and subordination.

5

Exploring Interlocking Systems of Oppression and Privilege

Undocuqueer Intersectionality

I am queer and undocumented – "undocuqueer." I began organizing five years ago with Orange County Dream Team, and I was captivated by that space, hungry to tell my undocumented story. Soon enough I was coming out as undocumented and sharing my story with friends and coworkers and in public spaces, but that process was heavy and painful, because I was leaving my queer story in the back seat. Every time I walked into a meeting, joined a rally or attended an event, I was making a painful negotiation: "Today I am only wearing my undocumented hat." I couldn't do that to myself, my community or movement. I needed to come out again, but his time as both queer and undocumented. The pain I felt no longer held me back; alliances via my undocuqueer identity. Jorge Gutierrez

I always feel that I am at the edge of two borders....It feels like I am fighting two different struggles. Whenever I come across LGBT folk that don't support immigrant rights, I feel marginalized and oppressed by my own community. Equally, when I am around people belonging to the immigrant community, I am saddened that some don't support equal rights for LGBT people. Jorge Gutierrez

The immigrant rights movement has been a little unwelcoming sometimes there is still some homophobia in the immigrant rights movement...I think we have to hold conversations about homophobia in the immigrant community, while at the same time have similar conversations with LGBT people about how they support undocumented immigrant people. Reyna Wences

The largest immigration youth-led organization in the country, United We Dream (UWD), has embraced its LGBTQ members and formed an alliance. Jorge Gutierrez and Reyna Wences are representatives of undocumented LGBTQ immigrant students who are at the forefront of the DREAM (Development, Relief, and Education for Alien Minors) Act Movement. The DREAM Act is legislation in the United States aimed at establishing a path to citizenship for the many high school graduates under 30 who came to the country as minors (Amaro 2010). In 2007, the DREAM Act failed to pass the Senate, and UWD began to build an immigrant youth movement that would shape and influence the broader immigrant rights movement. UWD's platform and twenty-point plan for immigration reform includes LGBTQ individuals in the leadership and recognizes their families and partners. In 2011, UWD established the Queer Undocumented Immigrant Project (QUIP) to secure the place of the LGBTQ community in the struggle for immigration reform. The Immigrant Youth Justice League (IYJL) had already joined the LGBTQ Immigrant Rights Coalition in Chicago. UndocuQueer, QUIP and other campaigns bring together the identity of LGBTQ undocumented immigrants who previously felt isolated in groups identifying only as LGBTQ or only as undocumented immigrants, such as those mentioned by Jorge Gutierrez and Reyna Wences at the beginning of the chapter (Nicholls 2013). By merging these identities in their advocacy for a path to citizenship, they are creating a space that empowers people to be both undocumented and LGBTQ.

Like LGBTQ people claiming their sexual and gender identity, the IYJL organized the National Coming Out of the Shadows in 2010, which became a significant strategy to call attention to the impact that immigration policy has on limiting their opportunities. Publicly telling their stories became an act of empowerment and expressed their commitment to come out of the shadows and live their lives openly. Coming-out events were the first form of civil disobedience in the immigrant youth movement, which was also marked with the slogan, "undocumented, unafraid." As undocumented LGBTQ immigrants, these activists come out twice to their family, friends and community. As immigrant youth activists planned their strategy for protests and rallies, they yielded to the famous quote from the late Harvey Milk (the first openly gay elected official in California, on the San Francisco Board of Supervisors): "Brothers and sisters, you must come out. Come out to your parents, Come out to your Friends, if indeed they are your friends. Come out to your neighbors. Come out to your fellow workers. Once and for all, let's break down the myths and destroy the lies of distortion" (Ramirez 2012). Milk recognized that winning public support to change discriminatory laws required putting a human face on the issue and allowing one's personal lives and pain to be visible.

One well-known person to use the tactic is Jose Antonio Vargas, a member of the *Washington Post* team that won the Pulitzer Prize for Breaking News Reporting in 2008 for their coverage of the Virginia Tech Shooting. Vargas received the Sidney Award for his 2011 *New York Times Magazine* essay, "My life as an undocumented immigrant," as "an outstanding piece of socially-conscious journalism." He describes how stepping out of the shadows and becoming visible among the many undocumented was more "daunting than coming out" as gay in high school. His story begins in the Philippines, when his mother sent him to live with his grandparents in Mountain View, California, when he was 12. Vargas recounts trying to live his life as a US citizen but with the constant reality of living in the shadows as an undocumented immigrant:

> And that means living a different kind of reality. It means going about my day in fear of being found out. It means rarely trusting people, even those closest to me, with who I really am. It means keeping my family photos in a shoebox rather than displaying them on shelves in my home, so friends don't ask about them. It means reluctantly, even painfully, doing things I know are wrong and unlawful. And it has meant relying on a sort of 21st-century underground railroad of supporters, people who took an interest in my future and took risks for me. (Vargas 2011)

His grandparents' plan was for him to marry a woman who is a US citizen and obtain legal residence through marriage. At the time, this option was not available to a gay man; the federal government only recently (2015) recognized gay marriage.

Outreach projects working with both populations addressed the significance of the intersection between the LGBTQ and the undocumented communities. For instance, Julio Salgado, co-founder of the collaborative media project DreamersAdrift.com in 2010, explains the intersection as follows:

> There's homophobia within our [immigrant] communities so what we need to do, the undocumented people who are also queer, [is] call out and say "hey if you're talking about social justice and you're trying to talk about treating everybody equally, we need to start with ourselves. How is our homophobia affecting certain things?" And likewise when

you're in queer spaces, a lot of the times [what's said is] we should focus on gay marriage, we should focus on joining the military but we don't focus on immigration. (Moreno 2013)

LGBTQ advocacy organizations are also recognizing the intersection of issues arising from shared identities and the impact that immigration legislation has on their broader community. As early as 2010, the Equality California Institute reached out to the immigrant community with the project "Equality Beyond Borders: LBGT Inclusive Immigration Reform," which shares the stories of LGBTQ immigrants and struggles to increase awareness for "a humane and inclusive approach to immigrant rights legislation" (Equality California 2010).

Immigration and LGBTQ issues had been debated for decades but the political movements kept each as separate issues. However, in the last few years, numerous individuals involved in advocacy for immigration reform and LGBTQ rights focused on the intersection of these movements. The Williams Institute at the University of California, Los Angeles, released a report, "LGBT adult immigrants in the United States," which further connected the two political issues – immigration reform and DOMA (Defense of Marriage Act):

An estimated 267,000 adult undocumented immigrants are LGBT-identified or 2.7% of undocumented adults; 71% of these are Hispanic and 15% are Asian or Pacific Islander.

An estimated 637,000 adult documented immigrants are LGBT-identified or 2.4% of documented adults; of which 30% are Hispanic and 35% are Asian or Pacific Islander.

An estimated 113,300 foreign born individuals are part of a same-sex couple; 54,600 of these individuals are not US citizens; an estimated 24,700 same-sex couples are binational, along with 11,700 same-sex couples comprised of two non-citizens; and an estimated 7,000 same-sex couples that include two non-citizens are raising an estimated 12,400 children under age 18. (Gates 2013: 1)

These statistics identify the intersection of changing immigration and marriage legislation to allow families and partners to be together. The US Supreme Court ruled in *Obergefell* v. *Hodges* in 2015 that all state laws had to recognize same-sex marriages, and QUIP remains committed to empowering the undocumented LGBTQ community and recognizing same-sex marriages.

I begin this chapter on interlocking systems of oppression and privileges by introducing immigration issues and employing intersectional analysis of citizenship status, age and sexuality, or more specifically the intersection of LGBTQ undocumented youth. This perspective on citizenship challenges the dominant narrative of undocumented immigrants in the US as Mexican heterosexual adult males employed as farmworkers. That image is one that dates back to the Bracero Program, a guest program negotiated between the US and Mexico in 1942 to cover the labor shortage experienced after World War II. Although the war ended in 1945, the program continued until 1964. During the program and afterwards, adult Mexican males continued to migrate to the agriculture areas to work in the fields (Molina 2014). However, some family members were also migrating, and many established homes and raised families in the US. In the last two decades of immigration scholarship, research points to the increasing number of women migrating with and without family members to work and begin new lives in the US (e.g., Hondagneu-Sotelo 1994; Flores-Gonzalez et al. 2013). The Dreamer generation makes visible the number of young children who migrated to be with their parents (Pallares 2015). Shifting attention from low-wage Mexican workers in agriculture to college campuses, the identities of undocumented immigrants of color becomes more fluid. Undocumented immigrants are included in all age categories; some are middle-class, young, old, disabled, and LGBTQ. Latino immigrants are from numerous countries; some are white, others Indian or Black, and many have a mixed-race background; all the possibilities make "Latino/Hispanic" a pan-ethnic category that is meaningless as a racial or cultural category. However, the Latino/Hispanic designation does serve to divide Whites of European ancestry from all other Whites and non-Whites from south of the US–Mexico border, including several Caribbean islands. Recent statistics also include the presence of undocumented Asian and Pacific Islander immigrants (Batalova et al. 2014).

This chapter focuses on citizenship status as defined by immigration legislation in order to examine interlocking systems of oppression and privilege. To begin, I review the ways in which immigration laws incorporate systems of domination by privileging or subordinating certain social identities. Certain types of citizenship status are allowed; others are denied. A closer review of immigration legislation and law enforcement illustrates the significance of an intersectional approach to understanding the complexities of citizenship that are too often analyzed as a single dimension based on the binary notion of documented versus undocumented status. A brief overview of immigration law immediately highlights the historical contextualization of race, ethnicity, class, gender, sexuality, ageism and disability. These laws established the legal structure for the social hierarchies surrounding citizenship privileges, opportunities and oppression that persons living in the US experience: "Immigration law has long been understood as an important site for regulation and production of class, ethnic, national, and race boundaries and hierarchies in the United States...but more recently scholars have examined how these dynamics intersected with the regulation and production of familial, gender, reproductive, and sexual boundaries and hierarchies" (Stein 2005: 507–8).

Examining immigration law enforcement and the policing of citizenship status further illustrates the significance of intersectionality in these processes of subordination and domination. Reframing the analysis of immigration to recognize the ways immigration law and enforcement construct citizenship, one can see how different social identities are at risk, while others are not suspect. I will conclude the chapter on interlocking systems of oppression and privilege by examining how immigrant movements have worked at the intersections of social identities to build important alliances.

Citizen Status, Immigration Law and Intersectionality

To get to the heart of the significance of intersectionality in citizenship status and immigration law enforcement, it is essential to recognize that the legal classification of "alien" and "citizen" is socially constructed. Legal scholar Kevin Johnson (2004: 154) describes the social processes in constructing "alien" as:

> Fabricated out of whole cloth, the "alien" represents a body of rules passed by Congress and reinforced by popular culture. It is society, with the assistance of the law, that defines who is an "alien," an institutionalized "other," and who is not. It is a society, through Congress and the courts, that determines which rights to afford "aliens."...Like the social construction of race, which helps to legitimize racial subordination, the construction of the "alien" has helped justify the limitation on noncitizen rights imposed by our legal system.

Thinking about citizenship as a social construct is necessary to identify and comprehend the intersections of systems of domination, particularly white supremacy, patriarchy and capitalism.

Citizenship status includes numerous identities but the three major social structural positions used by the state to construct "alien" are race, gender and class. The Constitution recognized white men with property. Citizenship status constructed around racial and ethnic identities is apparent by examining the ethnic groups defined as "white" and "non-white," as well as noting the changes in immigration law and legal cases that moved some groups from being legally defined as "non-white" to the legal designation of "white" (López 1996). Other social identities, such as religion, sexuality, colorism and age, have experienced citizenship privileges or subordination throughout US history. For instance, in 1776, not all the colonies recognized Catholic, Jew, and Quaker men with property as having voting rights (Chilton 1960). Systems of privilege and oppression determining citizenship rights are most evident when examining the intersection of citizenship and race.

Throughout US history, racialized immigration laws and citizenship have been a major theme, from the classification of slaves from Africa, to indigenous populations, to the treatment of immigrants from southern Europe, Asia and Latin and South America (López 2006). Citizenship status in the US has a long history of privileging certain social identities and oppressing others. Dating back to the Declaration of Independence, the phrase "all men are created equal" was not inclusive. The Articles of Confederation ratified in 1781 defined a slave as three-fifths of a person. This use of the word "men" did not mean all people, but rather meant that only white men with property had citizenship rights. Over time, a form of citizenship rights included women and Blacks. In 1868, the Fourteenth Amendment, passed in that year, allowed former slaves to be US citizens. In 1870, the Fifteenth Amendment gave Black men the right to vote by eliminating race, color and servitude restrictions. The Nineteenth Amendment gave *all* women the right to vote in 1919.

While Black men and women were citizens, their citizenship status was distinct from that of Whites. Even though they were citizens in 1868, the enforcement of state and local Jim Crow laws denied Black men and women freedom of movement and enforced segregation, and they were restricted to inferior schools, parks, libraries, drinking fountains and restrooms. They sat in segregated spaces of buses and trains, and were not permitted into restaurants serving Whites. Unlike white men or women, Blacks faced voting restrictions imposed by poll taxes, property requirements, literacy tests and other mechanisms. Several important legal cases slowly eroded legalized racial segregation. For instance, in *Morgan v. Commonwealth of Virginia* (1947), the Supreme Court decided against the segregated seating on interstate buses as a violation of the interstate commerce clause. In 1948, President Truman signed Executive Order 9981, which eliminated segregation in the military. Desegregation under President Eisenhower's administration expanded to include military schools, hospitals and bases (Nichols 2007). The most widely cited desegregation case is *Brown v. Board of Education* (1954), which declared school segregation as unconstitutional. The Voting Rights Act of 1965 was crucial in eliminating the use of poll taxes, literacy tests and other mechanisms to deny Black women and men the right to vote. Even though the law prohibited segregation and discrimination, the lack of enforcement protected white privilege. Issues around equal treatment before the law, such as racial profiling, continue to be an obstacle, particularly for Blacks living in poor and working-class communities.

Native peoples' unique legal status of "dependent sovereign nations" carried both privileges and liabilities. Recalling the treatment of Blacks who were first only counted as three-fifths of a person under slavery, the US did not recognize Native Americans as persons. However, the government did attempt to establish numerous treaties, which resulted in establishing Indian Territory on smaller areas of land. The 1879 Standing Bear trial (*Standing Bear v. Crook*) began with arguments over the status of Native Americans as either people or citizens, and what, if any, rights they had. Judge Dundy ruled that "an Indian is a person within the meaning of the law" and issued a "writ of habeas corpus," which declared Standing Bear to have been held illegally. However, this decision did not establish clarity in the citizenship status or rights of Native people. The Snyder Act of 1924 granted Native Americans the right to vote, but not necessarily the right to vote in state and local elections. Many state laws disenfranchised Native Americans, and in other cases states used poll taxes, literacy tests and similar strategies used against Blacks to deny voting rights. Many American Indian groups fought to keep their independence as nations, since the US government's decision to grant citizenship to indigenous groups was an attempt to absorb and assimilate them. Prior to this, Indian men had access to citizenship by joining the military, as well as through special treaties and statutes, while Indian women were able to become citizens by marrying white men. Federal courts acknowledged the property rights of white husbands married to indigenous women, which included her tribal property, but state courts usually disputed that men, white or indigenous, had any legal obligation to their indigenous wives. Gender and race were frequently determining factors in legal rulings involving property. Eventually, the Voting Rights Act of 1965 protected Native Americans' rights, and later legislation protected their rights as non-English-speakers. However, indigenous men and women have not always been able to claim the same rights or obligations as others in the US.

Immigration Laws

Turning specifically to immigration, the intersections of systems of domination – particularly white supremacy, patriarchy and capitalism – embedded in legislation appear throughout history and were central to developing immigration restrictions and limiting paths to citizenship. While race appears the most salient identity throughout the history of

US law, gender and class were important intersectional identities and were significant in lived experiences. To begin, let's turn to the writings of legal scholar Robert Chang (1999), who identifies the major obstacle to justice for immigrants of color as the exclusion of non-Whites in the Naturalization Act of 1790. This Act is one of many racialized immigration legislations over the next century and a half. Many laws enacted protected white citizens and immigrants. For instance, as the Chinese began migration to the US during the California Gold Rush of 1848–55, the Irish and German miners competed with the Chinese and Mexican miners in California. In response, the state enacted the Foreign Miners' Tax in 1852 against the Chinese miners, and applied the law to Mexican miners as well. Chinese leaders complained about the anti-Chinese violence and the lack of justice. An example of the violation of Chinese rights is illustrated in *People of the State of California* v. *George W. Hall* (1854), in which the California Supreme Court overturned the guilty verdict against George Hall for the murder of Ling Sing, on the basis that testimony from Chinese persons was not permissible. The court based its decision on the state statute prohibiting Blacks, "mulattos" or Indians from testifying against a white man.

The Page Act of 1875 prohibited the entry of immigrants deemed as "undesirable"; this included any forced labor, prostitutes and convicts, which served to exclude men and women arriving from China, Japan or any Asian country with a fixed term of service or for lewd and immoral purposes. Chinese male laborers worked to pay brokers for their trip to California. However, white male workers perceived them as slave labor and felt threatened by their low wages (Chang 1999; Johnson 2004). Government officials scrutinized Chinese women on arrival to determine whether they were prostitutes. There were attempts to identify Chinese women from respectable families, or they needed to prove their husbands had the means to support them (i.e., merchants' wives), or to have other visible evidence of wealth, such as their clothing. Marriage between Chinese women and white men was prohibited, and white men risked losing their citizenship if they violated the law. Essentially, the Page Act served to exclude Chinese women from the US (Luibhéid 2002). California passed laws prohibiting Chinese from entering the state in 1858. Eventually the federal government stepped in and established the Chinese Exclusion Act in 1882, which was the first law to exclude entry by race. Only Chinese who were able to prove they were not laborers were eligible to enter the US. The Scott Act (1888) expanded the Chinese Exclusion Act to deny re-entry to Chinese who left the US. Congress passed additional legislation in the following years to renew the exclusion. The Immigration Act of 1924 then prohibited *all classes* of Chinese from entering the US. The US repealed the Chinese Exclusion

Act in 1943 when China became a US ally against Japan in World War II. However, even then, entry was limited to a quota determined by the Immigration Act of 1924, which was 2 percent of the total number of Chinese residing in the US. The quota for Chinese did not increase until the Immigration and Nationality Services Act of 1965.

Unlike the Chinese, most Japanese migrated in family groups with the intent of settling in the US. They assimilated by wearing western clothing, and many converted to Christianity, and lived throughout cities rather than developing distinct areas like Chinatowns. Nevertheless, anti-Japanese sentiment began rising in 1905, and the Japanese and Korean Exclusion League campaigned for exclusion like that applied to the Chinese to be extended to Japanese and Koreans. The League pushed for closed borders, denying Japanese and Koreans employment, and the restriction of their children to segregated schools. After the 1905 San Francisco earthquake, fire destroyed many of the schools and the school board forced the Japanese students to attend the Chinese Primary School, which was renamed the Oriental Public School for Chinese, Japanese, and Koreans. Japanese parents complained to government officials in Tokyo, who responded to the act of segregation as an "insult to their national pride and honor." President Roosevelt convinced the San Francisco mayor and school board to drop the segregation plan in return for addressing the immigration issue. The informal agreement reached between Japan and the US, known as the Gentleman's Agreement of 1907, consisted of Japan agreeing not to approve passports for their citizens to migrate to the US unless they were joining family, which they had already begun to do in 1900. However, this essentially established the practice of "picture brides" who were Japanese women wanting to come to the US who arranged long-distance marriages using photographs. President Roosevelt further limited migration by signing Executive Order 589 (1907), which prohibited Japanese laborers from migrating from Hawaii, Mexico or Canada. The Immigration and Nationality Services Act of 1965 limited further Japanese entry into the US (Chang 1999).

In his book *White by Law*, Ian Haney López (1996) chronicles the legal history of immigrant groups becoming defined as "white" and thus eligible to become naturalized citizens. The legal construction of white identity demonstrates that the social construction of race is fluid, constructed relationally, against other categories, rather than in isolation. This is quite evident in reviewing the range of rationales given from the 1878–1944 law cases determining what ethnic immigrant groups were sufficiently white to be eligible for naturalization, or the degree of citizenship rights immigrants were granted. The rationales included scientific evidence, common knowledge, Congressional intent, legal precedent and, in one case, "ocular inspection of skin." López' review of prerequisite cases documents the changing constructions of various groups – once defined as white and later as non-white, as well as initially defined as non-white and later legally constructed as white. Some of these cases include legal decisions about persons of mixed ancestry.

The legal process of defining race is far from consistent but reflects difference in geography and history, and other factors such as colorism and religion. Here, we see the interaction of systems of domination is more evident. Regarding Syrians, in the case *In re Najour* (1909), the court granted Costa George Najour eligibility for citizenship based on "scientific evidence" that he was white. The court cited scientific evidence that "free white person" is a reference to race, not color, and in this case was based on Dr. Keane's claim in *The World's People* that Syrians are part of the Caucasian or white race. However, in both *Ex Parte Shahid* (1913) and *Ex Parte Dow* (1914), the court denied Syrian applicants were white, based on common knowledge. The judge argued that, while Caucasian and white are similar today, in 1790 the founding fathers meant "European" when referring to Whites. In *Dow v. United States*, the judge overturned the verdict and decided that George Dow was entitled to naturalize because he was Caucasian, and noted that Syria is geographically near the birthplace of Judaism and Christianity. Asian Indians were determined "probably not white" in *In re Balsara*, where the 1909 case was based on Congressional intent. In *US v. Dolla* (1910), they were determined to be white based on "ocular inspection of skin." In *United States v. Thind* (1923), the Supreme Court used common knowledge and Congressional intent to determine that Bhagat Singh Thind was not white and, therefore, ineligible for citizenship. Socially constructing race does not always include the privilege and disadvantages individuals may experience from colorism, which may present further barriers to attaining white privilege and the ability to access all citizenship rights. For example, Mexicans were legally defined as white but experienced a history of segregated housing and schools, denial of entrance to restaurants and theatres (unless there was segregated seating), and other forms of discrimination that were sanctioned by local governments (López 1996).

Many court cases determining racial eligibility for citizenship point to the intersectionality of religion and colorism in white supremacy. Peoples from ancient biblical lands of Moses, Jesus and the Apostles, near the roots of Christianity and Judaism, posed contradictions for constructing the white race. These cases demonstrate that immigrants from northern Africa, Asia Minor, and the Middle East in general posed a dilemma for a legal system that constructed Christianity as a European religion. Persons with ancestry from these holy lands, but who were not Christian – be they Sikhs, Muslims or Hindus – challenged the construction of whiteness. Later, southern Europeans who were largely Catholic further reinforced notions of whiteness as linked with Protestantism. They also experienced discrimination based on their darker skin color. All the racial prerequisite cases classified persons of "mixed blood" as not white. Colorism, particularly when intersected with class and religion advantages, helped individuals engaged in passing: individuals who were light-skinned could pass as white, which involved living one's public and private life so as to conceal one's heritage. Therefore, persons with light-enough skin and European features might avoid revealing their indigenous, African or Asian ancestry by avoiding social interaction in these communities and cutting off their ethnic family and community.

In addition to race, religion and colorism, gender is significant in analyzing the lived experiences of men and women granted or denied citizenship rights (Harty 2012). Gender oppression and privilege limited and constrained women's ability to acquire and maintain citizenship, particularly if they were not white or middle class (Glenn 2004). The ways in which marriage shaped women's citizenship status and rights in US legal history demonstrate the continued race and class privilege, and the domination of patriarchy. As mentioned in relation to indigenous women earlier in this chapter, coverture doctrine, which placed women under the control of their husbands, shaped women's access to citizenship rights and to legal entry into the US, as well as their ability to become naturalized citizens. Laws determining citizenship also limited who was eligible for marriage. Immigrant women became US citizens if they married a US male citizen or when their immigrant husbands became naturalized citizens. However, as noted earlier, white men could not marry Chinese women and keep their citizenship. "Until 1931, a woman could not naturalize if she was married to a foreigner racially ineligible for citizenship, even if she otherwise qualified to naturalize in every respect" (López 1996: 15). A woman with US citizenship lost her citizenship when she married a man racially excluded. These restrictions did not end until 1952.

Linking immigrant women to their husbands has had serious consequences for women in abusive marriages and limited their abilities to leave their husbands without facing deportation. Other exclusions of women from similar rights occurred because of prostitution laws (i.e., The Alien Prostitution Importation Act of 1875), failure to recognize gender-based asylum (i.e., cases of rape and genital mutilation) and assumptions of women lacking moral values (i.e., sexually active women, lesbians), and by incorporating the male privilege of coverture (Luibhéid 2002; Ono & Sloop 2002; Johnson 2004). "When citizens or residents are abuse partners, they tend to take advantage of their power to sponsor or not sponsor the immigrant spouse's USCIS [United States Citizenship and Immigration Services] application as a means of control" (Villalon 2015: 120). Eventually, domestic violence-based asylum became recognized (Cianciarulo 2009). The passage of the Victims of Trafficking and Violence Protection Act (VTVPA) in 2000 provided some protection for women. Circumstances of trafficking are now considered, and women arrested for prostitution are not immediately prosecuted and deported (Cianciarulo 2009). However, some women may not fit the image of the "iconic victim" (i.e., children, young girls) of a trafficked person, and others, such as older women or adolescent males, have other intersecting social identities that prevent them from gaining protection under the law (Srikantiah 2007).

Our previous discussion has not so far highlighted the class bias in citizenship construction that intersects with race and gender. However, class is an important system of domination in obtaining status as a US citizen. Beginning with giving citizenship rights to white men who were property owners, class continues to determine a person's eligibility for citizenship. Many early immigration laws integrated a class bias, but a closer look at class and citizenship makes this more evident, particularly in light of the phrase inscribed on the Statue of Liberty: "Give me your tired, your poor." However, US immigration law has consistently practiced the opposite of open borders to the poor. More accurately, the US established statutes and laws barring the entry of "paupers" that date back to the beginning of the nation-state (Johnson 2004). The terminology most frequently used against the poor is the exclusion of persons who are likely to become public charges. "Public charges" replaced the classification of paupers as a basis to deny entry into the US or as grounds for deportation. Frequently, the basis for classifying a person as a public charge intersected with race and gender (Johnson 2004). For instance, arguments for excluding or limiting immigration of Chinese, Japanese, and southern and eastern Europeans have relied on categorizing these populations as public charges.

The intersection of race and class explains the different paths of entry between workers. Low-skilled workers of color are limited to temporary entry through guest programs (i.e., the Bracero Program) and the use of H-2 Visa programs (i.e., used to bring in workers for clean-up after Hurricane Katrina). Today, class continues to be a significant axis by privileging immigrants with wealth and professional job skills. US companies can sponsor 85,000 skilled immigrant workers with H-1B visas. The majority of these visas (65,000) are for immigrants with a bachelor's degree, and the remaining 20,000 are given to foreign nationals with advanced degrees from US universities (Jordan 2015). The wealthy have always had special provisions for immigration to the US. Currently, the

EB-5 visa program allows wealthy foreigners access to green cards for themselves and family members if they invest $500,000 to $1 million in development projects (Oder 2015). Many wealthy foreigners are interested in relocating families to the US for their children to receive an education there. However, the disadvantages poor working immigrants face are particularly visible in legislative action taken to deny public assistance and healthcare, and attempts to exclude their children from an education. More contemporary examples include the provisions ensuring that individuals do not become public charges under the Immigration Reform and Control Act of 1986 (IRCA) (Chang 2000), and the Personal Responsibility and Work Opportunity Reconciliation Act of 1996 (Marchesvsky & Theoharis 2006).

Class also intersects with ageism and disability in defining populations classified as public charges. These populations are socially constructed as unable to work and "likely to become a public charge" (LPC) (Nielsen 2012). Early in the eugenics movement in the US, persons differently abled were perceived as inferior and it was feared they would pollute the "nation's gene pool" (Johnson 2004: 106). Disability was legally constructed to include persons perceived as "lunatic, idiot, maimed, aged, or infirm," which was easily applied to persons with any physical or mental impairment, particularly working-class immigrants denigrated as inferior races. As disabled persons gained more acceptability for residing in society rather than being institutionalized, the Americans with Disabilities Act was passed (1990). In 1994, Congress removed the naturalization requirements of English proficiency and knowledge of US history and civics for disabled immigrants. However, in 1996, disabled immigrants were no longer eligible for public benefits. Here, anti-immigrant sentiment was primarily targeted at older immigrants of color who were disabled (Weber 2004).

Sexuality is also an important identity in white supremacy and patriarchal systems of domination regulating immigration. Early cases of limiting immigration entry and naturalization based on sexuality (perceived or otherwise) involved Chinese women classified as prostitutes (Johnson 2004). Deportation of men engaging in homosexual acts was included under the regulation of denying entry to populations that may become public charges or legally defined as "aliens afflicted with psychopathic personality, epilepsy or a mental defect" (Johnson 2004: 142). Later, Congress added "sexual deviation" to the previous phrase. The history of excluding gay and lesbian immigrants does not officially begin until the 1950s when McCarthyism added them to the population of "undesirables." One of the major Supreme Court gay rights rulings on immigration rights involved the 1967 case of a Canadian immigrant, Clive Boutilier. He entered the US in 1955 with his family and became a permanent resident. In 1963, he applied for citizenship. In the application process, Boutilier mentioned his 1959 arrest for sodomy in the interview with the naturalization examiner in 1964. The government began deportation proceedings on the basis that he was gay. In 1967, the Supreme Court upheld his deportation to Canada on the basis that he should have been denied entry in 1955 because of the exclusion of gays under the psychopathic personality provision of the 1952 Immigration and Nationality Act. However, the court made no inquiries nor offered evidence that Boutilier identified as gay or was gay when granted entry to the US (Stein 2010). Justice William Douglas argued in his dissent that the exclusion under "psychopathic personality" was vague and did not take into consideration the number of gays in the larger US society, as well as the distinguished gays serving in Congress and the Executive Branch (Stein 2005). Eventually, the Immigration Act of 1990 removed homosexuality as a basis for exclusion. Later, gays faced barriers under the HIV exclusion until 2009 (Robinson & Moodie-Mills 2012).

Sexual orientation eventually was recognized as an eligible classification of "protected group" seeking asylum. In 1994, Attorney General Janet Reno granted a gay Cuban man relief from deportation on the basis of sexuality, which established a precedent for homosexuals as a "particular social group eligible for asylum" (McClure & Nugent 2000). However, "applicants must mold aspects of their life and identity to fit US norms and expectations of what it means to be LGBT" (Morgan 2006: 136) and "immigration officials and judges make decisions based on racialized sexual stereotypes and culturally specific notions of homosexuality" (Morgan 2006: 137). In her interview with asylum applicants, Morgan describes a case of an Iranian gay male who had experienced abuse by a male guard in a volunteer military force in Iran; when he escaped, the guard filed criminal charges that he was a homosexual, which is a crime punishable by death. In response, his father beat him and disowned him. He initially failed to gain asylum because he did not meet the immigration officer's expectations that gays are feminine. He was also living with his Iranian American lover under the pretense they were room-mates. The officer concluded that if he was able to pass for straight in the US, he would be able to do the same in his homeland. After he was denied asylum, attorneys advocating for LGBTQ rights took his case and reopened it to provide additional background information. His attorney advised him to "provide proof comporting with judicial stereotypes of what it means to be gay, his membership in gay organizations, subscriptions to gay publications, and participation in gay pride parades" (Morgan 2006: 147). Without an intersectional approach to analyzing sexual orientation, gay essentialism is assumed, along with rigid boundaries of sexual identity (Katyal 2002).

In excluding specific racial, gender, class and sexual orientation categories of persons from citizenship or legal entry into the US, physical appearance frequently becomes a proxy for citizenship. Consequently, the uniformity of types of persons denied citizenship reinforces gendered-racialized and class-based images of what an "illegal alien" looks like. In his examination of legal history, Robert Chang (1999: 29) captures the link between the racial experiences of citizenship and immigration when he observes "the dynamics of racial formation as immigrants enter the political/cultural/legal space of the United States and 'become' differentially racialized as Asian American, black, Latina/Latino, and White." Chang argues that persons racialized as non-white in the US carry a "figurative border" as they are stigmatized as "aliens." Even though US legal history establishes the identification and treatment of persons classified as "alien," the social construction of a specific racialized, gendered and class-based body as an "illegal alien" is reified in public discourse, media and the everyday practices of immigration policing and surveillance. Marc Stein (2010: 58) further observed: "U.S. immigration has helped form and regulate class, racial and religious hierarchies by favoring white Christians from northwestern Europe and Canada, and this has intersected with the formation and regulation of gender and sexual hierarchies through provisions and practices that favored heteronormative families." As we will see in the next section, policing citizenship status and rights relies heavily on assumptions about social identities made based on physical appearance.

Discussion questions

1 How does an intersectional analysis of immigration law identify the privileges that certain populations have had in migrating legally to the US?
2 What systems of domination shaped your family's citizenship history?

Immigration Policing, Surveillance and Intersectionality

Between 2010 and 2012, the federal government deported over 200,000 parents with children who were born in the US. The government deported more people in 2010 than between 1981 and 1990. Under current immigration laws, persons deported without criminal records become criminalized in the process, which eliminates legal options to reunite with their family (Golash-Boza 2012). Under the Obama administration, a record number of families were torn apart by Congress's mandate that required the immigration agency to detain 34,000 immigrants daily. Consequently, an estimated 2 million individuals have been deported. Civil rights organizations argue that, in order to meet quotas, law enforcement has incorporated racial profiling practices. While 37% of undocumented immigrants are from Mexico and Central America, 29% are from Asia, 14% are from Europe, Canada, Australia, New Zealand and the rest of the South West Pacific, 9% from Africa, 4% from the Caribbean, and 7% from South America (Rosenblum & Soto 2015). Yet Mexicans have become the political face of anti-immigrant sentiment and law enforcement. However, a closer look at reported policing practices points to the intersectionality of citizenship status with other identities – namely race, ethnicity, class, age and, frequently, gender.

Exclusion, detention and surveillance of non-citizens of color are central to counterterrorism legislation, which includes the USA PATRIOT Act, the Homeland Security Act (HSA) and the Enhanced Border Security and Visa Entry Reform Act (EBSVERA). The distinction between criminal aliens (deportable for their post-entry criminal conduct), illegal aliens (deportable for their surreptitious crossing of the US border) and terrorists (deportable for the grave risk they pose to national security) are blurred and all undocumented immigrants are treated as dangerous. Combining the traditional domains of immigration and criminal law enforcement under the umbrella of the Department of Homeland Security has further served to obscure differences between immigrants who are simply working illegally in the US and immigrants and non-immigrants engaged in murder, human smuggling, money laundering or child pornography. In 2003, the Department of Homeland Security released a ten-year detention and removal strategy. As a mission slogan, the Office of Detention and Removal (DRO) selected: "Promote the public safety and national security by ensuring the departure from the United States all removable aliens through the fair and effective enforcement of the nation's immigration laws." In framing the mission solely on public safety and national security, the government defined all unauthorized immigrants as security threats. Traditionally, immigration raids occurred at work sites employing low-wage male workers. However, since the beginning of the immigration program Operation Return to Sender, in 2006, news accounts and civil rights litigation report an unusually high number of immigration raids targeting low-income families of color.

One story to catch the headlines was "Child's civil rights were violated during immigration raid" (Hendricks 2007). Kebin Reyes, the 6-year-old son of a Guatemalan-born father, was arrested along with his father when immigration agents raided their home early in the morning. His father explained that his son was born in California and showed his son's passport as evidence of citizenship. Agents refused his father's plea to call relatives to come to pick up his son. Instead, agents held Kebin in a locked room all day and only gave him bread and water. A family member arrived at the detention center and requested Kebin's release but he was not released until the evening. Before the arrest, his father described Kebin as very friendly and active. Afterwards, he "turned to be very reserved and quiet and not as open to speak to anyone" (McKinley 2007).

During Return to Sender and Operation Endgame, reports of immigration agents entering residences unannounced or without warrants, particularly in pre-dawn raids, increased (Romero 2011b). Concerns about the civil rights violation of family members, frequently children, have emerged, particularly given the unprecedented number of poor and working-class immigrant women and children of color held in detention centers. The largest family detention center in 2015 was Dilly in Texas, which held 1,735 individuals, including about 1,000 children. Without an intersectional framework, immigration enforcement may appear to be one-dimensional, but race and class systems of domination intersect with citizenship to place communities of color at risk. A closer look at the way law enforcement inspects citizenship status reveals race, class, gender and other systems of domination.

Scholarly attention to the everyday practices of citizenship highlights the significance of social identities intersecting and placing certain groups at a higher risk of police scrutiny (Lugo 2000; Heyman 2001; Inda 2006; Romero 2011b). Similar experiences have been found in the racial profiling of Latinos and African Americans in the War on Drugs (Russell 2009 [1998]; Milovanovic & Russell 2001; Lundman & Kaufman 2003), and are evident in targeted citizenship inspections that occur away from the border. Among the most common aspects of immigration law enforcement is the targeting of persons with particular physical characteristics that mark race and class, rather than behavior, to trigger "probable cause" and "reasonableness" for citizenship inspection (Lugo 2000; Heyman 2001). Specific immigration enforcement practices place low-wage, racialized Latinos in harm's way of the law. Consequently, the heavy police surveillance in Latino communities results in immigration stops for many Latinos who are born US citizens, naturalized citizens, permanent residents, and immigrants with and without documentation. White racialized spaces, such as middle-class neighborhoods and upscale shopping malls, provide a bubble for Whites, regardless of their citizenship status, to move around without the burden of police questioning their right to be in the US. Middle-class Latinos experience more freedom of movement without policing in these white racialized spaces (Romero 2006). Therefore, as a heterosexual Mexican American woman born in the US and employed as a college professor, I do not face the same risk of having my rights violated by immigration law enforcement as if I were a working-class Mexican American male college student driving home from campus to a predominantly low-income community of color. If working-class white students are undocumented, they are at far less risk of being stopped than a person physically characterized as Latino/a, Asian, American Indian or of Middle Eastern descent. However, border patrol officers at immigration checkpoints along the highway in the southern area of Arizona are more likely to stop and question me than they are to stop my white male or female, straight or LGBTQ colleague driving through the same checkpoint. While the use of racial profiling relies on physical appearance as evidence of citizenship status, it intersects with social class, gender, and location.

Immigrant advocate organizations voiced concern about the civil rights violations of citizens of color when Congress passed draconian immigration policies, as well as the bills passed at the state and local levels. Along with researchers, they understood that the public responds to anti-immigrant laws by discriminating against people of color, particularly Latinos, Asians and Arabs, as well as ethnically identified persons speaking with an accent or having the ability to speak more than one language, regardless of their actual citizenship status (Davis & Moore 2014). As perceived foreigners, they are more likely to be denied employment, housing and access to quality healthcare. Low-income adults of color are questioned more than Whites when they attempt to vote or apply for government benefits. The intersections of race, ethnicity, class and gender increase the likelihood that darker-skinned low-wage Latino male workers will be stopped by police and Immigration and Customs Enforcement (ICE) agents for proof of citizenship on worksites or driving to and from work. For instance, the notorious Sheriff Joe Arpaio in Maricopa County in Arizona regularly raided workplaces, such as construction sites and factories, claiming a crime sweep of criminals on the basis of workplace fraud. However, white citizens also commit workplace fraud but are not targeted in these raids. Since 9/11, Arab Americans are more likely to be questioned when they are passengers waiting for a flight. Nafees Syed, a writer and attorney in New York, noted that "flying while Muslim" means extra screening, particularly when wearing a hijab or having an Arabic name. Understanding citizenship inspection and the privileges of citizenship requires an intersectional approach. Examining the context of immigration checkpoints, the degree of Transportation Security Administration (TSA) inspection, surveillance in low-income neighborhoods of color, employment sites hiring Latinos and Latinas, and the convenience of voting precincts highlights the interaction of race, gender and class systems of domination in restricting citizenship rights.

Discussion questions

1   How do systems of domination interact to restrict citizenship rights of certain populations?
2   How does an intersectional analysis identify the social inequities in immigration policing and surveillance?

The Significance of Intersecting Social Identities in Immigrant Organizing

Now that we've reviewed immigration legislation and law enforcement, the intersectionality of various systems of domination constructing citizenship is apparent. I will return to the young LGBTQ UndocuQueer immigrants living at the intersection of sexuality, gender identity and citizenship status. Embracing intersectional alliances, they demonstrate significant ways the LGBTQ and immigration reform movements converge on common issues. In an interview, Julio Salgado, a gay artist and co-founder of DreamersAdrift, described the inspiration found in intersectional activism:

> I've been queer since I was little, since I can remember. But one of the people that sort of created the spark in me about two years ago was Mo [Mohammad] Abdollahi. He was one of the people that did the sit-in in Tucson in 2010. He's from Iran. When I heard his story, I said – this dude is willing to say "I'm queer and undocumented." I mean, he was risking deportation back to Iran, a place where homosexuality is punished with death.
>
> So I was graduating from college at the time, and the first thing they would tell us was don't tell anyone you're undocumented. And here we have people revolutionizing that. It was Mo, and Yahaira Carillo, and Tania Unzueta from Chicago. So we have three queer folks who are huge parts of this movement. And I was like, "Oh my god I have to document this."

LGBTQ immigrant youth of color called attention to their presence in the US – some of them fleeing prosecution in their own countries, others who are married to US citizens but as same-sex couples do not necessarily have access to the "cancelation of removal" that heterosexual married couples enjoy. Undocumented LGBTQ immigrants in detention face sexual assault, arbitrary solitary confinement (used as the only safety measure), denial of medical care, harassment and discrimination

(National Immigrant Justice Center [NIJC] & Physicians for Human Rights [PHR] 2012). Recognizing the intersection of sexuality, gender identity and citizenship status, as well as race and class in the construction of immigration, the youth immigration movement works closely with the National Day Laborer Organizing Network in planning activities for the "Not1MoreDeportation" campaign aimed at protesting against deportations. They successfully called a National Day of Action on April 5, 2014, with thousands of demonstrators in more than 50 cities. LGBTQ and other youth activists in the immigration movement were active in hunger strikes in 2014. They have been at the forefront of civil disobedience, blocking buses carrying undocumented immigrants by forming a human chain or creating human blockades at detention centers and court entrances. However, while the campaigns for marriage equality and immigration reform intersect, media coverage and political pundits treat the activism and struggles as separate and distinct from each other.

Summary

This chapter has examined the interlocking systems of oppression and privilege by focusing on immigration to illustrate the significance of intersectional analysis. On the surface, immigration appears to be one-dimensional, only having to do with a person's citizenship status in the country in which they reside. This overview, however, addresses the necessity of an intersectional framework for explaining intra-group differences in obtaining and retaining citizenship rights. Like all social identities, citizenship status is socially constructed. A review of immigration policy demonstrates the way an immigrant's social identity links race, class, gender, ethnicity, sexuality, age and abilities. Access to citizenship rights is contingent on the intersectionality of these systems of domination, which are contextually rooted in history and geography. While citizenship status is primarily one constructed by the law and criminal justice system, practices in the media and other institutions perpetuate specific images of "aliens" that are racialized, class-based, gendered, and often include age and sexual orientation – all of which have real consequences.

6

Intersectional Approaches to Social Issues: The Wealth Gap, the Care Crisis and Black Lives Matter

In his book *The Sociological Imagination*, C. Wright Mills acknowledged that, in times of trouble and crises, there is an almost overwhelming sense of feeling trapped and a corresponding tendency to focus on individual change, responsibility and personal transformations. Mills' development of the sociological imagination addressed the duty that sociologists had in making visible the links between personal problems and social issues. He distinguished personal troubles from public issues by drawing our attention to the difference that an issue "involves a crisis in institutional arrangements" (Mills 1959: 9). A sociological imagination requires one to focus on the way in which biography and history connect within society. Every person is both the product of society and one of its producers. Mills' view resonates with critical scholars reframing traditional approaches to sociology to include and embrace the lived experiences of everyone, including those previously left out: people of color, the poor, LGBTQ, disabled, immigrants, and others who are not white, middle-class males. Intersectionality also asks citizens, not just sociologists, to begin with biography and history, which sociologists commonly refer to as positionality or standpoint. Understanding individuals' relations to power structures requires acknowledging multiple identities and recognizing the saliency of these identities in various social situations; it involves examining people's lived experiences. Intersectional approaches provide some tools for developing a greater understanding of domination and oppression that is connected to social issues from many positions.

Recognizing the relation between biography and history from intersectional approaches promises to generate new knowledge that creates comprehensive understandings for social justice. Intersectional approaches for researching and developing social policy are crucial to understanding the dynamics of social issues and ensuring that proposed solutions are comprehensive. This approach is not advocating traditional universality but rather "pluri-versalism" (Grosfoguel 2012), which incorporates positions, interests and lived experiences inside and outside systems of domination. Intersectional approaches not only analyze from the center to the periphery, but strive to identify how systems interact to create and maintain privilege and oppression. Social issues explored in this chapter are the racial wealth gap and the lack of caretaking (frequently referred to as the care crisis) in the US. I conclude by analyzing the use of intersectionality in the Black Lives Matter (BLM) Movement.

The Wealth Gap

In 1962, Michael Harrington published a slim volume called *The Other America* which became very influential in American politics. Part of the book examined the plight of coal miners and others living in Appalachia: eastern Kentucky, western Virginia, and the state of West Virginia are out-of-the-way places even today, with a peculiarly American intersection of race, gender and social class. When New England was being settled by Puritans fleeing religious persecution in Britain, Virginia was settled by corporations seeking profit in the new lands. Planters with large acreages of tobacco and cotton needed labor. They brought enslaved Africans, but also indentured white workers. Most were petty criminals, vagrants or just "surplus population" of Scottish/Irish descent. Magistrates or judges condemned them to seven or more years of unpaid servitude for the Tidewater Virginia corporations. Some ran away, west, into the mountains. They had a strong independent streak, relived in our folklore of Davy Crockett and Jim Bowie. They engaged in subsistence agriculture and practiced evangelical types of Protestantism. However, their story changed dramatically in the early 1800s.

While the land was still almost completely isolated by high peaks and deep hollers, surveyors came to explore the area. Prospectors discovered a wealth of untouched hardwood forests and some of the richest coal veins on the continent. Landholders were approached by "city slick-ers" offering cash for the trees and the rights to the underground coal. Since there was no way to get the timber or haul the coal, locals signed "broad form deeds," which guaranteed that they could keep their lands while selling the resources. The railroads penetrated the area, the moun-tains' old-growth forest was logged off to build the booming cities in the North, and underground mining began on a large scale. As a cash economy replaced subsistence farming, the boys went into the mines. Eventually more workers were imported from Southern and Eastern Europe to do the brutal labor of pick-and-shovel mining in underground tunnels.

Perhaps you know the song "Sixteen tons," with the line "Another day older and deeper in debt." That was the way of the mine families who "owed their souls to the company store." Miners were considered independent contractors, much like Uber drivers today. They had to buy their own tools, clothes, safety equipment, and supplies like blasting powder and fuel for the lamps on their hats. They borrowed the money for this from the mine company. They also rented their house from the company, and paid the company for electricity – when it finally arrived. They started in debt and some never escaped. Only men were allowed underground, and coal mining was the only job around, so women had to be the daughter, wife or mother of a miner if they were to survive. If the miner was killed by accident or explosion, the entire family became destitute.

Thus, the intersection of a particular extractive industry and Anglo-American female-headed households produced an isolated, rural and deeply impoverished community. Malnourished, uneducated, dirt-poor and white, these people had been hidden from American eyes in the hills and hollers of Appalachia. Perhaps due to his intelligence, or his own Scots/Irish roots, John Fitzgerald Kennedy was one of the first American politicians since Abraham Lincoln to visit the southern mountains. His administration brought in "the best and the brightest" to formulate "anti-poverty" programs, but he was murdered before most of them could be implemented. To this day, many poor people in Appalachia still have pictures of JFK hanging on the wall next to Jesus – and sometimes Mother Jones, the influential union organizer.

As Kennedy's successor, President Lyndon Johnson introduced the War on Poverty in 1964 in response to the fact that nearly one in five Americans lived in poverty: Appalachia was just one of the big swathes of deep poverty "discovered" in the early 1960s by Harrington and others. Whole sections of the nation, ranging from the Appalachians to rural New England, from Indian reservations to inner cities, were poor by any definition. The poor were white and Black, urban and rural, male and female, young and old, Native American, Mexican American and recent immigrants. Most worked steadily; they picked strawberries, mined coal, logged forests in the Pacific Northwest, and fished shrimp in the Gulf of Mexico – yet they did not have enough to eat, access to medical or dental care, or adequate educational opportunity. Antipoverty programs were intended to eliminate such destitution and end generational cycles of dependency.

Unfortunately, attempts to make poor people and communities more like white, middle-class, two-parent, and heterosexual families frequently failed. College-educated "social engineers" often ignored, or worse yet denigrated, strong local cultures ranging from "Hillbillies" to Black churches. Major initiatives were Head Start, Volunteers in Service to America (VISTA), TRiO (e.g., Upward Bound, Talent Search, Student Support Services), and Job Corps. At this time, the Economic Opportunity Act was passed and established the Office of Equal Opportunity (OEO). These programs worked to an extent.

Jump forward the next 50 years or so – which includes two decades of President Clinton's Personal Responsibility and Work Opportunity Act – and the intersections of poverty have changed. While eliminating the "Safety Net" decreased money for families and shifted emphasis onto employment, an entirely new group living in poverty is recognized as the working poor. In 1959, 41.7% of the poor in the US were working in their prime working years, 18–64; in 2012, that group constituted 57% of the poor. Thanks to Social Security and Medicare, far fewer elderly persons were among the poor – about 9% in 2012, and 8% in 2015 (US Census 2015a), whereas in 1966 more than 28% of persons 65 and over were poor (DeSilver 2014). Unfortunately, childhood poverty continues to be high. In 2015, about 14.5 million children, or 19%, were poor. In other words, about one child in every five lives in poverty. The National School Lunch Program provided lunches to 30.3 million poor children in 2016 (USDA 2016). Conservatives tend to attribute this to households being headed by women; however, married couples are also among the poor. In 1973, half of the families headed by a married couple (51.4%) and 45% headed by women were poor. In 2012, over half of the households headed by women were poor and 38.9% of families with married couples were poor.

The differences among the poor continue to be highlighted by race. For instance, looking at children by race, the poverty rate for some is much higher. One in every three African American children and one of every four Latino children live in poverty, which is two times higher than the figure among white children (Lin & Harris 2010). In 1966, four in ten African Americans were poor, a figure which has dropped over the decades but remains twice the rate of Whites (DeSilver 2014).

The highest rate by race in 2015 was found among Blacks (24.1%), and Latinos had the second-highest rate (21.4%). Asians had a poverty rate of 11.4% and Whites had the lowest poverty rate (9%) (US Census 2015a, 2015b). However, the differences are extended to public policy differences. States with the highest concentration of Blacks and Latinos on welfare are more likely to impose lifetime limits, family caps on benefits, and stricter sanctions for noncompliance (Lin & Harris 2010).

Traditionally, sociologists have approached issues of economic inequality as poverty – a single issue. They focused on job discrimination, poor education and wage disparities. Focusing on poverty led to numerous studies on the causes and consequences of being poor – the impact on parent–child relations, strains on marriage, lack of healthy food choices, lack of educational opportunity, and survival strategies. Sociologists have researched the lifestyle of the poor, their household arrangements, marital status, number of children, and other personal and social interactions. While the nation recognized poverty to be a social problem, the research focus tended to be on the ways the poor differed from the middle class, leading many sociologists to treat poverty as a personal defect rather than a crisis in institutional arrangements. Intersectional approaches are different. They examine the ways identities are linked to existing systems of power and produce structures of oppression and opportunity. When an intersectional approach is used, different research questions arise: Since poverty seems always to be present, what function does it serve? Does any person or social group benefit from the fact that other persons or groups are poor?

A major change in understanding poverty occurred when the emphasis shifted to *wealth inequality* rather than wages and employment rates. Researchers began to analyze how opportunity is structured into systems of social inequality. In the 1940s and 1950s, sociologists such as C. Wright Mills began to investigate wealth and power in America. Mills produced a trilogy: *New Men of Power* (1948) examined the role of labor leaders not in uniting workers but in maintaining and guarding the intersections of race, gender, job and nationality – which separated Black railroad porters from skilled white machinists, for example. In 1951, Mills published *White Collar: The American Middle Classes*, which was a detailed analysis of the post-war class of bureaucrats and managers with a "salesman" mentality. In *The Power Elite* (1956), Mills examined the connections among extremely wealthy families, the political class, and the military hierarchy, that operated together in Prep and Ivy League schools, social clubs and business relations.

In 1968, a journalist named Ferdinand Lundberg published *The Rich and the Super-Rich: A Study in the Power of Money Today*. Like Mills, Lundberg marshaled data to argue that the United States had become a plutocracy governed by political, military and economic elites – almost exclusively male and white – that were embedded in a social network of exclusive clubs, schools and corporations where social, economic and political policies were made. These authors argued that just as *poverty* is intersectional – in other words, generational, persistent and structured by race, class, gender, geographical location and other categories – so are *wealth* and *power*. Great wealth in families like the Rockefellers, Bushes or Trumps is concentrated by race and, to some extent, gender. Poverty is persistent but so is wealth. Today, the vast fortunes accumulated by the Gates and Walton families can never be given away – they are far too vast. The control these people have extends to the mass media, universities and politics through foundations like the Walton Family Fund and the Bill and Melinda Gates Foundations which, to an extraordinary extent, control public broadcasting and educational policy.

A book by Melvin Oliver and Thomas Shapiro (1995) was one of the first to explicitly examine the overall effect of *wealth*, as opposed to *income*, in race relations. *Black Wealth, White Wealth: A New Perspective on Racial Inequality* revealed structural causes for racial inequality by examining the creation, expansion and preservation of assets over generations. They highlighted three historical processes that contributed to the racial legacy of wealth, revealing the racialization of state policy, the economic detour, and the sedimentation of racial inequality. They examined the intersections by which government policy established barriers to purchasing land, housing and profitable businesses, and acquiring other assets to gain wealth. Inherited wealth from past discriminatory policies continues to have profound consequences for non-Whites today.

Structural and intersectional research shifted to the wealth gap, turning sociological analyses of poverty away from an individual's lack of education or income to systems of power and the overall structure of oppression and opportunities. New work re-affirmed Mills' notion that individual plight and social problems could not be separated. With United for a Fair Economy, Meizhu Lui et al. (2006) detailed the asset-building histories of racialized groups in their book *The Color of Wealth: The Story Behind the U.S. Racial Wealth Divide*. An intersectional approach to the wealth gap problem in the US has been crucial in shifting the focus from individual poverty and behavior toward the role that the state and banking industries play in perpetuating wealth inequality. This approach illuminates the way race, class and gender inequalities are socially constructed and the link between these systems of power. The historical approach explains the significance of past policies and practices in creating current advantages and disadvantages that accumulate in one's lifetime and are passed on to future generations. The history of racialized, and sometimes gendered, laws and policies assisted white men in both accumulating wealth and placing restrictions on non-white men and women's opportunities, debunking the myth of the "self-made man."

Historical Beginnings of the Wealth Gap

In the case of African Americans, state policies bequeathed enormous wealth to white slave owners through the legal practice of slavery. Wealth gained through slavery was not limited to Southern plantation owners but included northern cotton mill owners, the shipping trade and universities. Over the last decade, several universities have acknowledged their history in the slave trade, including Brown, Columbia, Harvard and the University of Virginia. Georgetown University is currently engaged in efforts to locate the descendants of 272 slaves sold by some of the most prominent Jesuit priests in 1838 to secure the future of the school. The college relied on the Jesuit plantations in Maryland that worked slaves donated by wealthy parishioners (Swarns 2016). After emancipation, Jim Crow laws limited access to opportunities for African Americans. Many states denied them the right to own land. Sharecropping and tenant farming kept Black families in debt. For decades, the Ku Klux Klan threatened Black landowners; some were forced to abandon their homes in fear for their lives. The Great Migration from the South offered opportunities, but in the North *de facto* residential segregation, red lining by banks, and sometimes violence restricted the Black middle class to living in the same communities as poor African Americans, again denying them the class privileges gained by white middle-class families. Black business owners suffered like everyone else in the Great Depression. However, programs under the New Deal that extended to African Americans were limited, and many programs favored Whites (Lui et al. 2006). Moreover, programs like Social Security and the minimum wage did not apply to domestic workers or farmworkers, which left out many workers of color. As noted by Oliver and Shapiro, the unequal treatment of Black GIs restricted their use of benefits to apply to the best universities and to purchase homes in the nicest communities offering access to public services. Segregation resulting from these policies and practices relegated Blacks to the poorest schools, and restricted access to public libraries, parks and other resources for acquiring cultural capital.

Federal and state policies that hindered indigenous peoples from gaining wealth began with the US appropriation of Indian assets by treaties, followed by relocation of tribes and the creation of reservations. The passing of several allotment acts, the Dawes Act (1887), the Curtis Act (1898) and the Burke Act (1906) opened lands to non-Indian

settlers. Most of the land and resources previously occupied by indigenous peoples were lost through treaties. The land and resources that
remain are "held in trust," which means the federal government regulates
leases of land, and determines the price of oil and gas extracted and
the distribution of money earned. Other assets lost were timber, vegeta-
tion, wild game and fish. The doctrine of trust responsibility "promoted
federal control of Indian assets, including land and natural resources"
and a wide range of destructive cultural practices in the process of
assimilation (Lui et al. 2006: 31). These practices further enhanced the
loss of asset-building capacity by forcing the sale of tribal lands for cash,
pressure to use western farming techniques, and removal of children
from their families during the era of boarding schools. Cultural genocide
replaced collective tribal property ownership with private landowner-
ship. Stripped of their assets, Native people have the highest rate of
poverty and the most dilapidated housing, increasing their dependency.
Presently, entrepreneurial ventures with the potential to generate tribal
wealth face special federal and state taxes crippling their businesses. The
Indian Gaming Regulatory Act limits the wealth opportunities through
gaming by specifying the use of funds. State governments have benefited
greatly from state and state income taxes. As long as legal restrictions
maintain American Indians as wards of state, they are vulnerable to the
mismanagement of tribal wealth (Lui et al. 2006).

In the case of Latinos, the wealth gap began with the Monroe Doctrine (1824) and the Manifest Destiny doctrine's (1858) position on
expansionism. Examining the two largest groups of Latinos, Mexican
Americans and Puerto Ricans, one can see the lasting legacy of colonialism and conquest – as well as established power relations of dominance
and subordination. The legacy encapsulates race, class, gender, colorism
and citizenship status that perpetuate the wealth gap. The intersections
of Puerto Ricans and Mexicans with the United States are very distinct
and different. These intersections are masked or obliterated by the census
terms of "Hispanic" or "Latino."

Puerto Rico is one of five US colonies; the island is neither state nor
independent nation. Puerto Ricans can serve in the armed forces, but
cannot vote. The US government offered companies tax incentives to
establish businesses on the island, but that disadvantaged local land
and business owners. "The Foraker Act reinforced the protection of
American interests" and "officially opened [Puerto Rico] to U.S. economic domination" (Lui et al. 2006: 118). Woodrow Wilson signed
the Jones Act in 1917, which granted citizenship to Puerto Ricans but
not the right to trial by jury. That year, the Selective Service Act passed
and conscripted Puerto Rican men into the military; more than 20,000
served in World War I. Federal government policies turned the island

into a one-crop export-producing economy, further establishing Puerto Rico's dependency on US interests. This interest did not encourage entrepreneurship but reduced most of the island's population to low-wage workers. After confirmation of commonwealth status in 1952, Operation Bootstrap restructured the island economy to increase foreign investments, which extended tax-exempt status to US firms but not to those owned by Puerto Ricans. Workers recruited to the mainland were offered low-skill, low-paying industrial jobs. The name "Nuyorican" recognizes the fact that there were more Puerto Ricans in New York City than in San Juan. The loss of manufacturing in the following decades resulted in high unemployment rates and poverty. Homeownership among Puerto Ricans is extremely low in comparison to Whites and even lower if they are Black (Lui et al. 2006).

One-third of Latinos of Mexican ancestry living in the Southwest before 1848 lost their land after the Mexican–American War, even though the Treaty of Guadalupe Hidalgo (1848–50) was supposed to protect their property rights. Under Mexican law, women had the right to inherit and own property; these rights were lost or limited under Anglo-American law. Anglo-Americans took by conquest 80 percent of Mexican land grants. Spanish and Mexican land grants provided for strips of personally owned land to live on and for farming. These lands were passed down from generation to generation, and in the arid Southwest were typically close to water sources. The land grants also established "common lands" to be used by all for grazing, to cut wood for building and heating, and as a source of everything from mushrooms to berries. The trout streams were there for all, as were pinion forests, deer and elk herds. Anglo-American law did not recognize common lands, so anyone could step in, fence the land and call it theirs. Subsistence farming became impossible without access to the commons. As the economy shifted from subsistence farming and ranching to cash, Mexicans lost more land from taxation on the land's market value, as opposed to the value of the land's yield. The dispossession of the land was furthered by threats of violence and legal trickery. Mob rule and sanctioned "gangs" like the Texas Rangers killed and lynched Mexican Americans who tried to assert their rights.

Like African Americans, Mexican Americans suffered serious financial consequences due to the exclusion of domestics and agricultural workers from the Social Security Act of 1933. Mexican immigrants were recruited to work in agriculture during World War II, a program called the Bracero Program that continued until 1964. But this program proved to be pure exploitation of cheap labor, as opposed to a path to citizenship. Many who had lived with their families and worked in the US for decades lost their property during the massive deportation in the federal program called Operation Wetback conducted in the mid-1950s. This process of importing – or looking the other way as employers imported – cheap Mexican labor, followed by round-ups and mass deportations, continues today. Mexican immigrants, like many other Latino immigrants, were unable to reap benefits from the economic boom of the 1990s.

Anti-immigrant sentiment, along with legislation like Proposition 187 in California requiring policing of citizenship status to receive social services, healthcare and education, resulted in a loss of opportunities for racialized Latinos, who became suspected of being undocumented. Denying and limiting access to education challenges children and youth, as well as future generations. Federal legislation of the Welfare Reform Act of 1996 similarly placed restrictions on immigrants based on their status. Recent practices during the Obama administration deported 2.5 million undocumented people between 2009 and 2015 (Romero 2006; Armenta 2017). The current president, Donald Trump, proposes to deport millions more. Most of those deported are identified by the intersection of race, class and colorism – Mexicans or other Latino immigrants. Undocumented persons who came from Europe and overstayed tourist or student visas have little to fear.

Like indigenous populations, many Latinos do not share the economic practices of individualism – families are central to surviving poverty and creating opportunities. Non-nuclear, extended and pseudo-kin family arrangements are important in pooling resources to sponsor relatives, contributing to household expenses and wealth accumulation. Economist Barbara Robles noted that "regressive sales and payroll taxes for those earning minimum wage and setting asset eligibility requirements for the Earned Income Tax Credit and other social service programs...do not take into account Latino families' communal asset building" (Lui et al. 2006: 162). Not considering collective strategies of wealth accumulation for families applying for mortgages or loans has negative consequences in assessing credit scores. Along with predatory lending, red-lining also limited Latinos' ability for asset-building by purchasing a home. These banking practices also restricted Latino entrepreneurs' opportunities for credit, while they faced the same challenges as other businesses. Microbusinesses that involve family members suffer when programs assisting community development decline or decrease. Microbusinesses were a major source of income and wealth for Latinas, regardless of whether they were first, second or third generation. The lack of pension funds, particularly among Latinas, remains a pressing issue for elderly Latinos.

The situation faced by "Asians" in the US lumps together peoples with vastly different histories. As the census term "Hispanic" obliterated differences between Puerto Ricans, Cubans and Mexicans, "Asians" made invisible the different intersections of Japanese, Chinese, Pacific Island-ers and others. Obviously, their intersections with each other, and with the multicultural American peoples, were distinct. As noted in chapter 5, the Foreign Miners Tax was only one of the many Asian-only taxes legislated. State and local laws prevented Asians from purchasing lands from the mid-1800s to the mid-1900s. Ineligibility for citizenship had a huge financial cost. From the 1870s, imported as cheap exploitable labor, Chinese workers mined gold in California, built the Central and Union Pacific Railroads, and labored in California's agricultural industry. Frequently ghettoized in "Chinatowns" and forced to live away from Whites, few lived outside these areas. When Chinese immigration was halted, Japanese workers were recruited, later Asian Indians, and Fili-pinos became one of many in what popular imagination thought of as the American "Melting Pot." Forced segregation created ethnic enclaves and many Asians turned to self-employment through small businesses. These included restaurants, markets and rooming houses. For instance, laundry work was an open market for Chinese but their accumulation of wealth was restricted through fees and the passing of statutes such as the Anti-Ironing Ordinance.

In one of the heinous acts perpetrated on people of color, after Decem-ber 7, 1941, Japanese Americans were suspected of spying for Japan. The 1949 Evacuation Claims Act dealt with the settlement of claims by Japanese Americans who had lost their property and been placed in internment camps. Whole families were placed in the camps: men, women and children. Many of them were *Nisei*, born in the United States to first-generation or immigrant Japanese, or *Issei*. Regardless of citizenship status, the intersection of race, location on the West coast, and ethnicity marked them as probable traitors. The internment camps were located far from the coast. *Issei*, *Nisei* and *Sansei* (the third genera-tion) lost everything. Only after the war were Japanese Americans able to begin acquiring assets again, and gained entrance into universities and colleges (Lui et al. 2006).

American wars overseas have always resulted in an influx of new refu-gees. At the cutting intersection of colonialism, class, race and political status, a new wave of Asian immigrants began entering the US in the early 1960s. Here again the conglomerate term "Asian" blurs intersectional differences. Some refugees fleeing Vietnam were middle-class educated professionals who may have collaborated with the American military and feared retaliation from the North Vietnamese and Vietcong, who won the war. Others fled Laos and Cambodia – sometimes from hill tribes who lived in communities scarcely different from the traditional way of living in the previous century. Working-class Vietnamese and Cambodian refugees from peasant backgrounds, like the Hmong people, experienced unimaginable culture shock when suddenly finding themselves thrust into suburban Minneapolis. They tried to hold to their traditions but experienced high rates of poverty and juvenile delinquency as the old ways of filial piety were tested. I am sure you can see how only an intersectional analysis has the possibility to untangle the wealth gap in what are called "Asian American" communities. Analysis is complicated by race, class, gender, community of origin, date and terms of immigration, religion and a trove of other identities. Asians tend to live in urban areas and have higher incomes. Their households comprise more employed persons, resulting in higher household incomes. A few Asians have accumulated enormous wealth. The most important factor is that "the distribution of income and wealth differs widely by nationality" (Lui et al. 2006: 211). That is to say the demographic "Asian Americans" includes a family of fourth-generation Japanese where the mother is a doctor, the father is a lawyer, and the children are in the Ivy Leagues. It also includes a Cambodian family who escaped the Khmer Rouge "killing fields," with a single female head of household and children who drop out of high school to work to support the family.

Beyond intersections of race and class, as well as ethnicity and citizenship status, there is also a gender wealth gap. Gendered federal and state laws have shaped the wealth gap between men and women. For instance, married women's property rights traditionally came under common law or coverture, which gave her husband control over her property, income and ability to engage in contracts and lawsuits. Changes in legislation granting women the right to own property, write a will or control their income were passed at the state rather than federal level, beginning in Mississippi with the 1839 Married Women's Property Act. Gradually, states passed laws allowing married women to file patents, enter contracts, collect rents, receive an inheritance, open their own bank accounts and file lawsuits (Speth 2011). Only in 1974 with the federal Equal Credit Opportunity Act were *all* single, widowed and divorced women able to apply for credit without a man co-signing. Not until 1981, in the Supreme Court decision *Kirchberg* v. *Feenstra*, were husbands denied the right to acquire a mortgage on property owned by his wife without her consent (Baer 2007). The fight for equal pay for women continues – more than 50 years after the Equal Pay Act in 1963 was passed. When signed into law, women earned 59 cents for every dollar men earned. In 2011, the gap had been narrowed by 18 cents, leaving a 23-cent wage gap (National Women's Law Center 2013). Delayed marriage, cohabitation and divorce or having a female partner further impact wealth accumulation (Addo & Lichter 2013). Women experience steeper declines in wealth after a divorce than men (DiPrete 2001). Women also pay a "motherhood wealth penalty that stems from the motherhood wage penalty, time spent out of the labor force or working part-time, and for single mothers, the financial burden of being a custodial parent" (Chang 2010: 9). Over a lifetime, the wage gap has serious consequences in retirement, social security benefits and pensions (Neelakantan & Chang 2010). Traditionally, marriage was the chief means to financial security for women; but today there are high rates of unmarried women and single mothers – moreover, women tend to live longer than men do.

An intersectional analysis that includes race, gender and class is crucial in understanding lived experiences. Marriage disruption or being a single woman is highly correlated with significantly less wealth, particularly true for older women of color (Addo & Lichter 2013). While the gendered wealth gap in retirement is a major concern for all women (Neelakantan & Chang 2010), women of color are the most vulnerable. They are more likely to be living in poverty and living longer than men. "Often, women of color lack access to fringe benefits because of the types of jobs they have" (Chang 2010: 17). Since many fringe benefits have tax advantages, these women are further disadvantaged in asset-building. The differences are stark. Single Black women report a median wealth of $100, Latinas a median wealth of $120, while single white women report having $41,500. For instance, out of 100 single women: 57 white women own their homes, 33 Black women do, while only 28 Latinas are homeowners. Most of the wealth held by Black women and Latinas is "in the form of vehicles, which is a depreciating asset" (Chang 2010: 7). The equity in their homes for women of color is 25–50 percent less than for white women (Chang 2010).

Housing & Wealth Accumulation

As Oliver and Shapiro pointed out, homeownership is the most significant means for families to accumulate wealth in the US. Shapiro identified housing policies as causing "hidden injuries" by setting barriers to accumulating wealth in communities of color. In previous generations, the Federal Housing Administration implemented policies that benefited Whites and negatively affected African Americans and Latinos. Whites received enormous opportunities for wealth accumulation from the Tennessee Valley Authority, the interstate highway system, and the GI Bill; these programs in effect subsidized the suburbanization of America. Alongside legal structures and federal policy were the *de facto* practices of red-lining, mortgage discrimination and residential segregation. Thus, legal and "extra-legal" practices denied African Americans and Latinos the ability to obtain and hand down inheritance as white families were able to do. Beginning in the 1950s, civil rights legislation went a long way toward eliminating legal discrimination and closing loopholes in housing practices that maintained segregation. Gradually, the Black and Latino middle class gained access to purchasing homes in neighborhoods offering better public services. Thanks to the federal Fair Housing Act of 1968 and the federal Fair Housing Act Amendments Act of 1988, housing segregation has slowly been declining for the past half-century. However, much of the progress made after the civil rights legislation eroded during the economic recession of 2008.

While the recession was difficult for many, the impact on African Americans and Latinos was devastating. The housing bubble in 2007 that triggered an economic recession hit Black and Latino middle-class homeowners harder than white homeowners: "In 2011 the foreclosure rate for African Americans was 9.8 percent, for Latinos was 11.9 percent, and for Asians was 6.6 percent, while the foreclosure rate for whites was 5.0 percent" (Weller et al. 2012). After home prices fell, 31 percent of homeowners of color were "underwater," meaning they owed more on the mortgage than the market value of their house and they lost their home equity (Rokosa 2012). "Between 2005 and 2009, Asian Americans lost 54 percent of their wealth, compared with a 16 percent decline for whites, much of it due to loss of home equity during the housing crisis" (Hasegawa & Duong 2015: 278). The elderly population in Asian American communities was particularly vulnerable to living in poverty and being weighed down with housing debt. Overall, US families lost 28.5 percent of their wealth but the loss for Black families was 47.6 percent (McKernan et al. 2014). As the government responded to the growing crisis, white families did not experience a continued loss during 2009–11, but Black families continued to lose 13 percent more of their wealth.

This devastation came as a result of subprime and predatory lending which involves attaching discriminatory and abusive terms to loans, such as charging excessive fees and higher interest rates, and making loans knowing that borrowers are unable to pay them back. Black and Latino borrowers were disproportionately targeted for predatory subprime lending. Examining the loan practices of 14 banks, one study found that only 17.8 percent of Whites received subprime loans, whereas, 30.9 percent of Latinos and 41.5 percent of African Americans received them. The housing crisis hit women of color homeowners particularly hard because banks targeted their communities for the high-cost and high-risk subprime loans. African American women were "256 percent more likely to have a subprime mortgage than a white man with similar financial profile" (Baker 2014b: 62). Even in one of the most affluent middle-class Black communities, Prince George county in Maryland, a quarter of all mortgages in 2009 were subprime. Like other people of color, banks gave Blacks subprime even when they qualified for a prime loan (Baptiste 2014).

Thus, continuing racial discrimination in banking was integral to the housing market crisis (Burd-Sharps & Rasch 2015): "Long histories of discriminatory lending practices that denied people of color access to traditional lending services left these communities vulnerable" (ARC 2009: 32–3). Looking beyond mortgage lending, a report on "State of the dream" (United for a Fair Economy [UFE] 2015) highlighted issues related to obstructions to wealth accumulation created by banks, companies granting student loans, and predatory fringe lenders such as payday lenders, check cashers and auto-title lenders. Obtaining a payday loan may cost anywhere from 391 percent to 521 percent yearly in interest, and car-title loans are 15 to 20 times more expensive than credit cards. There are eight times as many payday lenders in African American and Latino communities, compared to predominantly white neighborhoods. From 2008 to 2012, 93 percent of all bank branches closed in zip codes with low incomes. Most of these unbanked or underbanked individuals report not being able to meet minimum balance requirements, wanting to avoid overdraft fees, mistrusting banks, and privacy concerns about revealing credit and banking information. Monolingual Spanish-speakers faced difficulty accessing suitable banking services. Many of these problems were exacerbated in rural areas, particularly the poorest counties that are described as "banking deserts." Meanwhile, Wall Street gained over $103 billion, some of it from stripping families from equal banking services (UFE 2015), and, following the recession, poverty rates rose higher for households of color than for white households (Weller et al. 2012). The Great Recession increased the racial wealth gap and its legacy will continue for generations (Burd-Sharps & Rasch 2015).

By contextualizing racial and class identities in history and geography, the systems of power become transparent in analyzing the wealth gap. Generations of state policies assisting white wealth accumulation reveal the interconnectedness of racialized identities. Many social problems arise from the wealth gap. The inability to purchase a home in a middle-class neighborhood is a hidden cost of being poor. Educational opportunities linked to the location of your home underlie other problems related to housing segregation. In my state of Arizona, for example, former Governor Fife Symington suggested that if poor families did not like their local school, they should move to a better neighborhood, or send their children to a private "day school" that costs $10,000 dollars a year (Silverman 1994). Being the location for toxic dump sites is a common phenomenon in low-income communities of color in urban and rural areas. Traffic pollution is higher in low-income neighborhoods located under and around major city highways. Public transportation is inadequate and favors affluent neighborhoods. Workers living in predominantly white and higher-income areas have shorter commutes on public transportation than low-wage workers of color. The number of parks and recreation areas increases with the increased pricing of houses. The range of issues tied to the wealth gap includes access to fresh food at affordable prices, fair and just treatment in the criminal justice system, the healthcare crisis, and the erosion of democracy. Again to use my home state as an example, districts have been drawn to weaken the vote of Latinos and African Americans by either placing them all in one district – creating the very few Latino or African Representatives in an overwhelmingly white state legislature – or, conversely, by including a few neighborhoods of color in an overwhelmingly white district, thus making their vote impotent. Voter suppression tactics like this have ranked Arizona 39th among the states for democratic fairness (Buckwalter-Poza & Kennedy 2016). Understanding the interconnectedness of marginalized identities helps us to recognize that all Americans will gain by closing the wealth gap. Maintaining the wealth gap sets the overall US living standard below that of other western and industrialized countries.

Discussion questions

1   Identify the ways in which public policy has opened doors for or disadvantaged your family in wealth accumulation, based on race, class and gender or citizenship status.
2   How does the wealth gap challenge the idea of Americans as self-made individuals?

Seeking Intersectional Solutions

United for a Fair Economy (UFE) is a program that acknowledges that the concentration of wealth and power is a threat to a democracy that is inclusive and promotes equity; wealth disparity further deepens the race divisions in the country. UFE identified the development of two economies since the mid-1970s, when CEOs and others with monetary resources invested in the stock market and made spectacular gains, while worker salaries stagnated. In 1970, CEOs earned 79 times as much as the average worker's pay; but by 2013, CEOs took home 331 times as much. Wealth is generational – in other words, passed down in the family – and the consequence is that both wealth and opportunity are inherited by some children, while the children of workers may see their inheritance actually shrink. As discussed above, if the main thing one inherits is one's parents' house, and the value of that property decreases or is more heavily mortgaged, one's inheritance is lessened. Conversely, if one inherits a stock portfolio, the inheritance increases with the market. Protection of these growing assets is why some people in Congress wanted to abolish the "estate tax." In 2016, for example, the first $5.5 million one wills to one's descendants is tax-free. Only the wealthiest among us will have that much to leave. Moreover, the amount is indexed for inflation and will generally increase each year (Clifford 2016).

The estate tax falls very unevenly on different races and ethnicities in our society. As discussed above, government policy since World War II has increased white wealth through programs that did not benefit all equally. Specifically, the GI Bill for higher education, and housing policy that invested in suburbia rather than "inner cities" through red-lining and exclusive developments, left many Latinos and African Americans in urban ghettos, even as Italians, Jews and Anglo Americans moved to the suburbs. A GI's investment in a suburban "ranch-style" home in the 1950s was likely to multiply many times before being passed on to the baby boom generation in the twenty-first century. "For every dollar owned by the average White family in the US, the average family of color has less than a dime" (UFE 2015: 6). Since the 1970s, the country has experienced divestment, disrepair and privatization of services in many urban and rural communities, resulting in opportunity becoming a luxury. This is at the same time that the average worker began losing ground through the lack of cost-of-living (COLA) wage increases from the 1970s, rising job insecurity and growing debt. Wages have not kept pace with the rising cost of living. The UFE reaches out to workers organizing for higher wages, fair scheduling and the right to unionize. Local leaders and groups are part of the Inclusive Economy Network advocating for fair and progressive taxes, and capacity-building to alleviate poverty. In these initiatives, the wealthy have been recruited as allies to expand opportunities and work through media, legislative and fundraising campaigns. At the center of the vision for equal opportunity and equal justice are intersections of gender, sexual orientation, race, nationality and social class. Everyone wins when sustainability and equity are the goals.

In addressing the issue of underrepresented Americans having access to banking services, UFE (2015) considers race, class, age and citizen status in both rural and urban locations. One proposal is postal banking, previously advocated by Senators Elizabeth Warren and Bernie Sanders, and the US Conference of Mayors. All communities have postal services, and they are trusted institutions that adapt to fit the needs of the local area they serve. The ability for individuals to pay bills, cash checks and access small loans would provide underserved families with affordable financial services and help them to build a credit history. Post offices already have experience in providing financial services by offering electronic money transfers and prepaid gift cards: "In addition to handling money orders, transfers, and debit cards, postal window clerks have experience cashing checks, processing refunds, renting post office boxes, preparing bank depositions, and maintaining business accounts" (UFE 2015: 22).

Another proposal is to support further the development of lending circles that provide zero-interest and zero-fee loans to build credit. A successful program is the Mission Asset Fund Organization (MAF), which began in San Francisco in 2007 with a million-dollar investment from the sale of the Levi Strauss factory. Their aim was to serve the local residents who had previously relied on fringe financial services like "payday loans." MAF offers financial training and professional development. They built on the *tanda* model traditionally used in the Mexican immigrant community to lend and borrow money. Filipinos refer to the model as *paluwagan*, and in the Caribbean, the term is *susas*. Providing linguistically and culturally appropriate services has benefited both Latino and Asian Pacific American communities. Participants in the MAF Lending Circle in 2013 increased their credit scores and many were able to refinance high-cost debt: "In 2014, California Governor Brown signed Senate bill 896, a law that provides exempt status from the state's lender license laws to nonprofit organizations that provide zero-interest, credit-building loans" (Quinonez 2015: 288). Their success has generated similar programs across 19 states.

A program sharing similarities is Lakota Funds, the first Community Development Financial Institution (CDFI) located on an Indian reservation. The Native American Lending Study (NALS) found that "15 percent of Native communities are more than 100 miles from the nearest ATM or bank, and 86 percent of Native communities lack a single financial institution within their borders" (Meeks 2015: 273). Based on the needs of the Pine Ridge Reservation, Lakota Funds worked with Tribal colleges and schools to provide financial education, entrepreneurship and asset-building programs, and started the Lakota Federal Credit Union. The program includes working with youth and children in the "Generations of Wealth" program that matches savings for grade-school children. "South Dakota enacted a law that allows tribal identification cards to be used for opening bank accounts and cashing checks" which helps people "who do not have a state driver's license or identification card" (Meeks 2015: 275–6).

A program related to UFE is "Our Responsible Wealth," which consists of people in the top 5 percent of income or assets fighting for tax fairness and corporate responsibility. This network of business leaders, investors and inheritors recognizes that the increasing wealth gap in the US is not in their interest or in the interest of the country. Another initiative the program has joined is changing the banking system that denies services to 93 million individuals, forcing people to rely on payday lending, check cashing, rent-to-own, and auto-title lending. These predatory lending services cost an average household an additional $3,029 per year in fees – another way of looking at it is that predatory lenders drain $103 billion from these communities. The fees represent 10 percent of household incomes. As a part of the UFE, wealthy members understand that the wealth gap maintains social and economic inequality and erodes both the quality of life in the US and the democratic process. They lobby for a progressive tax system and limits on the amount of wealth that can be passed from one generation to another.

Among UFE's educational efforts is to call attention to the myth of the "self-made man," or the narrative of the American Dream as the "rags to riches" narrative. In most cases, the wealthy are aided and sheltered through tax and other government policies benefiting the rich. Most of the 1 percent who hold most of the wealth in the US were the recipients of the unearned privilege of being born to a rich family. The UFE conducted an analysis of the Forbes list of the 400 richest Americans in the year 2011. The study revealed that:

21.25% were born with enough wealth to include them on the list;
7% inherited "in excess of $50 million or a large and prosperous company";
11.5% inherited "a medium-sized business or wealth of more than $1 million or received substantial start-up capital";
22% were born into "an upper-class background and inherited less than $1 million or received some start-up capital";
35% are "from a lower- or middle-class background." (UFE 2012: 9)

One-tenth of 1% of Americans receives half of all net increases in capital gains. The tax laws were written so that capital gains are taxed at a lesser rate than income earned as salary. The 0.1% only pay a 15% tax on the first 60% of capital gains. Workers in the middle class, making $37,950 to $91,900, pay 25% in income tax. And those in the lowest tax bracket, making less than $10,000 a year, pay 10 percent of their income as tax (Pomerleau 2016).

As an example of inherited wealth: "Mary Janet Morse Cargill died in 2010 (when the estate tax was completely repealed) & saved her family $750 million in estate taxes.... Cargill-MacMillan family members inheriting just 1/18th of the family fortune are still inheriting enough wealth to put them on the Forbes 400" (UFE 2012: 13). The Forbes

400 is overwhelmingly white. Oprah Winfrey is the only African American on the list and 1 of the 40 women on the list. Born to an unwed teenage mother in rural Mississippi, she earned her wealth from a successful career in television, film, and publishing. Oprah is a statistical "outlier"; 87.5% of women on the Forbes 400 inherited their fortune from a deceased husband or family member. Members of "Our Responsible Wealth" recognize that wealth determined at birth rather than from achievement is a deterrent to a democratic society. Opportunities structured by systems of race, class and gender place enormous amounts of wealth in the hands of a small group of families, and threaten paths to opportunities to gain economic security.

I now turn to my second example, the structural issue of caregiving, frequently referred to as the care crisis. However, as I point out in the following section, access to care for children, the disabled, the sick and the elderly is beyond the crisis stage and is a long-term structural problem.

The Caregiving Social Issue

In South Carolina, a 46-year-old Black woman has been arrested for letting her daughter play in a nearby park while trying to earn a living. (Friedeersdorf 2014)

Shanesa Taylor, a mother living in Scottsdale, Arizona, was arrested in March after leaving her children, ages six months and two years old, in the car while she went to a job interview.... Taylor, who was homeless at the time, got a job interview with Farmers Insurance to be an insurance agent, which would have paid $39,000 with the ability to earn more.... even though she had arranged for a babysitter, no one answered the door at the babysitter's on the day of the interview. So she drove to the interview and left her children in the car with windows cracked and the car fan blowing. (Covert 2014)

A single mom was arrested at the Memorial City Mall in Houston, Texas, for allegedly "abandoning" her two six-year-old children who were waiting for her 30 feet away. Laura Browder has just moved to Houston from Chicago and was called in for a last-minute interview for a job...Because she was new in town, she didn't have anyone to watch her children, she said, so she took them with her and asked them to wait in the food court. She had just accepted the job when she was arrested. (Steiger 2015)

These are a few news stories drawing attention to the difficulty that single mothers encounter in finding reliable and affordable childcare. In the case of the mother in South Carolina employed at McDonald's, her daughter had been spending the days at work with her, sitting at one of the tables with her laptop. However, their home was robbed and the laptop was stolen. She had provided her daughter with a cell phone and agreed to let her go to the park nearby where about 40 other children were playing. The mothers in Scottsdale and Houston needed to obtain employment to be a position to find dependable childcare. Single mothers and mothers in situations where both partners have unstable but full-time jobs must make hard decisions to juggle finding and keeping a job while attending to the caretaking needs of their children. Their arrests highlight the irony of a society punishing mothers who try to gain and keep employment to fulfill their families' basic economic needs. The law holds them to a parenting standard that requires resources outside their reach. The care crisis in the US is a major issue that families and individuals face in fulfilling needs for childcare, elder care, and care for disabled or ill members. While the need has always existed, social and economic changes have worsened many women's circumstances. A closer look at some of these changes addresses the causes behind the crisis in current institutional structures. These problems do not just confront the working poor; care has become so expensive in the US that many middle-class mothers who work full-time end up paying more than half their income for child or elder care.

As noted in previous chapters, more mothers, wives and daughters work full-time outside the home and are thus no longer able to provide the unpaid labor that previous generations of women did. Women make up 47% of the total US labor force and this is expected to increase to 51% by 2018; 73% of these women work full-time and 27% work part-time (Women's Bureau 2010). Four in ten households with children have mothers who are the sole or primary provider; 37% of "breadwinner moms" are married and have incomes higher than their husbands, and 63% of them are single mothers (Wang et al. 2013). However, single breadwinner moms are more likely to be living in poverty. In 2010, 31% of single working white mothers, 41% of Black working mothers, and 44.5% of Latina working mothers lived in poverty (Ajinkya 2012). Women of color experience both gender and racial wage gaps: while women in general earn 77 cents on the dollar compared to white men, Black women earn 69.5% and Latinas 60.5% compared to white male workers (Kerby 2012). Unlike previous generations, most working mothers no longer take a leave from work after they have children. Many cannot afford to be stay-at-home mothers or may find that childcare is too expensive and work does not cover the cost.

Compounding the pressure on families are longer workdays resulting from mandatory overtime, demanding careers, and long commutes to and from work. Families are less likely to rely on kin-care since many of their adult family members, including grandparents (Meyer 2014), work outside the home. Family members are living farther away from each other, which is an added challenge to having kin available for childcare or elderly care. Day care centers are not always ideal solutions since parents may not be able to afford to enroll their children, the hours available may not correspond with working schedules, or children may be too young to qualify. Studies evaluating access to and quality of childcare report mediocre to dangerous environments, which are not regulated by national health and safety standards (National Institute of Child Health and Human Development [NICHD] 2006). Elementary and middle schools provide some relief for working parents but their schedules almost never correlate completely, requiring additional arrangements. Purchasing childcare and education is second to families' mortgage or rent payments. Parents with the financial means can hire in-home care by employing a nanny. Some professionals hire live-in nannies to be available during most of the child's waking hours and sometimes even during the night.

Along with changing family roles, there are important demographic shifts. Life expectancy began increasing in the US over the last century, and, worldwide, life expectancy has increased dramatically since World War II. In 2012, the Centers for Disease Control and Prevention's National Center for Health Statistics reported that that the average life expectancy for women in the US is 81.2 years, and for men, it is 76.4 years. Race and gender intersection in the average life expectancy is apparent by comparing white and Black men and women. For instance, in 1900 the average life expectancy for white men was 47 years, and only 33 years for Black men. For white women in 1900, the average life expectancy was 49, and Black women only had an average of 34 years. In 1950, the average for white men had increased to 67, and it was 59 for Black men. The average for white women in 1950 had increased to 72, and it was 63 years for Black women. The US has a growing elderly population who are likely to have health problems and impairments: "The erosion of paid healthcare benefits, welfare and paid assistance to the disabled has placed additional burdens on working family members, particularly those who do not have the financial means to take time off work or employ a care worker" (Romero & Perez 2015: 173). Caring for the elderly frequently falls on families first, usually daughters; many of them are employed full-time. State and federal assistance is secondary in caregiving for the elderly and remains limited. Needless to say, caring for disabled family members is difficult for working parents and partners. Without access to pay for leave, or sick pay, working adults may face losing their job or not being able to pay their bills if they stay home to be the caretaker. State assistance has proven to be inadequate and families without the financial means to afford for one adult to stay home or to be able to hire assistance piece together some day-to-day arrangement. The care crisis highlights gender, race, class, citizenship and ability status through privileges and oppression.

Unlike many countries, the US views elder- and child-care as "personal troubles" rather than as "social issues." Consequently, the US lags behind other countries in maternity and paternity leave, affordable childcare options, work flexibility, and other benefits assisting working families. In 2014, only three countries did not offer paid maternity leave and the US was one of these countries. The other two countries are Oman and Papua New Guinea. A few states offer paid leave, but there is no federal legislation mandating it. Some US companies provide paid leave to working mothers, fewer for fathers, but they are not legally obligated to do so. Countries with less economic strength than the US offer paid leave to working parents, including Mexico, Romania, South Korea and Turkey. Several European countries have offered paid parental leave for decades (OECD 2011). The US offers only one family-friendly policy, the Family and Medical Leave Act, which offers unpaid leave only, for up to 12 weeks. When family members need caring for, working mothers and daughters are more likely than husbands or sons to take the time off to provide care. When paid parental leave is available, working mothers are more likely to use the benefit than men are. A few workplaces offer the family-friendly policies of work flexibility like telecommuting, job sharing and sabbaticals. Unfortunately, work flexibility is available to only half of employees in the US (Matos & Galinsky 2014).

Most workers have caregiving responsibilities at some point in their lives and, if they have the income to purchase care work, the solution has usually been to hire low-wage immigrant women of color. Caring for children is not priceless in our society, but rather relies on the cheapest labor available. Immigration policies and declining welfare benefits ensure professionals a ready pool of low-wage workers. Current childcare policies and programs are not inclusive for all mothers. Instead of a system, the US has a market for childcare where purchasing power presents completely different options.

Individual solutions to the care crisis that involve hiring a low-wage immigrant woman of color to care for children or an elderly parent reproduce inequality. Frequently, caretakers are mothers too, which places their children at an enormous disadvantage. Growing numbers of mothers work abroad as caretakers to earn money for their own children and family. If you sit on a bench in New York's Central Park, for instance, you will notice many Caribbean and Latina women pushing carriages and tending to the needs of white children. These day workers have their lives shaped by low wages, lack of healthcare or childcare benefits, inflexible work schedules, mandatory overtime and citizenship restrictions. As we know from several high-profile political cases, frequently employers do not even pay the mandatory social security and Medicare for the mothers they employ. This means that domestic workers may not receive benefits when they reach retirement age. In the case of the children of migrant workers employed as domestics and nannies abroad, they experience more than just the loss of a parent or parents. Having a mother working in a different city or country can lead to family instability. Frequently, gifts and remittances that mothers send home to their children become symbols of parent–child attachment, which results in the commodification of their mother's love. In globalized care work, the workers' children remain invisible to families who purchase private care in their own country.

All working mothers face the problem of childcare and elder care later in life. As we have already seen, as a nation, we continue to address care as a personal problem rather than a public issue. Consequently, employers are unwilling to pay very much for the labor, and they are reluctant to accept their home is a site of employment in compliance with federal and state laws or the norms of modern work culture. Like so many social issues, the need for care did not become a crisis until families with more privilege experienced the consequences of living in a country with few benefits to help working parents. Addressing the gender wage gap is important in helping working parents, particularly single mothers; however, families of color and single mothers of color also need race discrimination to be eliminated. Policies only focused on the gender wage gap and not the race wage gap maintain white privilege. Immigrant policies that keep some workers vulnerable as undocumented provide cheap labor for families with financial resources. However, too often people fail to grasp the way intersections can offer public solutions.

Examining the scandals that arose in the nomination of attorney generals in the 1990s demonstrates the tendency to analyze problems from a one-dimensional perspective. "Nannygate" was the first national scandal over childcare. The term refers to scandals over the childcare arrangements of people President Clinton had nominated for attorney general. The nannygate scandals demonstrate lost opportunities to have a public discussion about the care crisis in the US. This is painfully obvious during each nannygate scandal. The public debate surrounding these events revealed not only a great deal about American social norms and values relating to gender and work, but also the disregard for these issues when race, ethnicity and citizenship are submerged under the topic of immigration.

Limitations to One-Dimensional Perspectives

The first nannygate occurred in 1993 when the Clinton administration attempted to nominate the first woman attorney general, Zoe Baird. Baird and her Yale law professor husband had hired an undocumented Peruvian couple to care for their household, including childcare, and had failed to pay for social security, Medicare or unemployment insurance. Although she paid back taxes and fines, she withdrew her nomination in response to the public outrage. Clinton then nominated Kimba Wood, who had hired an undocumented Trinidadian woman at a time when it was legal to do so, and she had paid taxes. However, she too eventually withdrew because the general public made no distinction between her situation and Zoe Baird's. Clinton then nominated Janet Reno, who was single and had no children. Nannygate sheds light on how feminist issues framed from the position of women in professional positions do not necessarily include the needs of the mothers who clean their homes and care for their children (Romero 2002).

Controversies arising from the nannygate scandals were missed opportunities for a national conversation over the care crisis. The absence of an intersectional approach pitted against one another groups that should have been allies. Each of the scandals involved two issues: (1) the hiring of undocumented workers; and (2) the failure to pay taxes. Public opinion clustered around two major criticisms: one emphasizing gender, and the other, class. A gender analysis proposed by Zoe Baird and Kimba Wood supporters cited a double standard operating that discriminated against women nominees. They argued that male nominees were not questioned about their childcare arrangements. Furthermore, if a woman is ever going to be nominated, she is likely to be a mother with childcare concerns. The other sentiment was class-based. Outrage against the nominees' hiring of undocumented women crystallized around the class distinction in law breaking and the leniency of the government toward white-collar crime. Class politics characterized "nannygate" as a "Yuppie" white-collar crime and resisted attempts to sweep it under the rug. Gender politics constructed the response to the issue of white-collar crime by arguing that laws pertaining to hiring undocumented nannies were rarely enforced. Further, they argued that enforcement in this case had the effect of discriminating against women, namely working mothers. In addition, they noted that these laws were out of step with the needs of the nation (Romero 2002).

Nannygate represents the family and work dilemma presented by more women entering the labor force. An intersectional analysis of nannygate identifies existing systems of power, privileges and oppression.

As a personal trouble rather than a social issue, the care dilemma relies on working families using their existing privileges to hire marginalized groups. Fathers can allocate the care of their children and elderly parents to their wives. Some working couples might take opposite shifts to cover the caregiving responsibilities, or take lower-paid positions that allow more flexibility. Working women with disposable income can hire other women at low wages who are vulnerable because of age, class, race or citizenship status. Most domestics and nannies are paid poorly, and lack benefits or sick leave. Frequently they are "on call" and expected to be available 24/7. Many of these women are themselves mothers and have to negotiate their own caregiving arrangements, such as leaving their children alone or with kin during the day or in their home country. Welfare "reform" eroded assistance and resources for poor families and increased the vulnerability of poor women of color in the labor force. Congress' unwillingness to pass immigration reform providing pathways to citizenship maintains the vulnerability of undocumented immigrant women, ensuring that class, race and citizenship status continue to influence working conditions and ability to fulfill caregiving responsibilities. Undocumented women of color are the most vulnerable to low wages, harsh working conditions and employer theft. The use of undocumented and immigrant labor to fill the market for paid caregivers devalues women's traditional work, denies the recognition of it as "real work," and ignores domestic workers' rights as workers. If you think about it, it is very odd to entrust our most valuable family members – aging parents and young children – to the lowest-paid workers. If you were old, wouldn't you want the person helping you to bathe, to change your clothes, and making sure you got your medicine to be a happy, stable and secure worker, instead of just the opposite?

Drawing on the metaphor of the Rubik's cube, the intersection of gender and class captures the need for childcare that is flexible enough to accommodate working parents with long hours and changing work schedules. Working parents need affordable childcare that is reliable and of high quality. Moving the face of the cube to include colors representing gender, class and race, the needs of middle- and working-class mothers and parents of color are exposed. These needs incorporate the previous characteristics and add the requirement for racially and culturally knowledgeable caretaking services. Shifting the colors to represent the intersection of gender, class, race and citizenship status, we are pushed to consider the needs of immigrant mothers of color working as domestics and nannies who are also in need of affordable childcare. In addition, as careworkers, their needs as vulnerable workers require higher pay, benefits, sick leave, and vacations, as well as employment stability. Intersectional approaches to caregiving call for incorporating the needs of all working mothers and domestics, nannies, and caregivers for the elderly.

Discussion questions

1 Explain why a gender or a class analysis is not sufficient in understanding the care crisis.
2 How does the care crisis affect your life? How is it different for other individuals?

Intersectional Solutions to the Structural Issue of Caregiving

There exist campaigns based on an intersectional analysis with an understanding that gender, race, class, age, citizenship status and other forms of subordination and privilege must be included in a comprehensive program to resolve the care crisis. A campaign incorporating the intersectional identities of employees and employers appears in organizing efforts by the National Domestic Workers Alliance (NDWA). Their slogan underlines the significance of interconnectedness for all working families: "Domestic work is the work that makes all other work possible" (www.domesticworkers.org/who-we-are). The NDWA's mission statement goes on to characterize the workers as follows:

> Domestic workers care for the things we value the most: our families and our homes. They care for our children, provide essential support for seniors and people with disabilities to live with dignity at home, and perform the home care work that makes all other work possible. They are skilled and caring professionals, but for many years, they have labored in the shadows, and their work has not been valued. These workers deserve respect, dignity and basic labor protections.

While race, class, gender and immigration issues shape their interest in decent work for fair wages, they have organized around three themes: community, dignity and care. Since many of their members are immigrant women of color, including undocumented women, they have two initiatives addressing immigration and trafficking. The initiative "We Belong Together" is a joint program with the National Asian Pacific American Women's Forum, other women's organizations, and immigrant advocacy organizations, working toward immigration reform that includes broad and clear paths to citizenship and keeping families together. As domestics are one of the largest categories of workers that are trafficked, the NDWA established the "Beyond Survival" campaign to work with communities to identify human trafficking and establish the structures to assist victims and work with survivors. They aim to protect and assist survivors of violence and trafficking. Recognizing the previous organizing and the number of Black women currently employed as domestics, NDWA has built on the work of their Atlanta-based chapter in the "We Dream in Black" initiative. This campaign works with Black communities to expand efforts to organize Black women employed as domestics, and Afro-Caribbean workers in New York City.

An NDWA campaign aimed at meeting the needs of employers who are elderly or disabled, or members of working families, is "Caring Across Generations." This campaign promotes "Changing the Way We Care, Quality Care and Support and a Dignified Quality of Life for all Americans." Recognizing that the elderly constitute a growing population in the US that prefers independent living, and that the current care choices are inadequate, the NDWA is working to promote a change to our "out-of-date" and "out-of-touch" approach to caring for the elderly and disabled people. Nursing homes are expensive but, without home- and community-based services, living independently is not an option for many. Family members who are also engaged in caring for children provide an estimated 80 percent of elderly care. Without state-mandated sick leave, vacations, personal time and flexible working schedules, being overburdened with caregiving impacts the family's economic and social well-being. This campaign for improving care for the elderly and disabled identifies five goals:

- the creation of new, quality jobs in home care;
- labor standards and improved job quality for the existing jobs and new jobs;
- training and career ladders for home care workers;
- a new visa category and path to citizenship for care workers;
- support for individuals and families in need of support and care, including a matching register and maintaining and creating new funding streams.

Rather than speaking only from the perspective of the worker and focusing on what we usually consider as workers' issues, such as higher wages, overtime, social security, sick leave and benefits, their intersectional strategy is inclusive of both the giver and receiver of care. The "Caring Across Generations" campaign uses an intersectional analysis to identify the care crisis and proposes policies that bring together the various interests of the working parents providing caregiving, those purchasing care, and their family members receiving care.

The NDWA works closely with Hand-in-Hand, which is a national network of employers of nannies, housecleaners and home attendants, to establish working conditions that benefit the employer and worker. They began as allies to the NDWA's efforts to pass the New York State Domestic Worker Bill of Rights in 2010. This domestic employers' association recognizes the interdependence of employers and workers in collaborative efforts to transform care in the US by changing cultural norms, public policies and labor regulations. Rather than pitting affluent or disabled communities against working-class white women and women of color providing the care, they collaborate to educate employers about fair employment relationships based on mutual respect and well-being. They launched a Code of Care that established standards for domestic employment, and provide resources to respond to employers' needs and questions. As one nanny-employer testified at a Human Rights Tribunal for the California Domestic Workers' Bill of Rights, "Having clear guidelines helps employers understand what to do. We want to provide the best working environment possible for people caring for our children." Education and raising public awareness are important activities to gain support for programming and legislation assisting employers and workers. Bringing together domestic employers, seniors and disabled people, Hand-in-Hand is an active partner in the "Caring Across Generations" campaign. The association works with workers to organize strategies in developing legislation conceived from an intersectional perspective.

Black Lives Matter

We close this chapter by taking a look at the incorporation of intersectionality in the fast-growing movement Black Lives Matter. This grassroots movement demonstrates the challenges of developing intersectional strategies for organizing and the strength in bringing coalitions together.

From its inception, the BLM Movement embraced intersectionality. Beginning an online campaign with the hashtag #BlackLivesMatter, the movement responded to the neighborhood watch volunteer George Zimmerman being acquitted for fatally shooting the unarmed 17-year-old Trayvon Martin. After the police shooting of Michael Brown in Ferguson, Missouri, BLM held their first protest and demonstration against police and vigilante killings of Black people. However, the initial attention overemphasized Black men as victims of police violence, and the deaths of women and transgender people of color were invisible. This was not intentional, as the founders of the movement, Alicia Garza, Opal Tometi and Patrisse Cullors, identify as Black queer women. As they engaged in public discourse and social media, clarifications appeared. The hashtag #SayHerName was a rallying point around the police shootings and killing of Black women. Soon BLM's mission statement on the website stated that BLM "affirms the lives of Black queer and trans folks, disabled folks, Black-undocumented folks, folks with records, women and Black lives along the gender spectrum" (http://blacklivesmatter.com/herstory).

That BLM's decentralized network of 30 chapters across the country made an intentional shift to an intersectional approach is apparent as the movement grew. Along with links to previous Black liberation movements, the attention to local and state issues kept identities historically and geographically rooted. The founders developed a comprehensive intersectional statement about the movement, as the following quote demonstrates:

> When we say Black Lives Matter, we are talking about the ways in which Black people are deprived of our basic human rights and dignity. It is an acknowledgement Black poverty and genocide is state violence. It is an acknowledgment that 1 million Black people are locked in cages in this country – one half of all people in prisons or jails – is an act of state violence. It is an acknowledgment that Black women continue to bear the burden of a relentless assault on our children and our families and that assault is an act of state violence. Black queer and trans folks bearing a unique burden in a hetero-patriarchal society that disposes of us like garbage and simultaneously fetishizes us and profits off of us is state violence; the fact that 500,000 Black people in the US are undocumented immigrants and relegated to the shadows is state violence; the fact that Black girls are used as negotiating chips during times of conflict and war is state violence; Black folks living with disabilities and different abilities bear the burden of state-sponsored Darwinian experiments that attempt to squeeze us into boxes of normality defined by White supremacy is state violence. And the fact is that the lives of Black people – not ALL people – exist within these conditions is consequence of state violence.
> *When Black people get free, everybody gets free.*

When all Black people are included, intersectional identities are necessary to being inclusive. Race does not exist without gender, sexuality, citizenship status, abilities and age. State violence against Black people is inseparable from their other identities. By accepting and embracing the slogan #BlackLivesMatter, connections to other struggles across systems of inequality are made by affirming Black lives.

The counter-slogan #AllLivesMatter ignored the point of intersectionality in BLM's organizing and ideology. The counter-slogan perpetuated color-blind racism by depoliticizing and erasing racism from state violence against Blacks in the US: "While the claim that all human life is valuable is not 'wrong,' it intentionally erases the complexities of race, class, gender, and sexuality in the lives of people who suffer from systematic police brutality" (Carney 2016: 185). Similar to theorizing about gender as a universal experience, the result of #AllLivesMatter is to collapse the uniqueness of differences as experienced along the axes of structural racism and white supremacy. The counter-slogan fails to recognize situated knowledge.

BLM arose at the same time young youth of color were engaged in other struggles for racial justice. Activists protesting against police violence in Ferguson joined the predominantly fast-food workers of color protesting in New York City in the Fight for 15, which is a campaign to raise the minimum wage to $15 an hour. Activists fighting for labor and economic justice were already involved in BLM and the impact of the low-wage economy on Black lives was evident. Previously viewed as a white issue, the labor movement now presented African Americans an opportunity to participate in decision-making, access to resources and organizational structure. White labor activists became more aware of the racial aspect of the Fight for 15 progressives (Teuscher 2015). As the alliance developed between BLM and the fight to increase the minimum wage, the need to incorporate immigrant rights groups became evident. Latino workers would also benefit greatly from wage increases. To avoid setting one group in opposition to the other, a further coalition was necessary. Immigration issues also connected to the racial justice issue surrounding prison reform. The growing industry of detaining undocumented immigrants posed similarities as another incident of incarcerating people of color in the US.

The Movement for Black Lives (M4BL) brought over 50 organizations and over 2,000 activists to Cleveland in 2015 to build coalitions with a unifying platform. Keeping their focus on ending state-sanctioned violence against Black communities, the issues raised included criminalization and incarceration of Black people; reparations for harms against Black people; investing in health, education and safety; economic justice; community control; Black political power and self-determination. Strategies for addressing these issues are inclusive of race, class, gender, sexuality, ableism and citizenship status. Returning to where we started this chapter, if we are to address these concerns as sociologists, with a sociological imagination, as Mills advocated, these issues are not personal but social issues, which need structural solutions.

Conclusion: Intersectionality and Social Justice

Capturing the nuances of intersectionality demands a rethinking of how we approach social issues and conceptualize social inequality. The academic norm has traditionally leaned toward examining a single issue that appears to be the dominant system of oppression. This is evident in the university departments of "Gender Studies," "Africana Studies," "Chicano Studies" and so on. It is not surprising that marginalized scholars, particularly women of color, were at the forefront of pushing intersectional research and theorizing. Marginalized groups previously absent and invisible in academia confronted mainstream scholarship that did not include them. As more men and women of color, working-class, LGBTQ, disabled and racialized immigrant scholars gained entrance into the academy and became engaged in activist scholarship, intersectional approaches in sociology appeared more often. Many scholars from marginalized communities took lessons from participation in social movements organizing against social inequality (e.g., Cole 2008). These experiences in coalition building offered new ways to define social issues from a range of social positions proposing inclusive solutions. Legal scholar Mari J. Matsuda offered an example of such a process:

> The way I try to understand the interconnection of all forms of subordination is through a method I call "ask the other question." When I see something that looks racist, I ask, "Where is the patriarchy in this?" When I see something that looks sexist, I ask, "Where is the heterosexism in this?" When I see something that looks homophobic,

I ask, "Where are the class interests in this?" Working in coalition forces us to look for both the obvious and nonobvious relationships of domination, helping us to realize that no form of subordination ever stands alone. (Matsuda 1991: 1189)

Matsuda depicts a strategy that involves approaching a social issue from multiple perspectives. Analytically, we might think of using the Rubik's cube I introduced in the first chapter. Each color representing a marginalized group, we can turn each color into various configurations capturing different colors representing intersectional systems of power, and then ask another question to identify an inclusive understanding of social issues. For example, consider mass incarceration of boys and young men of color tracked in the school-to-prison pipeline.

The American Civil Liberties Union (ACLU) and Amnesty International cite that 5% of the world's population lives in the US but the nation has imprisoned 25% of the world's inmates. Many inmates are serving long sentences for non-violent crimes – especially for drug possession or "intent to sell." Policies introduced in New York by Governor Nelson Rockefeller and nationwide by President Nixon during the 1960s and 1970s increased the rate of incarceration generated from the "tough on crimes" policy, which included the War on Gangs and the War on Drugs. Both "wars" targeted communities of color, particularly those overlapping with immigrant communities. Racialization of the War on Drugs is evident in the incarceration of Blacks, which is 10 times greater than for Whites even though the amount of drug usage in both groups is similar. The 2010 US Census reported Whites are 64% of the population and only 39% of the incarcerated population; Hispanics are 16% overall, but 19% of those incarcerated; and Blacks, 13% of the US population, but 40% of the incarcerated population. The analysis of the mass incarceration of young Black men requires a discussion of the school-to-prison pipeline. Several campaigns have not used an intersectional approach but have organized solely around Black men and boys in this pipeline. President Obama and numerous organizations identified the welfare of Black boys and young men to be in crisis and have called for programs to address the problem. The White House report *My Brother's Keeper 2016 Progress Report, Two Years of Expanding Opportunity and Creating Pathways to Success* exemplified this turn. Focusing on linking young Black men to schools and colleges, the initiative provided state and local communities with funding for programing educational and career opportunities for this population. But the Presidential Commission views the problem with a non-intersectional analysis.

If Americans are going to understand mass incarceration, as well as to propose solutions, there is a need to include African American girls and women to capture the intra-gender racial disparities. The plight of Black girls in school and the increasing number of Black women incarcerated reveal the importance of an intersectional approach to identifying gender and racial disparities. Attention to Black male youth has ignored the impact of the surveillance, punishment and criminalization of other youth of color, including poor and working-class girls. The report *Black Girls Matter: Pushed Out, Overpoliced and Underprotected* (Crenshaw 2015) documents the need for an intersectional approach to the school-to-prison pipeline. Data collected in New York City and Boston point to areas in which racial disparity between girls is greater than between boys: "Although males are suspended in greater numbers than females overall, race and ethnicity turn out to be substantial risk factors of black girls when they are compared to their white counterparts" (Crenshaw 2015: 16).

Data from the Department of Education support Crenshaw's argument. They found that Black boys are treated as suspects three times more often than white boys; Black girls are suspected six times more often than white girls. This type of intra-gender comparison is important because it highlights that only 2% of white girls are treated as suspects, but 12% of all Black girls are. Let's look at the Boston and New York school districts to examine the intersection of race and class. In the case of the Boston school district, 28% of their enrollment of girls was Black, 41% was Hispanic, and 15% were white girls; however, Black girls made up 61% of those disciplined, Hispanics 34% and only 5% white girls. Among boys, Hispanics made up 40%, Blacks 28% and Whites were 15% of the enrollment. Yet the rates of students disciplined do not correspond to the number enrolled, particularly for Blacks and Whites. Hispanics made up 36% of the disciplined, but Blacks made up 57% and Whites were 7%. In 2011–12, the New York City school district reported similar racial discrepancies between students enrolled and students disciplined. Black girls made up 34% of the enrollment but 56% of those disciplined; whereas Black boys were 34% of the enrollment but 48% of those disciplined. Black girls were disciplined ten times more than white girls were, and Black boys six times more than white boys were in New York. Black girls were disciplined eleven times more than white girls, and Blacks boys eight times more than white boys, in Boston.

Discipline is one step toward the expulsion of students, which leads to poor employment opportunities and places them at risk as adults for prison, teenage pregnancy, and a life of poverty. Examining the different expulsion rates for Black and White girls and boys is alarming. Black girls were expelled at 53 times the rate of white girls, and Black boys were expelled at 10 times the rate of white boys in New York City. Boston reported Black girls expelled 10 times more than white girls, and Black boys six times more than white boys. Programs focusing on the educational and career opportunities of Black boys imply that Black girls are similar to White girls and there is no need for concern. Both Black girls and boys are at greater risk for punishment but "Black girls face a statistically greater chance of suspension and expulsion compared to other students of the same gender" (Crenshaw 2015: 23). Assumptions about Black girls' and women's encounters with the criminal justice system also overlook the severe sentencing they face, and they are the fastest-growing population in the juvenile justice system. Girls and women of color need to be visible in the discussions on excessive surveillance and police violence in communities of color.

The White House report and recommendations focusing exclusively on males erased the disadvantages and lack of opportunities for girls of color. Successful program design needs to understand the intersections of race, gender, class and other factors impeding high school graduation rates. The school-to-prison pipeline also affects girls of color. They too need counseling and other types of interventions to steer them away from contact with the juvenile justice system. These girls also need protection from bullying and sexual harassment. School personnel need to be able to identify indicators of sexual abuse. In addition, school programming needs to provide adequate assistance and support for pregnant students and young mothers. Girls may also have caretaking responsibilities that may be hindering their educational opportunities.

Defining an issue from an intersectional approach is tricky since problems arise among certain groups more quickly or affect them in ways that are more visible. Traditionally, problems intersecting race and class have focused solely on race or solely on class, rather than understanding the lived experience of both factors. However, another way of approaching social issues is offered by Lani Guinier and Gerald Torres (2002: 171), who argued that "experiences which converge around a racial minority are often a diagnostic tool. Starting with the experience of people of color, we can begin to identify the crucial missing elements of American democracy – missing elements that make the systems fail, not just for blacks or Latinos but for many other groups that are similarly situated." Using the metaphor of the canary in the mine, they call for a political race project: "The canary serves both a diagnostic and an innovative function.... What the canary lets us see are the hierarchical arrangements of power and privilege that have naturalized this unequal distribution" (2002: 259). Therefore, Guinier and Torres propose that we consider the experiences of the most vulnerable population very seriously, because they are the first to exhibit difficulties arising from structural problems. Returning to the issue of mass incarceration and the school-to-prison pipeline, there is a high cost in working-class and poor communities of color dealing with over-policing and surveillance, interactions with a militarized police force, and the incarceration of the mentally ill, drug offenders and others for non-violent crime, and the list goes on. But white middle-class communities are also impacted. They too share part of the burden of losing civil liberties, shifting budgets further away from social benefits and improving schools, increasing the cost of state colleges and universities, and eroding the infrastructure of highways and bridges.

Guinier and Torres suggest that inclusive solutions are found when an approach to an issue is explicitly intersectional. This approach identifies marginalized groups that are most vulnerable to the issue at hand, examines their experiences and considers them as the canaries in the mine, rather than attempting to identify only one or two causal characteristics. As Guinier and Torres remind us, "All canaries bear watching. Our democratic future depends on it."

I began this book using the example of Take Our Daughters to Work Day to illustrate the problem with assuming gender was the only difference in an educational program to inspire girls to enter male-dominated occupations. Take Our Daughters to Work Day assumes that gender is a universal experience and that girlhood does not differ by race, ethnicity, class, disability or sexuality. A one-dimensional framework used to develop an educational program excludes children and parents who do not fit the universal idea of gender. Rethinking the program from an intersectional approach, one might consider empowering daughters and sons by challenging the way that work is organized around difference in US society. An intersectional program would send our daughters and sons to work with:

- women and men who are developing legislation to promote social and economic justice: increasing the minimum wage; achieving funding for apprenticeship, training and scholarship programs; gaining childcare benefits and healthcare coverage for all families;
- union members bargaining for flexible work options including: part-time work options with benefits; flextime; job sharing; telecommuting; shorter work weeks with no loss of pay; and no mandatory overtime;
- activists who are organizing communities to support living-wage campaigns, fight for environmental justice, direct funding to public schools, aid the homeless, stop deportations, and increase democratic participation in political life;
- working people from diverse class backgrounds and job descriptions so that all our daughters and sons can get a first-hand glimpse of the

way work is organized, the way workers are differently empowered and fulfilled by their work, and the way employment is often segregated by race, class, gender, ability and citizenship status.

Rethinking the program does not begin with the assumption that all daughters, sons and parents share the same life experiences and have the same opportunities. The program instead shifts from highlighting individual pioneers in prestigious positions and to a focus on political action, collective organizing, and other efforts by working women and men, which help the next generation of children and adults to be strong, confident and bold.

Thinking about the social world as intersectional invites students, researchers and activists to examine the dynamics of power relations, both privileges and oppression. In discussing the racial wealth gap, contextualizing race, class and gender in history was essential in identifying the legacy of policies that structured disadvantages and opportunities for accumulating assets and increasing family wealth. Recognizing the unearned privileges passed from one generation to the next begins to reveal the ways wealth and power are structured by race, ethnicity, class, gender and citizenship status. Like the canary in the mine, the housing and financial crises experienced by communities of color were early signs of a recession fueled by the housing bubble and subprime loans. However, not until white middle-class families faced unemployment and the inability to pay mortgages were government efforts made to stem the tide. Black and Latino communities will bear the burden of the recession for generations. Solutions for reversing the wealth gap need to focus on the most vulnerable populations and shift the analysis to various intersections of power to be an inclusive plan of action.

Intersectionality helps us understand troubling conditions and circumstances as social issues rather than simply personal problems requiring individuals to change their behavior. As I presented in the previous chapter, society treats care work as a personal problem that is the burden of family members. Yet all of us face a time in our life when we are dependent on others to care for us. At birth and during childhood, individuals need care. When we are sick, disabled or become physically limited by age, people experience dependency. Even though dependency and the need for caretaking are needs we share, there are no comprehensive government programs or policies to assist all parents or individuals requiring care. An intersectional approach to the care issue considers not only those in need of care but also those providing the care. The National Domestic Workers Alliance is attempting to use an intersectional approach in defining the problem and the solution by building coalitions that cross generations, class, race, ethnicity and gender.

Unlike most conceptual frameworks in academic work, intersectionality has its roots and evolution in collective struggles. Consequently, studying multiple dimensions of inequality is only one aim of this intellectual project. To grasp the ongoing evolution of this powerful tool, we must recognize that identifying and understanding inequality must occur alongside the struggle to resist and actively challenge all forms of oppression.

References

Abdul-Jabbar, K. (2015) "Body shaming Black female athletes is not just about race," *Time* (July 20), http://time.com/3964758/body-shaming-black-female-athletes.

Abraham, M. (1995) "Ethnicity, gender, and marital violence: South Asian women's organizations in the United States," *Gender & Society* 9(4): 450–68. (2015) "The intersectionalities of protest suicides, oppression and social justice," *Sociologies in Dialogue* 1(1), www.sociologiesindialogue.com.

Acker, J. (1990) "Hierarchies, jobs, and bodies: A theory of gendered organizations," *Gender & Society* 4: 139–58.

Acuesta, B. (2016) "Conservatives criticize Michelle Obama for bare arms, stay silent on Melania Trump's nude poses," *True Activist* (March 8), www.trueactivist.com/conservatives-criticize-michelle-obama-for-bare-arms-stay-silent-on-melania-trumps-nude-poses.

Adams, A. (2011) " 'Josh wears pink cleats': Inclusive masculinity on the soccer field," *Journal of Homosexuality* 58: 579–96.

Addo, F. R. & Lichter, D. T. (2013) "Marriage, marital history, and black–white wealth differentials among older women," *Journal of Marriage and Family* 75: 342–62.

African American Policy Forum (AAPF) (2013) "Intersectionality," www.aapf.org/2013/2013/01/intersectionality.

Agular, L. (2001) "Doing cleaning work 'scientifically': The reorganization of work in the contract building cleaning industry," *Economic and Industrial Democracy* 22(2): 239–69.

Ahmed, S. (2012) *On Being Included: Racism and Diversity in Institutional Life.* Durham: Duke University Press.

Ajinkya, J. (2012) "Unequal pay day for Black and Latina women, the gender wage gap is even worse for many women of color," *Center for American Progress,*

https://www.americanprogress.org/issues/women/news/2012/04/16/11437/
unequal-pay-day-for-black-and-latina-women.

Alexander, J. M. (2005) *Pedagogies of Crossing: Mediations on Feminism, Sexual Politics, Memory, and the Sacred*. Durham: Duke University Press.

Alimahomed, S. (2010) "Thinking outside the rainbow: Women of color redefining queer politics and identity," *Social Identities* 16(2): 151–68.

Allen, K. R. & Demo, D. H. (1995) "The families of lesbians and gay men: A new frontier in family research," *Journal of Marriage and Family* 57(1): 111–27.

Almaguer, T. (2007) "Looking for Papi: Longing and desire among Chicano gay men," in R. Rosaldo & J. Flores (eds.) *A Companion to Latina/o Studies*. New York: Blackwell Publication.

Amaro, J. (2010) "LGBT activists at forefront of DREAM Act movement," *Hispanicla*,   www.hispanicla.com/lgbt-activists-at-forefront-of-dream-act-movement-16512.

Anderson, Elijah. (1990) *Streetwise: Race, Class, and Change in an Urban Community*. University of Chicago Press.

Anderson, Eric. (2005) *In the Game: Gay Athletes and the Cult of Masculinity*. Albany: State University of New York Press.

(2009) *Inclusive Masculinity: The Changing Nature of Masculinities*. New York: Routledge.

Anderson, E. & McCormack, M. M. (2010a) "Comparing the Black and gay male athlete: Patterns in American oppression," *Journal of Men's Studies* 18(2): 145–58.

(2010b) "Intersectionality, critical race theory, and American sporting oppression: Examining Black and gay male athletes," *Journal of Homosexuality* 57(8): 947–67.

Anderson, M. L. & Collins, P. H. (eds.) (2006) *Race, Class, and Gender: An Anthology*, 6th edn. Belmont: Wadsworth Publishing.

Andrews, J. & Jordon, D. (1993) "Minority and minority deaf professionals," *American Annals of the Deaf* 138: 388–96.

Applied Research Center (ARC) (2009) "Race and recession: How inequity rigged the economy and how to change the rules," Oakland: Applied Research Center, https://www.raceforward.org/sites/default/files/downloads/2009_race_recession_0909.pdf.

Arditti, J. A., Kennington, M., Grzywacz, J. G., et al. (2014) "Fathers in the fields: Father involvement among Latino migrant workers," *Journal of Comparative Family Studies* 45(4): 537–57.

Armenta, M. (2017) "Racializing crimmigration: structural racism, colorblindnesss, and the institutional production of immigrant criminality," *Sociology of Race & Ethnicity* 3(1): 82–95.

Aronowitz, S. (2003) *How Class Works: Power and Social Movements*. New Haven: Yale University Press.

Asencio, M. (2009) "Migrant Puerto Rican lesbians negotiating gender, sexuality, ethnonationality," *NWSA Journal* 21(3): 1–23.

Baca Zinn, M. (1980) "Employment and education of Mexican-American women: The interplay of modernity and ethnicity in eight families," *Harvard Education Review* 50(1): 47–62.

Baca Zinn, M. & Dill, B. T. (1996) "Theorizing difference from multicultural feminism," *Feminist Studies* 22: 321–31.

Baer, J. A. (2007) "Women's rights and the constitution," *Social Science Journal* 44: 57–66.

Bajaj, V. & Fessenden, F. (2007) "What's behind the race gap?" *New York Times* (Nov. 4).

Baker, A. (2014a) "Women in foreclosure: How we got here," Women's Media Center, www.womensmediacenter.com/feature/entry/women-in-foreclosure-how-we-got-here.

(2014b) "Eroding the wealth of women: Gender and the subprime foreclosure crisis," *Social Science Review* 88(1): 59–91.

Bannerji, H. (2000) *The Dark Side of the Nation: Essays on Multiculturalism, Nationalism and Gender*. Toronto: Canadian Scholars Press.

Baptiste, N. (2014) "Them that's got shall get," *American Prospect*, October 12, http://prospect.org/article/staggering-loss-black-wealth-due-subprime-scandal-continues-unabated.

Barnartt, S. (2006) "Deaf women and inequality in educational attainment and occupational status," in B. J. Brueggemann & S. Burch (eds.) *Gendering Disability*. New Brunswick: Rutgers University Press.

Batalova, J., Hooker, S. & Capps, R. (2014) *DAVA at the Two-Year Mark: A National and State Profile of Youth Eligible and Applying for Deferred Action*. Washington, DC: Migration Policy Institute.

Battle, J. & Ashley, C. (2008) "Intersectionality, heteronormativity, and Black lesbian, gay, bisexual, and transgender (LGBT) families," *Black Women, Gender, and Families* 2(1): 1–24.

Beale, F. (1970) "Double jeopardy: To Be Black and female," in T. Cade (ed.) *The Black Woman: An Anthology*. New York: The New American Library, Inc.

Bell, E. L., Edmonson, J. & Nkomo, S. (1998) "Armoring: Learning to withstand racial oppression," *Journal of Comparative Family Studies* 29: 285–95.

Berkowitz, D. (2009) "Theorizing lesbian and gay parenting: Past, present, and the future scholarship," *Journal of Family Theory and Review* 1: 117–32.

Beyer, D. (2015) "What makes a woman? A trans woman responds to a mid-20th century era feminist," *Huffington Post*, June 8, www.huffingtonpost.com/dana-beyer/what-makes-a-woman-a-tran_b_7533324.html.

Bhavnani, K. & Talcott, M. (2012) "Interconnections and configurations: Toward a global feminist ethnography," in S. N. Hesse-Biber (ed.) *The Handbook of Feminist Research Theory and Praxis*. Thousand Oaks: Sage.

Biblarz, T. J. & Savci, E. (2010) "Lesbian, gay, bisexual, and transgender families," *Journal of Marriage and Family* 72: 480–97.

Bigner, J. J. & Bozett, F. W. (1990) "Parenting by gay fathers," in F. W. Bozett & M. B. Sussman (eds.) *Homosexuality and Family Relations*. Philadelphia: The Haworth Press.

Billingsley, A. (1968) *Black Families in White America*. Englewood Cliffs: Prentice Hall.

Blank, S. & Torrecilha, R. S. (1998) "Understanding the living arrangements of Latino immigrants: A life course approach," *International Immigration Review* 32(1): 3–19.

Bowen, A. (2000) "Black Feminism," in B. Zimmerman (ed.) *Encyclopedia of Lesbian and Gay Histories and Cultures.* New York: Garland Publications.

Bowleg, L. (2013) " 'Once you've blended the cake, you can't take the parts back to the main ingredients': Black gay and bisexual men's descriptions and experiences of intersectionality," *Sex Roles* 68: 754–67.

Brewer, R. M. (1993) "Theorizing race, class and gender: The new scholarship of Black feminist intellectuals and Black women's labor," in S. M. James & A. P. A. Busia (eds.) *Theorizing Black Feminisms: The Visionary Pragmatism of Black Women.* New York: Routledge.

Broadus, K. B. (2015) "Vanity fair publishes Caitlyn Jenner cover photo," www.thetaskforce.org/vanity-fair-publishes-caitlyn-jenner-cover-photo.

Buckwalter-Poza, R. & Kennedy, L. (2016) "Preventing problems at the polls: Arizona," Center for American Progress, October 25, https://www.americanprogress.org/issues/democracy/reports/2016/10/25/290985/preventing-problems-at-the-polls-arizona.

Burd-Sharps, S. & Rasch, R. (2015) "Impact of the US housing crisis on the racial wealth gap across generations," Social Science Research Council, https://www.aclu.org/files/field_document/discrimlend_final.pdf.

Burkett, E. (2015) "What makes a woman?" *New York Times* (June 6), www.nytimes.com/2015/06/07/opinion/sunday/what-makes-a-woman.html.

Cade, T. B. (1970) *The Black Woman: An Anthology.* New York: Simon & Schuster.

Cahill, S., Battle, J. & Meyer, D. (2003) "Partnering, parenting, and policy: Family issues affecting Black lesbian, gay, bisexual, and transgender (LGBT) people," *Race and Society* 6: 85–98.

Cantú, L. (1999) "Entre hombres / between men: Latino masculinities and homosexualities," in P. Nardi (ed.) *Gay Masculinities.* Thousand Oaks: Sage Publications.

Carby, H. V. (1987) *Reconstructing Womanhood: The Emergence of the Afro-American Novelist.* Oxford University Press.

Carlson, S. (1992) "Black ideals of womanhood in the late Victorian Era," *Journal of Negro History* 77(2): 61–73.

Carney, N. (2016) "All lives matter, but so does race: Black Lives Matter and the evolving role of social media," *Humanity & Society* 40(2): 180–99.

Carrillo, H. (1999) "Cultural change, hybridity, and contemporary male homosexuality," *Culture, Health, and Sexuality* 1(3): 223–38.

Castello, C. (2001) "The (re)production of social stratification in professional school settings," in E. Margolis (ed.) *The Hidden Curriculum in Higher Education.* New York: Routledge.

Chang, G. (2000) *Disposable Domestics, Immigrant Women Workers in the Global Economy.* Boston: South End Press.

Chang, M. L. (2010) "Lifting as we climb: Women of color, wealth, and America's future," Insight Center for Community Economic Development, www.mariko-chang.com/LiftingAsWeClimb.pdf.

Chang, R. S. (1999) *Disoriented: Asian Americans, Law and the Nation-State.* New York University Press.

Chant, S. & Craske, N. (2003) *Gender in Latin America*. New Brunswick: Rutgers University Press.

Chapple, R. (2012) "Being a deaf woman in college is hard. Being Black just adds: Understanding the complexities of intersecting the margins," Ph.D. dissertation, Justice Studies, Arizona State University.

Chaudry, A. (2004) *Putting Children First: How Low-Wage Working Mothers Manage Child Care*. New York: Russell Sage Foundation.

Chesley, N. (2011) "Stay-at-home fathers and breadwinning mothers: Gender, couple dynamics, and social change," *Gender & Society* 25(5): 642–64.

Chilton, W. (1960) *American Suffrage: From Property to Democracy, 1760–1870*. Princeton University Press.

Chow, E. N., Wilkinson, D. & Baca Zinn, M. (1996) *Race, Class & Gender: Common Bonds, Different Voices*. Thousand Oaks: Sage Publications.

Cianciarulo, M. S. (2009) "U.S. immigration law: Where antiquated views on gender and sexual orientation go to die," *Wayne Law Review* 55(1): 1897–910.

Ciano-Boyce, C. & Shelley-Sireci, L. (2002) "Who is mommy tonight? Lesbian parenting issues," *Journal of Homosexuality* 43(2): 1–13.

Clifford, D. (2016) "Estate tax: Will your estate have to pay?," NOLO, https://www.nolo.com/legal-encyclopedia/estate-tax-will-estate-have-29802.html.

Cohen, D., Livingston, G. & Wang, W. (2014) "After decades of decline, a rise in stay-at-home mothers," Washington, DC: Pew Research Center's Social & Demographic Trends project, April. Moms-At-Home_04-08-2014.pdf.

Cole, E. R. (2008) "Coalitions as a model for intersectionality: From practice to theory," *Sex Roles* 50: 443–53.

Cole, E. R. & Zucker, A. N. (2007) "Black and white women's perspectives on femininity," *Cultural Diversity and Ethnic Minority Psychology* 13(1): 1–19.

Collins, P. H. (1990) *Black Feminist Thought: Knowledge, Consciousness, and the Politics of Empowerment*. New York: Routledge.
(2000) "Gender, Black feminism, and Black political economy," *Annals of the American Academy of Political and Social Science* 568: 41–53.
(2004) *Black Sexual Politics: African Americans, Gender, and the New Racism*. New York: Routledge.

Coltrane, S. (2000) "Research on household labor: Modeling and measuring the social embeddedness in routine family work," *Journal of Marriage and Family* 62: 1208–33.

Coltrane, S. & Galt, J. (2000) "The history of men's caring, evaluating precedents for fathers' family involvement," in M. Harrington Meyer (ed.) *Care Work: Gender, Class, and Welfare State*. New York: Routledge.

Coltrane, S. & Valdez, E. O. (1993) "Reluctant compliance," in J. Hood (ed.) *Men, Work, and Family*. Newbury Park: Sage Publication.

Connell, R. W. 2005. *Masculinities*, 2nd edn. Cambridge: Polity.

Cooper, A. J. (1990 [1834]) *A Voice from the South*. New York: Oxford University Press.

Coston, B. M. & Kimmel, M. (2012) "Seeing privilege where it isn't: Marginalized masculinities and the intersectionality of privilege," *Journal of Social Issues* 68(1): 97–111.

Covert, B. (2014) "Homeless mother arrested for leaving kids in car during job interview won't go to prison," *ThinkProgress*, July 21, https://thinkprogress. org/homeless-mother-arrested-for-leaving-kids-in-car-during-job-interview-wont-go-to-prison-256806fb0ff3#.5zhffud8h.

Cox, L. (2015) "Official Laverne Cox tumblr," June 2, http://lavernecox.tumblr. com/post/120503412651/on-may-29-2014-the-issue-of-timemagazine.

Crenshaw, K. W. (1989) "Demarginalizing the intersection of race and sex: A Black feminist critique of antidiscrimination doctrine, feminist theory and antiracist politics," *University of Chicago Legal Forum* 140: 139–67.

(1991) "Mapping the margins: Intersectionality, identity politics, and violence against women of color," *Stanford Law Review* 46: 1241–99.

(2015) *Black Girls Matter: Pushed Out, Overpoliced and Underprotected*. New York: African American Policy Forum and Center for Intersectionality with Social Policy Studies.

Culp, J. S. Jr. (1993) "Notes from California: Rodney King and the race question," *Denver University Law Review* 70(2): 199–212.

The Daily Show (2015) "Brave new girl," June 10, http://thedailyshow.cc.com/ videos/oekklq/brave-new-girl.

Davis, A. Y. (1981) *Women, Race and Class*. New York: Random House.

(1996) "Gender, multiculturalism, and class: Rethinking 'race' politics," in A. Gordon & C. Newfield (eds.) *Mapping Multiculturalism*. Minneapolis: University of Minnesota Press.

Davis, M. (1990) *Mexican Voices, American Dreams*. New York: Henry Holt.

Davis, T. Y. & Moore, W. L. (2014) "'Spanish not spoken here': Latinos, race, and the racialization of the Spanish language in the United States," *Ethnicities* 14(5): 676–97.

De Beauvoir, S. (1973) *The Second Sex*. New York: Vintage Books.

DeSilver, D. (2014) "Who's poor in America? 50 years into the 'war on poverty': A data portrait," Pew Research Center, www.pewresearch.org/fact-tank/2014/ 01/13/whos-poor-in-america-50-years-into-the-war-on-poverty-a-data-portrait.

Desmond, M. (2007) *On the Fireline: Living and Dying with Wildland Firefighters*. University of Chicago Press.

DeVault, M. L. (1991) *Feeding the Family: The Social Organization of Caring as Gendered Work*. University of Chicago Press.

Dewaele, A., Cox, N., Van den Berghe, W. & Vincke, J. (2011) "Families of choice? Exploring the supportive networks of lesbians, gay men, and bisexuals," *Journal of Applied Social Psychology* 41(2): 312–31.

Díaz, R. (1997) *Latino Gay Men and HIV: Culture, Sexuality, and Risk Behavior*. New York: Routledge Press.

Dill, B. T. (1980) "The means to put my children through: Child rearing goals and strategies among Black female domestic servants," in L. Rogers-Rose (ed.) *The Black Woman*. Beverly Hills: Sage Publication.

(1988) "Our mother's grief: Racial ethnic women and the maintenance of families," *Journal of Family History* 13(1): 415–31.

Dill, B. T. & Kohlman, M. L. (2012) "Intersectionality: A Transformative paradigm in feminist theory and social justice," in S. N. Hesse-Biber (ed.) *The*

Handbook of Feminist Research, Theory and Praxis. Thousand Oaks: Sage Publications.

Dill, B. T. & Zambrana, R. (2009) *Emerging Intersections: Race, Class and Gender in Theory, Policy, and Practice.* New Brunswick: Rutgers University Press.

DiPrete, T. A. (2001) "Losers and winners: The financial consequences of separation and divorce for men," *American Sociological Review* 66: 246–68.

Dottolo, A. L. & Stewart, A. J. (2008) " 'Don't ever forget now, you're a Black man in America': Intersections of race, class and gender in encounters with the police," *Sex Roles* 59: 350–64.

Doucet, A. (2006) *Do Men Mother? Fatherhood, Care, and Domestic Responsibilities.* University of Toronto Press.

Downing, J., Richardson, H., Kinkler, L. & Goldberg, A. (2012) "Making the decision: Factors influencing gay men's choice of an adoption path," *Adoption Quarterly* 12: 247–71.

Dreby, J. (2010) *Divided by Borders: Mexican Migrants and Their Children.* Berkeley: University of California Press.

DuCille, A. (1993) *The Coupling Convention: Sex, Text and Tradition in Black Women's Fiction.* New York: Oxford University Press.

Dudden, F. (1983) *Serving Women: Household Service in Nineteenth-Century America.* Middletown: Wesleyan University Press.

Eastman, S. T. & Billings, A. C. (2001) "Biased voices of sports: Racial and gender stereotyping in college basketball announcing," *Howard Journal of Communications* 12: 183–201.

Edin, K. & Kefalas, M. (2005) *Promises I Can Keep: Why Poor Women Put Motherhood Before Marriage.* Berkeley: University of California Press.

Embrick, D. G., Walther, C. S. & Wickens, C. M. (2007) "Working-class masculinity: Keeping gay men and lesbians out of the workplace," *Sex Roles* 56: 757–66.

Emmons, L. & Marcus, D. (2015) "How the hypersexual trans movement hurts feminism," *The Federalist*, June 3, http://thefederalist.com/2015/06/03/how-the-hypersexual-trans-movement-hurts-feminism.

Equality California (2010) EQCA Launches Equality beyond Borders Project, http://www.eqca.org/site/apps/nlnet/content2.aspx?c=kuLRJ9MRKrH&b=4990109&ct=8927445.

Ferguson, R. A. (2012) "Reading intersectionality," *Trans-Scripts* 2: 91–9.

Fine, M. & Weis, L. (1998) "Crime stories: A critical look through race, ethnicity and gender," *International Journal of Qualitative Studies in Education* 11: 435–59.

Fine, M., Weis, L. Adelston, J. & Marusza, J. (1997) "(In)secure times constructing white working-class masculinities in the late 20th century," *Gender & Society* 11(1): 52–68.

Flores, L. Y. & Deal, J. Z. (2003) "Work-related pain in Mexican American custodial workers," *Hispanic Journal of Behavioral Sciences* 25(2): 254–70.

Flores-Gonzalez, N., Guevarra, A. R., Maura Toro-Morn, M. & Chang, G. (2013) *Immigrant Women Workers in the Neoliberal Age.* Urbana: University of Illinois Press.

Freire, P. (1973) *Pedagogy of the Oppressed*. New York: Seabury Press.

Friedeersdorf, C. (2014) "Working mom arrested for letting her 9-year-old play alone at park," *The Atlantic* (July 15), https://www.theatlantic.com/national/archive/2014/07/arrested-for-letting-a-9-year-old-play-at-the-park-alone/374436.

Fung, R. (1991) "Looking for my penis: The eroticized Asian in gay video porn," in Bad Object-Choices (ed.) *How Do I Look? Queer Video and Film*. Seattle: Bay Press.

Gair, M. & Mullins, G. (2001) "Hiding in plain sight," in E. Margolis (ed.) *The Hidden Curriculum in Higher Education*. New York: Routledge.

Gandbhir, G. & Foster, B. (2015) "A conversation with my Black son," *New York Times* (March 17), www.nytimes.com/2015/03/17/opinion/a-conversation-with-my-black-son.html?_r=1.

Garelick, R. (2015) "The price of Caitlyn Jenner's heroism," *New York Times* (June 3), https://www.nytimes.com/2015/06/03/opinion/the-price-of-jenners-heroism.html?_r=0.

Gates, G. J. (2013) "LGBT adult immigrants in the United States," The Williams Institute, University of California, Los Angeles, Law School, http://wiliamsinstitute.law.ucla.edu/wp-content/uploads/LGBTImmigrants-Gates-Mar-2013.pdf.

Gerschick, T. (1998) "Sisyphus in a wheelchair: Men and physical disability confront gender domination," in J. O'Brien & J. Howard (eds.) *Everyday Inequalities: Critical Inquiries*. Malden: Blackwell.

Gerschick, T. & Miller, A. (1994) "Gender identities at the crossroads of masculinity and physical disability," *Masculinities* 2: 34–55.

Gerson, K. (1993) *No Man's Land: Changing Commitments to Family and Work*. New York: Basic Books.

Gines, K. T. (2011) "Black feminism and intersectional analysis: A defense of intersectionality," *Philosophy Today* 55: 275–84.

Glenn, N. E. (1986) *Issei, Nisei, War Bride: Three Generations of Japanese American Women in Domestic Service*. Philadelphia: Temple University Press.

(1999) "The social construction and institutionalization of gender and race: An integrative framework," in M. M. Ferree, J. Lorber & B. B. Hess (eds.) *Revisioning Gender*. Thousand Oaks: Sage Publications.

(2004) *Unequal Freedom: How Race and Gender Shaped American Citizenship and Labor*. Cambridge, MA: Harvard University Press.

(2009) *Shades of Difference: Why Skin Color Matters*. Stanford University Press.

(2010) *Forced to Care: Coercion and Caregiving in America*. Cambridge, MA: Harvard University Press.

Golash-Boza, T. (2012) *Due Process Denied: Detentions and Deportations in the United States*. New York: Routledge.

Goldberg, A., Mover, A. M. & Richardson, H. B. (2012) "'When you're sitting on the fence, hope's the hardest part': Challenges and experiences of heterosexual and same-sex couples adopting through the child welfare system," *Adoption Quarterly* 15(4): 288–315.

González, M. A. (2007) "Latinos on *da down low*: The limitations of sexual identity in public health," *Latino Studies* 5(1): 25–52.

Gottzén, L. (2011) "Involved fatherhood? Exploring middle-class fathers' educational work," *Gender & Education* 23: 619–34.

Gottzén, L. & Kremer-Sadlik, T. (2012) "Father and youth sports: A balancing act between care and expectations," *Gender & Society* 26(4): 639–64.

Grant, J. M. (2000) "Combahee River Collective," in B. Zimmerman (ed.) *Encyclopedia of Lesbian and Gay Histories and Cultures*. New York: Garland Publications.

Gray, H. S. (2005) *Cultural Moves: African Americans and the Politics of Representation*. Berkeley: University of California Press.

Greene, B. (1992) "Racial socialization: A tool in psychotherapy with African American children," in L. A. Vargas & D. J. Koss-Chioino (eds.) *Working with Culture: Psychotherapeutic Interventions with Ethnic Minority Youth*. San Francisco: Jossey-Bass.

Grinberg, E. (2015) "Why Caitlyn Jenner's transgender experience is far from the norm," CNN (June 3), www.cnn.com/2015/06/03/living/caitlyn-jenner-transgender-reaction-feat/index.html.

Grindstaff, L. and West, E. (2011) "Hegemonic masculinity on the sidelines of sport," *Sociology Compass* 5(10): 859–81.

Grosfoguel, R. (2012) "Decolonizing western uni-versalisms: Decolonial pluri-versalism from Aimé Césaire to the Zapatistas," *Transmodernity: Journal of Peripheral Cultural Production of the Luso-Hispanic World* 1(3), http://escholarship.org/uc/item/01w7163v.

Guinier, L. & Torres, G. (2002) *The Miner's Canary: Enlisting Race, Resisting Power, Transforming Democracy*. Cambridge, MA: Harvard University Press.

Guy-Sheftall, B. (1986) *Words of Fire: An Anthology of African American Feminist Thought*. New York: New Press.

Guzmán, M. (2006) *Gay Hegemony / Latino Homosexualities*. New York: Routledge.

Haberman, C. (2015) "Beyond Caitlyn Jenner lies a long struggle by transgender people," *New York Times* (June 14), www.nytimes.com/2015/06/15/us/beyond-caitlyn-jenner-lies-a-long-struggle-by-transgender-people.html?emc=&_r=0.

Hall, S. (1992) "New ethnicities," in J. Donald & A. Rattansi (eds.) *Race, Culture and Difference*. London: Sage Publication.

Halpern, G. (2003) *Harvard Works Because We Do*. New York: The Quantuck Lane Press.

Hamer, J. (2001) *What It Means to Be Daddy: Fatherhood for Black Men Living Away from Their Children*. New York: Columbia University Press.

Han, Chong-suk (2009) "Asian girls are prettier: Gendered presentations as stigma management among gay Asian men," *Symbolic Interaction* 32(2): 106–22.

Hancock, A. (2005) "W. E. B. Du Bois: Intellectual forefather of intersectionality?" *Souls* 7(3–4): 74–84.

Haraway, D. (1988) "Situated knowledges: The science question in feminism and the privilege of partial perspective," *Feminist Studies* 14: 575–99.

Harrington, M. (1962) *The Other America: Poverty in the United States*. New York: Simon & Schuster.

Harris, A. P. (2000) "Gender, violence, race, and criminal justice," *Stanford Law Review* 52: 777–807.

(2009) "Economies of color," in E. Nakano Glenn (ed.) *Shades of Difference: Why Skin Color Matters*. Stanford University Press.

Harty, A. S. (2012) "Gendering crimmigration: The intersection of gender, immigration and the criminal justice system," *Berkeley Journal of Gender, Law & Justice* 27(1): 1–27.

Hasegawa, L. & Duong, J. (2015) "Financial insecurity in Asian American Pacific Islander communities: An untold story of racial wealth inequality," in L. Choi, D. Erickson, K. Grifin, A. Levere & E. Sidman (eds.) *What It's Worth: Strengthening the Financial Future of Families, Communities and the Nation*, CFED & Federal Reserve Bank of San Francisco, www.strongfinancialfuture.org/wp-content/uploads/2015/12/What-its-Worth_Full.pdf.

Hays, S. (1996) *Cultural Contradictions of Motherhood*. New Haven: Yale University Press.

Hendricks, T. (2007) "Child's civil rights were violated during immigration raid, lawsuit says," *SFGate* (April 26), www.sfgate.com/politics/article/Child-s-civil-rights-were-violated-during-2599486.php.

Hequembourg, A. (2004) "Unscripted motherhood: Lesbian mothers negotiating incompletely institutionalized family relationships," *Journal of Social and Personal Relationships* 21: 739–62.

Herrnstein, R. J. & Murray, C. (1994) *The Bell Curve: Intelligence and Class Structure in American Life*. New York: Free Press.

Heyman, J. M. (2001) "Class and classification of the U.S.–Mexico border," *Human Organization* 60: 128–40.

Hill, M. (2004) *After Whiteness: Unmaking an American Majority*. New York University Press.

Hill, R. B. (1977) *Informal Adoption among Black Families*. Washington, DC: National Urban League.

(1993) *Research on the African-American Family: A Holistic Perspective*. London: Auburn House.

Hobson, B. (ed.) (2002) *Making Men into Fathers: Men, Masculinities and the Social Politics of Fatherhood*. New York: Cambridge University Press.

Hondagneu-Sotelo, P. (1994) *Gendered Transitions: Mexican Experiences of Immigration*. Berkeley: University of California Press.

Hughes, M. and Hertel, B. (1990) "The significance of color remains: A study of life changes, mate selection, and ethnic consciousness among Black Americans," *Social Forces* 68(4): 1105–20.

Human Rights Watch (2014) "Tobacco's hidden children: Hazardous child labor in US tobacco farming," http://hrw.org/node/125316.

Inda, J. X. (2006) *Targeting Immigrants: Government, Technology, and Ethics*. Malden: Blackwell Publishing.

Johnson, H. L. (2016) "Pipelines, pathways, and institutional leadership," Washington DC: American Council on Education, www.acenet.edu/newsroom/Documents/Higher-Ed-Spotlight-Pipelines-Pathways-and-Institutional-Leadership-Status-of-Women.pdf.

Johnson, K. R. (2004) *The "Huddled Masses" Myth: Immigration and Civil Rights*. Philadelphia: Temple University Press.

Jordan, M. (2015) "Visa demand for high-skilled foreigners is likely to prompt lottery, employers are expected to exhaust H-1B quota for workers in tech, science," *Wall Street Journal*, www.wsj.com/articles/visa-demand-for-high-skilled-foreigners-is-likely-to-prompt-lottery-1427921906.

Katyal, S. (2002) "Exporting identity," *Yale Journal of Law and Feminism* 14: 97–176.

Kazyak, E. (2012) "Midwest or lesbian? Gender, rurality, and sexuality," *Gender & Society* 26(6): 825–48.

Keith, V. M. (2009) "A colorstruck world: Skin tone, achievement, and self-esteem among African American women," in E. Nakano Glenn (ed.) *Shades of Difference: Why Skin Color Matters*. Stanford University Press.

Keith, V. M. & Herring, C. (1991) "Skin tone and stratification in the Black community," *American Journal of Sociology* 97: 760–78.

Kelly, R. D. G. & Lewis, E. (2000) *To Make Our World Anew: A History of African Americans*. New York: Oxford University Press.

Kendall, D. (2002) *The Power of Good Deeds: Privileged Women and the Social Reproduction of the Upper Class*. Lanham: Rowman and Littlefield.

Kerby, S. (2012) "Pay equity and single mothers of color," Center for American Progress, April 16, https://www.americanprogress.org/issues/race/news/2012/04/16/11436/pay-equity-and-single-mothers-of-color.

Kielburger, C. & Kielburger, M. (2011) "Child labour is Canada's invisible crisis," *Huffington Post*, November 14, www.huffingtonpost.ca/craig-and-marc-kielburger/child-labour-is-canadas-i_b_1087892.html.

Kim, S. A. (2011) "Skeptical marriage equality," *Harvard Journal of Law & Gender* 34: 37–80.

Kimmel, M. S. (1996) *Manhood in America: A Cultural History*. New York: The Free Press.

(2000) *The Gendered Society*. New York: Oxford University Press.

King, D. (1988) "Multiple jeopardy, multiple consciousness: The context of Black feminist ideology," *Signs: Journal of Women in Culture and Society* 14: 88–111.

Kristof, N. (2015) "From Caitlyn Jenner to a Brooklyn High School," *New York Times* (June 11), www.nytimes.com/2015/06/11/opinion/nicholas-kristof-from-caitlyn-jenner-to-a-brooklyn-high-school.html?_r=0.

Lang, N. (2016) "Gay and voting for Donald Trump? It's not as crazy as it seems," *Salon* (October 26), www.salon.com/2016/10/26/gay-and-voting-for-donald-trump-it-is-not-as-crazy-as-it-seems.

Lareau, A. (2003) *Unequal Childhoods: Class, Race, and Family Life*. Berkeley: University of California Press.

LaRossa, R. (1997) *The Modernization of Fatherhood: A Social and Political History*. University of Chicago Press.

LaSala, M. C., Jenkins, D. A., Wheeler, D. P. & Fredriksen-Goldsen, K. I. (2008) "LGBT faculty, research, and researchers: Risks and rewards," *Journal of Gay & Lesbian Social Services* 20(3): 253–67.

Lawler, S. (2014) *Identity: Sociological Perspectives*, 2nd edn. Cambridge: Polity.

Lee, F. R. (1997) "Young and in fear of the police: Parents teach children how to deal with officers' bias," *New York Times* (October 23), www.nytimes.

com/1997/10/23/nyregion/young-fear-police-parents-teach-children-deal-with-officers-bias.html.

Lewin, E. (2009) *Gay Fatherhood: Narratives of Family and Citizenship in America*. Chicago University Press.

Lewis, J. (1997) "Gender and welfare regimes: Further thoughts," *Social Politics: International Studies in Gender, State, and Society* 4(2): 160–77.

Lin, A. C. & Harris, D. R. (eds.) (2010) *The Colors of Poverty: Why Racial & Ethnic Disparities*, National Poverty Center Series on Poverty and Public Policy. New York: The Russell Sage Foundation.

Littleton, C. (2015) "The secret mastermind behind Caitlyn Jenner's transformation," *Variety* (June 5), http://variety.com/2015/tv/news/bruce-jenner-caitlyn-jenner-transition-new-york-times-story-1201513335.

López, I. H. (1996) *White by Law: The Legal Construction of Race*. New York University Press.
     (2006) *White by Law: The Social Construction of Race*. Revised and Updated: 10th Anniversary edn. New York: NYU Press.

Lorber, J. (1994) *Paradoxes of Gender*. New Haven: Yale University Press.

Lorde, A. (1984) *Sister Outsider: Essays and Speeches*. Berkeley: Crossing Press.

Lugo, A. (2000). "Theorizing border inspections," *Cultural Dynamics* 12(3): 353–73.

Lui, M., Robles, B., Leonadar-Wright, B., Brewer, R. & Adamson, R. (2006) *The Color of Wealth: The Story Behind the U.S. Racial Wealth Divide*. New York: The New Press.

Luibhéid, E. (2002) *Entry Denied: Controlling Sexuality at the Border*. Minneapolis: University of Minnesota Press.

Lundberg. F. (1968) *The Rich and the Super-Rich: A Study in the Power of Money Today*. New York: L. Stuart.

Lundman, R. J. & Kaufman, R. J. (2003) "Driving while Black: Effects of race, ethnicity, and gender on citizen self-reports of traffic stops and police actions," *Criminology* 41(1): 195–220.

Lury, C. (2004) "The united colors of diversity," in S. Franklin, C. Lury & J. Stacey (eds.) *Global Nature, Global Culture*. London: Sage.

Marable, M. & Mullings, L. (eds.) (2009) *Let Nobody Turn Us Around: An African American Anthology*, 2nd edn. Lanham: Rowman & Littlefield Publishers.

Marchevsky, A. & Theoharis, J. (2006) *Not Working: Latina Immigrants, Low-wage Jobs and the Failure of Welfare Reform*. New York University Press.

Margolis, E. & Soldatenko, M. (2016) "Higher education and the capitalist turn: Research and reflections," in J. L. DeVitis & P. A. Sasso (eds.) *Higher Education & Society*. New York: Peter Lang.

Margolis, E., Soldatenko, M., Acker, S. & Gair, M. (2001) "Hiding and outing the curriculum," in E. Margolis (ed.) *The Hidden Curriculum in Higher Education*. New York: Routledge.

Matos, K. & Galinsky, E. (2014) "National study of employers," Families and Work Institute, http://familiesandwork.org/downloads/2014NationalStudyOf Employers.pdf.

Matsuda, M. J. (1991) "Beside my sister, facing the enemy: Legal theory out of coalition," *Stanford Law Review* 43(6): 1183–92.

May, M. (1982) "The historical problem of the family wage: The Ford Motor Company and the five dollar day," *Feminist Studies* 8(2): 399–424.

McClure, H. & Nugent, C. (2000) "Preparing sexual orientation-based asylum claims: A handbook for advocates and asylum seekers," Midwest Human Rights Partnership for Sexual Orientation and Lesbian and Gay Immigration Rights Task Force, http://lgbtbar.org/annual/wp-content/uploads/sites/3/2014/07/Preparing-Sexual-Orientation-Based-Asylum-Claims.pdf.

McKernan, S., Ratcliffe, C., Steuerle, E. & Zhang, S. (2014) "Impact of the Great Recession and beyond: Disparities in wealth building by generation and race," Working Paper, Urban Institute, www.urban.org/sites/default/files/alfresco/publication-pdfs/413102-Impact-of-the-Great-Recession-and-Beyond.PDF.

McKinley, J. (2007) "San Francisco Bay area reacts angrily to series of immigration raids," *New York Times* (April 28), www.nytimes.com/2007/04/28/washington/28immig.html.

McLoyd, V. C., Cauce, A. M., Takeuchi, D. & Wilson, L. (2000) "Marital processes and parental socialization in families of color: A decade review of research," *Journal of Marriage and the Family* 62: 1070–1193.

Meeks, E. (2000) *Driving While Black. Highways, Shopping Malls, Taxicabs, Sidewalks: What to Do if You Are a Victim of Racial Profiling.* New York: Broadway Books.

Meeks, E. M. (2015) "The Lakota Funds story, how indian country is building financial capability," in L. Choi, D. Erickson, K. Grifin, A. Levere & E. Sidman (eds.) *What It's Worth: Strengthening the Financial Future of Families, Communities and the Nation,* CFED & Federal Reserve Bank of San Francisco, www.strongfinancialfuture.org/wp-content/uploads/2015/12/What-its-Worth_Full.pdf.

Messerschmitt, J. (2004) "Varieties of 'real men,'" in M. S. Kimmel & A. Aronson (eds.) *The Gendered Society Reader.* New York: Oxford University Press.

Messner, M. A. (1992) *Power at Play: Sports and the Problem of Masculinity.* Boston: Beacon Press.

(2009) *It's All for the Kids: Gender, Families and Youth Sports.* Berkeley: University of California Press.

Meyer, D. (2012) "An intersectional analysis of lesbian, gay, bisexual and transgender (LGBT) people's evaluations of anti-queer violence," *Gender & Society* 26(6): 849–73.

Meyer, M. H. (2014) *Grandmothers at Work: Juggling Families and Jobs.* New York University Press.

Meyers, K. (2004) "Ladies first: Race, class, and the contradictions of a powerful femininity," *Sociological Spectrum* 24: 11–41.

Michel, S. (1999) *Children's Interests / Mother's Rights.* New Haven: Yale University Press.

Mills, C. W. (1951) *White Collar: The American Middle Classes.* New York: Oxford University Press.

(1956) *The Power Elite.* New York: Oxford University Press.

(1959) *The Sociological Imagination*. New York: Oxford University Press.

(2001 [1948]) *New Men of Power: America's Labor Leaders*. Champaign: University of Illinois Press.

Milovanovic, D. & Russell, K. (eds.) (2001) *Petit Apartheid in the U.S. Criminal Justice System: The Dark Figure of Racism*. Durham: Carolina Academic Press.

Mohanty, C. T. (2003) *Feminism without Borders: Decolonizing Theory, Practicing Solidarity*. Durham: Duke University Press.

Molina, N. (2014) *How Race Is Made in America: Immigration, Citizenship, and the Historical Power of Racial Scripts*. Berkeley: University of California Press.

Moor, L. (2007) *The Rise of Brands*. Oxford: Berg.

Moore, M. R. (2008) "Gendered power relations among women: A study of household decision making in Black, lesbian stepfamilies," *American Sociological Review* 73: 335–56.

(2010) "Black and gay in L.A.: The relationships Black lesbians and gay men have with the racial and religious communities," in D. Hunt & A. Ramon (eds.) *Black Los Angeles: American Dreams and Racial Realities*. New York University Press.

(2011) *Invisible Families: Gay Identities, Relationships, and Motherhood among Black Women*. Berkeley: University of California Press.

Moraga, C. & Anzaldúa, G. (eds.) (1981) *This Bridge Called My Back: Writings by Radical Women of Color*. New York: Kitchen Table Women of Color Press.

Moreno, C. (2013) "Julio Salgado's 'UndocuQueer billboard' explores intersection of LGBTQ and undocumented communities," *Huffington Post*, June 21, www.huffingtonpost.com/2013/06/21/julio-salgado-undocuqueer_n_3480327.html.

Morgan, D. A. (2006) "Not gay enough for the government: Racial and sexual stereotypes in sexual orientation asylum cases," *Law & Sexuality Review: Lesbian Gay Bisexual & Legal Issues* 15: 135–62.

Morris, A. D. (2015) *The Scholar Denied: W. E. B. Du Bois and the Birth of Modern Sociology*. Berkeley: University of California Press.

Morris, J. F., Balsam, K. F. & Rothblum, E. D. (2002) "Lesbian and bisexual mothers and nonmothers: Demographics and the coming-out process," *Journal of Family Psychology* 16(2): 144–56.

Moynihan, D. (1965) *The Negro Family: The Case for National Action*. Washington, DC: Office of Policy Planning and Research, United States Department of Labor.

Nash, J. (2008) "Re-thinking intersectionality," *Feminist Review* 89: 1–18.

National Immigrant Justice Center (NIJC) and Physicians for Human Rights (PHR) (2012) "Invisible in isolation, the use of segregation and solitary confinement in immigration detention," www.immigrantjustice.org/sites/immigrantjustice.org/files/Invisible%20in%20Isolation-The%20Use%20of%20Segregation%20and%20Solitary%20Confinement%20in%20Immigration%20Detention.September%202012_2.pdf.

National Institute of Child Health and Human Development (NICHD) (2006) "The NICHD study of early child care and youth development, findings for children up to age 4½ years," NIH Pub. No. 05–4318, https://www.nichd.nih.gov/publications/pubs/documents/seccyd_06.pdf.

National Women's Law Center (NWLC) (2013) "50 years & counting: The unfinished business of achieving fair pay," www.nwlc.org/sites/default/files/pdfs/final_nwlc_equal_pay_report.pdf.

NBC (2016) "NBC News exit poll: Trump dominates among working-class whites," November 9, www.nbcnews.com/storyline/data-points/nbc-news-exit-poll-trump-dominates-among-working-class-whites-n681146.

Neelakantan, U. & Chang, Y. (2010) "Gender differences in wealth at retirement," *American Economic Review* 100: 362–7.

Nelson, M. K. (2010) *Parenting Out of Control: Anxious Parents in Uncertain Times*. New York University Press.

Newman, K. S. (1999) *No Shame in My Game: The Working Poor in the Inner City*. New York: Russell Sage Publication.

Nicholls, W. J. (2013) *The Dreamers: How the Undocumented Youth Movement Transformed the Immigrant Rights Debate*. Stanford University Press.

Nichols, D. A. (2007) *A Matter of Justice: Eisenhower and the Beginning of the Civil Rights Revolution*. New York: Simon and Schuster.

Nielsen, K. E. (2012) *A Disability History of the United States*. Boston: Beacon Press.

NIOSH (National Institute for Occupational Safety and Health) and ASSE (American Society for Safety Engineers) (2015) "Overlapping vulnerabilities: The occupational health and safety of young immigrant workers in small construction firms," www.asse.org/assets/1/7/NIOSHreport_FinalDraft.pdf.

Nixon, C. A. (2011) "Working-class lesbian parents' emotional engagement with their children's education: Intersections of class and sexuality," *Sexualities* 14(1): 79–99.

Ocampo, A. (2012) "Making masculinity: Negotiations of gender presentation among Latino gay men," *Latino Studies* 10(4): 448–72.

Oder, N. (2015) "What's really at stake in the EB-5 investor visa overhaul: honesty," *PBS News Hour*, December 15, www.pbs.org/newshour/making-sense/column-whats-really-at-stake-in-the-eb-5-investor-visa-overhaul-honesty.

Organisation for Economic Co-operation and Development (OECD) (2011) "Doing better for families," OECD Publishing, www.oecd-ilibrary.org/social-issues-migration-health/doing-better-for-families_9789264098732-en.

Oliver, M. L. & Shapiro, T. (1995) *Black Wealth, White Wealth: A New Perspective on Racial Inequality*. New York: Routledge.

Omi, M. & Winant, H. (1986) *Racial Formation in the United States: From the 1960s to the 1990s*. New York: Routledge Press.

Ono, K. A. & Sloop, J. M. (2002) *Shifting Borders: Rhetoric, Immigration and California's Proposition 187*. Philadelphia: Temple University Press.

Orloff, A. S. & Monson, R. A. (2002) "Citizens, workers or fathers? Men in the history of US social policy," in B. Hobson (ed.) *Making Men into Fathers: Men, Masculinities and the Social Politics of Fatherhood*. New York: Cambridge University Press.

Owen, D. (2007) "Toward a critical theory of whiteness," *Philosophy & Social Criticism* 33(2): 203–22.

Paap, K. (2006) *Working Construction: Why White Working-Class Men Put Themselves – and the Labor Movement – in Harm's Way*. Ithaca: ILR Press / Cornell University Press.

Packer, G. (2016) "Head of the class: How Donald Trump is winning over the white working class," *New Yorker* (May 16), www.newyorker.com/magazine/2016/05/16/how-donald-trump-appeals-to-the-white-working-class.

Padavic, I. & Reskin. B. (2002) *Women and Men at Work*. Thousand Oaks: Pine Forge Press.

Painter, N. I. (1996) *Sojourner Truth: A Life, A Symbol*. New York: W. W. Norton & Company.

Pallares, A. (2015) *Family Activism: Immigrant Struggles and the Politics of Noncitizenship*. New Brunswick: Rutgers University Press.

Parasnis, I. & Fischer, S. D. (2005) "Perceptions of diverse educators regarding ethnic-minority deaf college students, role models, and diversity," *American Annals of the Deaf* 150(4): 343–49.

Park, L. (2005) *Consuming Citizenship: Children of Asian Immigrant Entrepreneurs*. Stanford University Press.

Patterson, C. J. (2000) "Family relationships of lesbians and gay men," *Journal of Marriage and Family* 62(4): 1052–69.

Perna, L. W. (2010) "Understand the working college student," American Association of University Professors (AAUP), https://www.aaup.org/article/understanding-working-college-student#.WGEybH2XksA.

Petitt, B. (2008) "Academe maid possible: The lived experiences of six women employed as custodial workers at a Research Extensive University located in the Southwest," Ph.D. dissertation, Educational Administration, Texas A&M University.

Pimentel, D. (2012) "Criminal child neglect and the 'free range kid': Is overprotective parenting the new standard of care?" *Utah Law Review* 3: 947–1000.

Pomerleau, K. (2016) "2017 tax brackets," Tax Foundation, http://taxfoundation.org/article/2017-tax-brackets.

Pribilsky, J. (2007) *La Chullah Vida: Gender, Migration & Family in Andean Ecuador and New York City*. Syracuse University Press.

Purkayastha, B. (2010) "Interrogating intersectionality: Contemporary globalization and racialized gendering in the lives of highly educated South Asian Americans and their children," *Journal of Intercultural Studies* 31: 29–47.

Pyke, K. D. & Johnson, D. L. (2003) "Asian American women and racialized femininities: 'Doing' gender across cultural worlds," *Gender & Society* 17(1): 33–53.

Quinonez, J. (2015) "Latinos in the Financial Shadows," in L. Choi, D. Erickson, K. Griffin, A. Levere & E. Sidman (eds.) *What It's Worth: Strengthening the Financial Future of Families, Communities and the Nation*, CFED & Federal Reserve Bank of San Francisco, www.strongfinancialfuture.org/wp-content/uploads/2015/12/What-its-Worth_Full.pdf.

Ramirez, H. (2011) "Masculinity in the workplace: The case of Mexican immigrant gardeners," *Men and Masculinities* 14(1): 97–116.

Ramirez, R. (2012) "Undocumented activists follow LGBT tactics," *National Journal*, www.nationaljournal.com/thenextamerica/immigration/undocumented-activists-follow-lbgt-tactics-20120724.

Reardon, M. J. (2012) "The bonds of manhood: Public life, homosociality, and hegemonic masculinity in Massachusetts, 1630–1787," Ph.D. dissertation, University of Iowa, http://ir.uiowa.edu/etd/2969.

Reynolds, G. (2007) "The impact of facilities on recruitment and retention of students," *Facilities Manager* 135: 63–80.

Richardson, D. (1996) "Constructing lesbian sexualities," in S. Jackson & S. Scott (eds.) *Feminism and Sexuality: A Reader*. Edinburgh University Press.

Richardson, M. (1987) *Maria W. Stewart, America's First Black Woman Political Writer*. Bloomington: Indiana University Press.

Rios, V. M. (2009) "The consequences of the criminal justice pipeline on Black and Latino masculinity," *Annals of the American Academy of Political and Social Science* 623: 150–62.

Roberts, D. (1997) *Killing the Black Body: Race, Reproduction, and the Meaning of Liberty*. New York: Pantheon.

Robinson, R. & Moodie-Mills, A. C. (2012) "HIV-AIDS inequality: Structural barriers to prevention, treatment, and care in communities of color," *Center for American Progress*, https://www.americanprogress.org/wp-content/uploads/issues/2012/07/pdf/hiv_community_of_color.pdf.

Rodino-Colocino, M. (2012) "Geek jeremiads: Speaking the crisis of job loss by opposing offshored and H-1B labor," *Communication and Critical/Culture Studies* 9(1): 22–46.

Rodríguez, R. T. (2006) "Queering the Homeboy aesthetic," *Aztlán* 31(2): 127–37.

Roediger, D. R. (1999) *The Wages of Whiteness: Race and the Making of the American Working Class*. New York: Verso.

Roer-Strier, D., Strier, R., Este, D., Shimoni, R. & Clark, D. (2005) "Fatherhood and immigration: Challenging the deficit theory," *Child & Family Social Work* 10: 315–29.

Rohmer, S. (1965 [1913]) *The Insidious Dr. Fu Manchu*. New York: Pyramid Books.

Rokosa, J. (2012) "Latinos bearing the brunt of the foreclosure crisis," Center for American Progress, April 19, https://www.americanprogress.org/issues/housing/news/2012/04/19/11416/latinos-bearing-the-brunt-of-the-foreclosure-crisis.

Rollins, J. (1985) *Between Women: Domestics and Their Employers*. Philadelphia: Temple University Press.

Romero, M. (1992) *Maid in the USA*. New York: Routledge.

(2001) "State violence, and the social and legal construction of Latino criminality: From el bandido to gang member," *Denver University Law Review* 78(2): 1089–1127.

(2002) "Introduction to the 10th anniversary edition," in M. Romero, *Maid in the USA*. New York: Routledge.

(2006) "Racial profiling and immigration law enforcement: Rounding up of usual suspects in the Latino community," *Critical Sociology* 32(2–3): 449–75.

(2011a) *The Maid's Daughter: Living Inside and Outside the American Dream*. New York University Press.

(2011b) "Are your papers in order? Racial profiling, vigilantes and 'America's toughest sheriff,'" *Harvard Latino Review* 14: 337–57.

Romero, M. & Perez, N. (2015) "Conceptualizing the foundation of inequalities in care work," *American Behavioral Scientist* 60(2): 172–88.

Rondilla, J. L. (2009) "Filipinos and the color complex: Ideal Asian beauty," in E. Nekano Glenn (ed.) *Shades of Difference: Why Skin Color Matters*, Stanford University Press.

Root, L. S. & Wooten, L. P. (2008) "Time out for family: Shift work, fathers, and sports," *Human Resource Management* 47(3): 481–99.

Rosaldo, R. (1989) *Culture & Truth: The Remaking of Social Analysis*. Boston: Beacon Press.

Rosenblum, M. R. & Soto, A. G. R. (2015) "An analysis of unauthorized immigrants in the United States by Country and Region of Birth," Washington, DC: Migration Policy Institute.

Ross, L. J. (2006) "Frances Beale interview," Sophia Smith Collection, https://www.smith.edu/library/libs/ssc/vof/transcripts/Beale.pdf.

Rothenberg, B. (2015) "Tennis's top women balance body image with ambition," *New York Times* (July 10), www.nytimes.com/2015/07/11/sports/tennis/tenniss-top-women-balance-body-image-with-quest-for-success.html?action=click&contentCollection=Sports&module=RelatedCoverage&region=Marginalia&pgtype=article&_r=0.

Rothman, B. K. (1989) *Recreating Motherhood: Ideology and Technology in a Patriarchal Society*. New York: W. W. Norton.

Russell, K. (2009 [1998]) *The Color of Crime: Racial Hoaxes, White Fear, Black Protectionism, Police Harassment and Other Macroaggressions*. New York University Press.

Ryan, S. (2007) "Parent–child interaction styles between gay and lesbian parents and their adopted children," *Journal of GLBT Family Studies* 3(2–3): 105–32.

Ryan, W. (1976) *Blaming the Victim*. New York: Vintage.

Sartre, J. P. (1963 [1960]) *Search for a Method*, trans. from the French and with an introduction by Hazel E. Barnes. New York: Alfred A. Knopf.

Saucedo, L. M. & Morales, M. C. (2010) "Masculinities narratives and Latino immigrant workers: A case study of the Las Vegas residential construction trades," *Harvard Journal of Law and Gender* 33: 625–59.

Scott, J. W. (1999) *Gender and the Politics of History*. New York: Columbia University Press.

Segal, L. (1990) *Slow Motion: Changing Masculinities, Changing Men*. New Brunswick: Rutgers University Press.

Segura, D. A. (1989) "Chicana and Mexican immigrant women at work: The impact of class, race, and gender on occupational mobility," *Gender & Society* 3(1): 37–52.

Seidler, V. J. (1988) "Fathering, authority and masculinity," in R. Chapman & J. Rutherford (eds.) *Male Order, Unwrapping Masculinity*. London: Lawrence & Wishart.

Sennett, R. & Cobb, J. (1973) *The Hidden Injuries of Class*. New York: Random House.

Shelton, B. A. (1992) *Women, Men, and Time: Gender Differences in Paid Work, Housework, and Leisure*. New York: Greenwood Press.

Shelton, J. & John, D. (1993) "Ethnicity, race, and difference: A comparison of White, Black, and Hispanic men's household labor time," in J. Hood (ed.) *Men, Work and Family*. Newbury Park: Sage.

Shows, C. & Gerstel, N. (2009) "Fathering, class, and gender: A comparison of physicians and emergency medical technicians," *Gender & Society* 23(2): 161–87.

Shuttleworth, R., Wedgwood, N. & Wilson, N. (2012) "The dilemma of disabled masculinity," *Men and Masculinities* 15(2): 174–94.

Silverman, A. (1994) "Fife's double talk on education, Governor Symington's school-voucher plan is a gift for conservatives – not the poor," *Phoenix New Times* (February 23), www.phoenixnewtimes.com/news/fifes-double-talk-on-educationgovernor-symingtons-school-voucher-plan-is-a-gift-for-conservatives-not-the-poor-6425637.

Silverstein, L. B., Auerbach, C. F. & Levant, R. F. (2002) "Contemporary fathers reconstructing masculinity: Clinical implications of gender role strain," *Professional Psychology: Research and Practice* 33: 361–9.

Singh, A. A. (2012) "Counseling gay, lesbian, bisexual, and transgender culturally-diverse adolescents," in E. C. Lopez, S. G. Hanari & S. Proctor (eds.) *Handbook of Multicultural School Psychology: An Interdisciplinary Perspective*. Mahwah: Lawrence Erlbaum & Associates.

Smith, B. & Smith, B. (1981) "Across the kitchen table: A sister-to-sister dialogue," in C. Moraga & G. E. Anzaldúa (eds.) *This Bridge Called My Back: Writings by Radical Women of Color*. New York: Kitchen Table, Women of Color Press.

Smith, D. E. (1987) *The Everyday World as Problematic: A Feminist Sociology*. Boston: Northeastern University Press.

(1990) *The Conceptual Practices of Power: A Feminist Sociology of Knowledge*. Boston: Northeastern University Press.

Somaiya, R. (2015) "Caitlyn Jenner, formerly Bruce, introduces herself in *Vanity Fair*," *New York Times* (June 1), www.nytimes.com/2015/06/02/business/media/jenner-reveals-new-name-in-vanity-fair-article.html.

Speth, L. E. (2011) "The married women's property acts, 1839–1865: Reform, reaction, or revolution?" in J. R. Lindgren, N. Taub, B. Wolfson & C. M. Palumbo (eds.) *The Law of Sex Discrimination*. Belmont: Wadsworth.

Srikantiah, J. (2007) "Perfect victims and real survivors: The iconic victim in domestic human trafficking law," *Boston University Law Review* 87: 157–212.

Stacey, J. (2004) "Cruising to family land: Gay hypergamy and rainbow kinship," *Current Sociology* 52: 181–97.

(2005) "The families of man: Gay male intimacy and kinship in a global metropolis," *Signs* 30: 1811–933.

(2006) "Gay parenthood and the decline of paternity as we knew it," *Sexualities* 9: 27–55.

Stack, C. B. (1974) *All Our Kin: Strategies for Survival in a Black Community*. New York: Harper and Row.

Stanley, A. (2014) "Wrought in Rhimes's image: Viola David plays Shonda Rhimes's latest tough heroine," *New York Times* (September 18), www.nytimes.com/2014/09/21/arts/television/viola-davis-plays-shonda-rhimess-latest-tough-heroine.html?_r=0.

Stanley, T. L. (2007) "The specter of Oprah Winfrey: Critical Black female spectatorship," in J. Harris & E. Watson (eds.) *The Oprah Phenomenon.* Lexington: University Press of Kentucky.

Steiger, K. (2015) "Mom gets arrested for 'abandoning' kids in nearby food court while at job interview," Think Progress, https://thinkprogress.org/mom-gets-arrested-for-abandoning-kids-in-nearby-food-court-while-at-job-interview-7885a9c55b8a#.4fvlbee7f.

Stein, M. (2005) "Boutilier and the U.S. Supreme Court's sexual revolution," *Law and History Review* 23(3): 491–536.

(2010) *Sexual Injustice: Supreme Court Decisions from Griswold to Roe.* Chapel Hill: University of North Carolina Press.

Stell, E. (2015) "Bruce Jenner's transgender announcement draws 16.8 million on ABC News," *New York Times* (April 25), www.nytimes.com/2015/04/26/business/media/bruce-jenners-transgender-announcement-draws-16-8-million-on-abc-news.html?_r=0.

Sue, D. W. (2010) *Microaggressions in Everyday Life: Race, Gender and Sexual Orientation.* Hoboken: John Wiley & Sons, Inc.

Swarns, R. L. (2016) "272 slaves were sold to save Georgetown. What does it owe their descendants?" *New York Times* (April 16), www.nytimes.com/2016/04/17/us/georgetown-university-search-for-slave-descendants.html.

Takaki, R. (1993) *A Different Mirror: A History of Multicultural America.* Boston: Little, Brown and Company.

Terkel, S. (1974) *Working: People Talk About What They Do All Day and How They Feel About What They Do.* New York: Pantheon Books.

Teuscher, A. (2015) "The inclusive strength of #BlackLivesMatter," *The American Project*, August 2, http://prospect.org/article/inclusive-strength-blacklivesmatter.

Thangaraj, S. (2010) "Ballin' Indo-Pak style: Pleasures, desires, and expressive practices of 'South Asian American' masculinity," *International Review for the Sociology of Sport* 45(3): 372–89.

(2012) "Playing through differences: Black–white racial logic and interrogating South Asian American identity," *Ethnic and Racial Studies* 35(6): 988–1006.

(2013) "Competing masculinities: South Asian American identity formation in Asian American basketball leagues," *South Asian Popular Culture* 11(1): 243–55.

(2015) *Desi Hoop Dreams.* New York University Press.

Tonso, K. (2001) "Producing public and private on an engineering campus," in E. Margolis (ed.), *The Hidden Curriculum in Higher Education.* New York: Routledge.

Truth, S. (1999 [1851]) "Look at me! Ain't I a woman," *The New Crisis* (Jan./Feb.).

Tung, I., Lathrop, Y. & Sonn, P. (2015) "The growing movement for $15," National Employment Law Project, www.nelp.org/content/uploads/Growing-Movement-for-15-Dollars.pdf.

United for a Fair Economy (UFE) (2015) "State of the dream 2015, underbanked and overcharged," http://www.faireconomy.org/dream15.

(2012) "Born on third base: What the Forbes 400 really says about economic equality & opportunity in America," http://files.faireconomy.org/sites/default/fiiles/BornOnThirdBase_2012.pdf.

US Census (2015a) *Income, Poverty, and Health Insurance Coverage in the United States: 2015*. Washington, DC: US Census Bureau.

(2015b) *The Research Supplemental Poverty Measure: 2015*. Washington, DC: US Census Bureau.

US Department of Agriculture (USDA) (2016) "National School Lunch Program", https://www.ers.usda.gov/topics/food-nutrition-assistance/child-nutrition-programs/national-school-lunch-program.aspx.

US Department of Education National Center for Education Statistics (2010) "Digest of education statistics," http://nces.ed.gov/fastfacts/display.asp?id=98.

Utall, L. (2002) *Making Care Work: Employed Mothers in the New Childcare Market*. New Brunswick: Rutgers University Press.

Van Maanen, J. (1998) *Tales of the Field: On Writing Ethnography*. University of Chicago Press.

Vargas, A. J. (2011) "My life as an undocumented immigrant," *New York Times* (June 22), www.nytimes.com/2011/06/26/magazine/my-life-as-an-undocumented-immigrant.html.

Villalon, R. (2015) "Violence against immigrants in a context of crisis: A critical migration feminist of color analysis," *Journal of Social Distress and the Homeless* 24(3): 116–39.

Vinjamuri, M. (2015) "'It's so important to talk and talk': How gay adoptive fathers respond to their children's encounters with heteronormativity," *Fathering: A Journal of Theory, Research, and Practice about Men as Fathers* 13(3): 245–70.

Walker, M. A. (2005) "Black coaches are ready, willing…and still waiting: By all accounts, there are no shortage of qualified Black coaches to lead Division I teams, so why are there so few?" *Black Issues in Higher Education* 22(6): 26–30.

Walter, N., Bourgois, P. & Loinaz, H. M. (2004) "Masculinity and undocumented labor migration: Injured Latino day laborers in San Francisco," *Social Science & Medicine* 59: 1159–68.

Wang, W., Parker, K. & Taylor, P. (2013) "Breadwinner moms, mothers are the sole or primary provider in four-in-ten households with children; Public conflicted about the growing trend," Pew Research Center, May 29, www.pewsocialtrends.org/2013/05/29/breadwinner-moms.

Weber, L. (2010) *Understanding Race, Class, Gender, and Sexuality: A Conceptual Framework*. New York: Oxford University Press.

Weber, M. S. (2004) "Opening the golden door: Disability and the law of immigration," *Journal of Gender, Race, and Justice* 1(8): 153–75.

Weller, C. E., Ajinkya, J. & Farrell, J. (2012) "The state of communities of color in the U.S. economy," Center for American Progress, https://cdn.americanprogress.org/wp-content/uploads/issues/2012/04/pdf/comm_of_color.pdf.

West, C. M. (2004) "Mammy, Jezebel, and Sapphire: Developing an 'oppositional gaze' toward the images of black women," in J. C. Chrisler, C.

Golden & P. D. Rozee (eds.) *Lectures on the Psychology of Women*. Boston: McGraw Hill.

The White House (2013) "Remarks by the President on Trayvon Martin," Office of the Press Secretary, July 19, www.whitehouse.gov/the-press-office/2013/07/19/remarks-president-trayvon-martin.

——— (2016) *My Brother's Keeper 2016 Progress Report: Two Years of Expanding Opportunity and Creating Pathways to Success*, https://www.whitehouse.gov/sites/whitehouse.gov/files/images/MBK-2016-Progress-Report.pdf.

Wilder, J. & Cain, C. (2011) "Teaching and learning color consciousness in Black families: Exploring family processes and women's experiences with colorism," *Journal of Family Issues* 32(5): 577–604.

Williams, M. E. (2015) "Even the New York Times is body-shaming Serena Williams now: It's time to break this absurd and insulting habit once and for all," *Salon* (July 13), www.salon.com/2015/07/13/stop_body_shaming_serena_williams_its_time_to_break_this_absurd_and_insulting_habit_once_and_for_all.

Williamson, C. E. (2007) *Black Deaf Students: A Model for Education Success*. Washington, DC: Gallaudet University Press.

Wilson, G., Dunham, R. & Alpert, G. (2004) "Prejudice in police profiling," *American Behavioral Scientist* 47: 896–909.

Wilson, P. and Yoshikawa, H. (2004) "Experiences of and responses to social distinction among Asian and Pacific Islander gay men: Their relationship to HIV risk," *AIDS Education and Prevention* 16(1): 68–83.

Wilson, V. & Rodgers, W. M., II (2016) "Black–White wage gaps expand with rising wage inequality," Washington, DC: Economic Policy Institute, www.epi.org/files/pdf/101972.pdf.

Women's Bureau (2010) "Women in the labor force in 2010," US Department of Labor, https://www.dol.gov/wb/factsheets/qf-laborforce-10.htm.

Yoshikawa, H. (2012) *Immigrants Raising Citizens: Undocumented Parents and Their Children*. New York: Russell Sage Foundation.

Young, A. A., Jr. (2004) *The Minds of Marginalized Black Men*. Princeton University Press.

Yuval-Davis, N. (2006) "Intersectionality and feminist politics," *European Journal of Women's Studies* 13(3): 193–209.

Index